# Education
## for All

# Education for All

## Critical Issues in the Education of Children and Youth with Disabilities

Terese C. Jiménez

Victoria L. Graf

Foreword by Michael M. Gerber

**JB** JOSSEY-BASS
A Wiley Imprint
www.josseybass.com

Published by Jossey-Bass
A Wiley Imprint
989 Market Street, San Francisco, CA 94103-1741   www.josseybass.com

Jossey-Bass books and products are available through most bookstores. To contact Jossey-Bass directly call our Customer Care Department within the U.S. at 800-956-7739, outside the U.S. at 317-572-3986, or fax 317-572-4002.

Jossey-Bass also publishes its books in a variety of electronic formats. Some content that appears in print may not be available in electronic books.

**Library of Congress Cataloging-in-Publication Data**

Education for all : preparing for the next 30 years of special education / Terese C. Jimenez, Victoria L. Graf ; foreword by Michael M. Gerber.
     p. cm.
   Includes bibliographical references and index.
   ISBN-13 : 978-0-7879-9522-5 (cloth)
  1. Special education–United States. I. Jimenez, Terese C., 1970- II. Graf, Victoria L., 1951-
  LC3981.E374 2008
  371.90973–dc22
                                                                                    2007044096

Printed in the United States of America
FIRST EDITION

HB Printing        10 9 8 7 6 5 4 3 2 1

# Contents

# Foreword

This book is a celebration of the Education for All Handicapped Children Act of 1975 (P.L. 94–142), later reauthorized and now known as the Individuals with Disabilities Education Act (IDEA). Although many ideas, practices, and institutions related to disabilities were more than two hundred years old in 1975, this was the first time that special education became national policy. In some ways, modern special education is now defined by national policy. Prior to P.L. 94–142, special education was a collection of teaching practices for different kinds of disabilities. Each disability was a separate field, with different histories and traditions of professional preparation and practices. These fields and practices were united only by a common concern of parents and professionals for educating children with disabilities who were excluded from public schools or received only inconsistent educational opportunities.

Public Law 94–142 guaranteed access to public schools for students with disabilities wherever they lived in the United States. It established the specific right to a free, individually tailored public education at public expense and in the least restrictive environment that would be consistent with their needs. It also established a unified view of special education that did not depend on the kind of disability a child might have. Under the new national policy, special education became a set of processes and procedures by which schools would respond thoughtfully and appropriately to the unique needs of their students with disabilities. The law required processes for identification, referral, assessment, planning, and programming, and it made the children and their parents equal partners with educators in decision making. Taken together, the guarantee of access to public education, the establishment of a unified understanding of special education that did not depend on any specific disabilities, and the granting of equal participation by families in decision making all made P.L. 94–142 revolutionary in the history of special education.

Like the Elementary and Secondary Education Act of 1965 (now known as the No Child Left Behind Act of 2001) a decade earlier, P.L. 94–142 aimed to promote educational opportunity. However, the problem presented by children with a range of disabling conditions required a new way of thinking about opportunity. First, students with disabilities faced more than the barrier of social discrimination. They also had unique needs and sometimes significant limitations. Second, "equality of opportunity" seemed to suggest identical amounts and qualities of teaching. But special education requires that different (that is, unequal) amounts and qualities of teaching must be provided depending on the unique needs of individual children with disabilities.

In recognizing these facts, the United States set into motion a series of dramatic changes in education across the country that forever altered how schools boards, teachers, administrators, and families would think about special education, the potential (and problems) of public schools, and the value of all human beings. Research on assessment and instruction exploded. New knowledge was produced about specific disabilities, their educationally relevant characteristics, techniques for teaching, and strategies for organizing school programs. New training programs developed to meet the demand for specialists. Parents learned their rights and how to exercise them. Lawsuits were litigated and constitutional issues raised. School officials, policymakers, and advocates began to rethink how schools are built, equipped, staffed, and operated. And in each of these ways, millions of individual lives were affected: those of children, those of parents, and those of teachers. Children who a decade before would have stayed home or gone to special private or state-sponsored schools were now in class with their peers, in their own neighborhoods, and having a chance to be just another one of the kids in a classroom, in assemblies, and on the playground. Families who a decade before could not conceive of their children going to school, or the transition from school to employment, postsecondary education, or independent living were now watching their children grow, learn, make friends, and live fulfilling lives.

The purpose of this celebratory volume is to capture and consider the dramatic effects this change of policy thirty-three years ago had on the daily lives of administrators, teachers, the families of millions of children with disabilities, and, of course, the children themselves. Quite simply but profoundly, the authors of these chapters reflect on their professional and personal experiences with the new special education and movingly demonstrate its lasting impact.

To be sure, even after thirty-three years, there is much to do. We are constantly learning more about how to design and deliver effective instruction in the same classrooms and within the same curriculum experienced by students who do not have disabilities. We struggle to understand how poverty, as well as cultural and linguistic differences, continue to make students so vulnerable and how and when special education may or may not be appropriate. It is clear too that special education can be very costly. We continue to puzzle over how to fund it properly and how to design programs and schools that deliver high-quality education, social integration, and greater successes for children with disabilities.

However, if P.L. 94–142 has changed American education, it has done so not only by changing the rules of education but also by changing the lives of all those touched by it. Important laws *should* change people's lives. They should influence as well as reflect the beliefs, aspirations, and behaviors of common people who live under them and by them. They are only momentarily the dry words written on a page. Once enacted, laws like P.L. 94–142 come alive. They become the lived histories of real people, such as those whose reflections from the field are shared in this book.

Michael M. Gerber
University of California, Santa Barbara

# Acknowledgments

This book would not have been possible without a true spirit of collaboration and cooperation among the many people who assisted in its development. We acknowledge the financial and moral support of Ernest Rose, chief academic officer, and Shane Martin, dean of the School of Education, both at Loyola Marymount University. Both provided significant support for the commemorative conference in 2005 that was the inspiration for this book. Loyola Marymount University also provided funding for the college fellowship that helped provide release time for the first author to devote significant time to the writing and editing of the book with its many contributors. We also thank our contributing authors for their willingness to tell their stories as a parent, professional, practitioner within the field, or individual with a disability. Finally, we thank our friends and family for their support during this journey over the past three years, from the beginning of our dream of holding a commemorative, interdisciplinary conference to the realization of this book. We hope this book will draw attention to the issues that educational professionals, families, and community and legal advocates still face as they continue to support children and youth with disabilities in our schools and communities.

# The Editors

**Terese C. Jiménez, Ph.D.,** is an assistant professor in the School of Education's Special Education Program at Loyola Marymount University in Los Angeles. She obtained her special education and bilingual resource specialist credentials at Loyola Marymount University. In 2004 she received her Ph.D. in Special Education, Disabilities, and Risk Studies and a master's degree in school psychology from the University of California, Santa Barbara. Before initiating her doctoral studies, Jiménez taught as a bilingual resource specialist in southern California. Her research interests include examining the development, application, and evaluation of problem-based pedagogy for professional education; the early intervention and identification of children at risk for reading failure; teacher responsiveness during early reading instruction with English language learners; and family advocacy. Jiménez collaborates with various parent organizations in educating parents and professionals to advocate for children with disabilities.

**Victoria L. Graf, Ph.D.,** is the director of the Special Education Program at Loyola Marymount University. Prior to her extensive career in the preparation of teachers for students with mild to moderate disabilities, Graf was a teacher of students with learning disabilities, autism, mild mental retardation, and emotional disturbance. She has written and administered many grants for the preparation of teachers for culturally and linguistically diverse students with exceptional needs. A highlight of her career has been the development of preparation programs for teachers and administrators of students with exceptional needs in the parochial school system. Graf's research interests include school reform and policy, public and parochial school inclusion, student success teams, and the intersection of gender and disability.

# The Contributors

**Marlene Canter** has served as an elected board member of the Los Angeles City Board of Education since 2001 and as president of the board from 2005 to 2007. She began her career as a special education teacher and went on to cofound a successful teacher training company.

**Olegario D. Cantos VII, Esq.,** has been a community leader for more than seventeen years. In addition to serving in leadership positions within small and large nonprofit organizations, he has been special counsel to the assistant attorney general for civil rights in the U.S. Department of Justice and completed two terms of service as associate director of the White House Domestic Policy Council in the Executive Office of the President.

**Katharine W. Clemmer, M.A.,** is the program director for the Math and Science Teaching program at Loyola Marymount University in Los Angeles, California. She holds a single-subject secondary teaching credential in mathematics and teaches secondary math methods and math and science methods for special education candidates.

**Richard Cohen, M.F.A.,** is a documentary film producer and distributor in Culver City, California. His work has been screened around the world and includes such films as *Taylor's Campaign* about homelessness and poverty and *Hurry Tomorrow* about involuntary psychiatric treatment.

**Sandi Drinkward, M.A.,** is an English teacher and codirector of the Academic Leadership Community, a small learning community at Miguel Contreras Learning Complex in Los Angeles. She taught high school special education for seven years before working as an Advancement Via Individual Determination coordinator to help underrepresented culturally and linguistically diverse students prepare for college.

**Alnita Rettig Dunn, Ph.D.,** is director of psychological services in the Los Angeles Unified School District. She has worked on initiatives that expand school psychological services delivery models to include educational intervention, decrease disproportional placement of students of color in special education, and increase community involvement in schools.

**Elizabeth J. Erwin, Ed.D.,** is a professor of early childhood special education at Montclair State University, Montclair, New Jersey. Her scholarly interests include inclusive education, family and professional partnerships, and self-determination in the early years.

**Mary A. Falvey, Ph.D.,** is the dean of the Charter College of Education at California State University, Los Angeles. She was coordinator of the master's and credential programs in inclusive education and moderate/severe disabilities for twenty-five years at the same university. Her scholarly interests are inclusive education, school reform, and collaboration.

**Robert W. Farran, M.A.,** is director of the Southwest Special Education Local Plan Area (SELPA) and Family Resource Center for the Los Angeles County Office of Education. He has been a special education local plan area director since 1989. He has held various special education and advisory leadership positions and is involved in curriculum development, legislative work, and parent-community projects.

**Michael M. Gerber, Ph.D.,** is a professor of education at the University of California, Santa Barbara. His research interests include information processing barriers to acquisition and performance of basic skills by individuals with cognitive disabilities, and using tolerance theory to explain how schools accommodate extreme individual differences associated with disabilities and risk for school failure. Earlier in his career, he taught as a K-6 elementary school teacher in Oakland, California.

**Diane Haager, Ph.D.,** is a professor at California State University, Los Angeles, where she instructs teachers in methods for teaching students with high-incidence disabilities. She has worked in urban public schools as a reading specialist and special educator. She is the author of several books and articles on reading instruction for English learners, students with learning disabilities, and students at risk for reading failure.

**Nancy E. Huerta, Esq.,** is an attorney and owner of Equal Chance Education Consulting, LLC in Shawnee, Kansas. She specializes in special education law and focuses her practice on representing parents in Kansas, Missouri, Maryland, Virginia, and the District of Columbia.

**Jo Ann Isken, M.A.,** is an elementary school principal at Moffett Elementary School in Lennox, California. She has worked as a principal for twenty years and has approximately thirty years of experience in the field of education. She has taught in the administrative and teacher education programs at Loyola Marymount University in Los Angeles and the University of California, Los Angeles.

**Janette Klingner, Ph.D.,** is a professor in bilingual special education at the University of Colorado, Boulder. She was a K–8 bilingual special education teacher for ten years before earning her doctorate in reading and learning disabilities from the University of Miami. One of her many research areas is the disproportionate representation of culturally and linguistically diverse students in special education.

**Greg Knotts, Ph.D.,** is an assistant professor of elementary education at California State University, Northridge. His scholarly interests include gender and sexuality issues in elementary education, social studies education, and cross-cultural dimensions of identity formation.

**Holly Menzies, Ph.D.,** is an assistant professor of special education at California State University, Los Angeles. She is program coordinator for mild/moderate disabilities in the Division of Special Education and Counseling. Her scholarly interests include schoolwide behavior support and inclusive education.

**Marianne Mitchell, M.A.,** is the assistant director of special education at Loyola Marymount University in Los Angeles, California. Her scholarly interests include the use of assistive technology in differentiating instruction for children with disabilities, positive behavior support, and social and emotional deficits in children with autism.

**Sandra Rentería** is the mother of three children (Richard, Brandy, and Maya Sofia) and the wife of her supportive husband, Ralph. Sandra is also a liaison coordinator for the Complaint Response Unit/Parent Resource Network for the Los Angeles Unified School District.

**Ernest Rose, Ph.D.,** is senior vice president and chief academic officer at Loyola Marymount University in Los Angeles, California. He is also professor of special education, with scholarly interests in the transition of students with disabilities to postsecondary education and adult life and the full inclusion of students in pre-K–12 schools.

**Sue Rubin** is a college student at Whittier College majoring in history. She is a board member of the human rights organization TASH and an advocate for people with disabilities.

**Robert Rueda, Ph.D.,** is a professor in the area of Psychology in Education at the Rossier School of Education, University of Southern California. His research interests are sociocultural aspects of learning and motivation, with a special focus on English learners and literacy.

**Nicole Sager, M.A.,** is a doctoral candidate at the University of Colorado at Boulder. Her scholarly interests include bilingual education, native language maintenance, biliteracy development, and the cognitive aspects of bilingualism.

**Tanya Santangelo, Ph.D.,** is an assistant professor in the Department of Special Education at Rowan University in Glassboro, New Jersey. Prior to earning her doctorate in learning disabilities from the University of Maryland, she was a special education teacher, working with elementary and middle school students in inclusive settings. Her research focuses on strategy instruction, effective practices in inclusive classrooms, and collaborative problem-solving teams.

**Gina Semenza** is a field representative for U.S. senator Barbara Boxer, working directly with southern California communities. She is the statewide liaison on disability issues. She is active in the disability youth movement and was previously chair of the Youth Advisory Committee to the National Council on Disability.

**Leslie C. Soodak, Ph.D.,** is a professor of special education at Pace University in New York City. Her research has focused on factors promoting inclusive education in elementary and secondary schools, the politics of school discipline in inclusive settings, and the role of trust in effective parent-professional partnerships.

**Janeen Steel, Esq.,** is the executive director and founder of the Learning Rights Law Center in Los Angeles, California. Steel, a graduate of the UCLA School of Law, is an expert in the area of education law specifically regarding special education.

**Alejandra Velasco, Ed.M.,** is a doctoral student at the University of Southern California. Her research interests include literacy, particularly issues related to English language learners and teacher education.

**Virginia M. Victorín** is commissioner for the City of Los Angeles in the Department on Disability. She also serves as first vice president and senior community affairs relationship manager for Washington Mutual, a company that supports the community with financial support to the nonprofit community in K-12 public education and affordable housing and that embraces employee volunteerism at its core. Victorín is a member of the advisory board for LA's BEST after-school program, a longtime advisor to Fiesta Educativa, a recent former board member of Families in Schools, and a child advocate working to improve the quality of life for low-income and underrepresented families.

**Savina Woodyard, M.A.,** is a high school English teacher in Los Angeles. She completed her undergraduate work at the University of California, Los Angeles. She has a master's degree in secondary education, is pursuing a reading specialist certificate, and is planning to pursue her doctorate in linguistic development.

# Introduction

*Education for All* is the outcome of a commemorative conference held in 2005 at Loyola Marymount University in Los Angeles, California, marking the thirtieth anniversary of important special education legislation in the United States. For this event, we convened students, teachers, university faculty, researchers, filmmakers, policymakers, legal professionals, parents, and individuals with disabilities as they reflected on the history and implementation of the Education for All Handicapped Children Act (Public Law 94–142), currently known as the Individuals with Disabilities Education Act (IDEA).

The chapters in this book were written primarily by conference presenters and panelists on various topics related to the education of students with disabilities and their families. The authors include well-known researchers and respected teacher-educators in the field of general and special education, individuals with disabilities, and educational advocates. They provide a historical backdrop to their individual topics and review current research and practices, while proposing implications for the future.

Each chapter ends with a short reflection essay, "From the Field," written by someone living or working in the trenches: an individual with a disability, a parent, or a practitioner in the field. These pieces, which address the issues raised in their respective chapters from a very personal point of view, were included to reflect the format and intent of the original conference. For the conference, we designed several sessions to include the perspectives of individuals with disabilities, parents, and educational professionals to discuss the realities of implementing special education legislation in the schools. By sharing their experiences, these practitioners brought forth a personal yet critical voice to these discussions. Ultimately, the conference prompted the development of the present volume for the purpose of capturing this unique collaborative dialogue and desire to support children and youth with disabilities and their families.

## Who Should Read This Book

Those who support the education of students with disabilities and their families will find the topics addressed in this book enlightening and useful in informing their work in the schools. Preservice and in-service educational professionals will become knowledgeable about critical historical and instructional issues related to special education from a variety of perspectives, including those of parents, whose voices are often silent in standard textbooks. University faculty, researchers, and policymakers will gain an understanding of important topics that challenge the field of special education and their respective work with the added insight of practitioners and families. Legal professionals, who typically do not reside in schools except in situations related to litigation, will gain from the educational issues presented as they relate to the rights of families and students with disabilities. Finally, parents and individuals with disabilities may identify with the experiences of practitioners, parents, and other individuals with special needs who share their personal journeys and insights regarding the supports and services within general and special education.

## Preview of the Chapters

This book contains nine chapters, all concluding with a personal essay, "From the Field." It is important that each chapter be read with its corresponding practitioner perspective in order to fully appreciate the multiple points of view presented within each topic. Chapters can also be read out of sequence given that they complement one another yet are able to stand alone.

Chapter One discusses the background of the initial passage of Public Law 94–142 and its evolution. Given the book's original purpose of commemorating the law, the author provides a detailed review. The author, an attorney and advocate, calls attention to critical areas of the current reauthorized law of 2004. "From the Field" for this chapter is written by a school board member of a large urban school district charged with overseeing the law's implementation. She addresses the challenges the law presents her district and shares recommendations to protect the original intent of the law.

Chapter Two provides a historical timeline of events and the significant role of families in the education of children with disabilities. It focuses on what we believe is the foundation of special education today: the families of children and youth with disabilities. Throughout the chapter, the authors describe parents as partners rather than adversaries in the education of students with disabilities. They include suggestions regarding how to maximize positive collaborative relationships between schools and families. "From the Field" is written by a parent of a child with autism who describes her journey navigating the often complex system of doctors and service providers to obtain adequate supports for her son while advocating for other parents in the process.

Chapter Three focuses on the development of successful inclusive practices involving students with disabilities in general education programs. The authors, both university faculty, review the history of inclusive policy and practices, discuss current research on inclusive education, and describe possible models of inclusion for elementary, middle, and high school settings. "From the Field," written by a director of special education services for a consortium of school districts, reflects on the topic of inclusion given his previous experiences as a special education teacher and long-time professional in the field.

Chapter Four examines the topics of inclusion and the importance of families more formally than in the previous two chapters, now through the eyes of a filmmaker and his documentary on the inclusion of students with disabilities in the Los Angeles Unified School District. The filmmaker answers a series of questions posed by the first author of this book where he discusses his efforts to capture firsthand accounts from teachers, parents, administrators, and students describing their experiences within special education. "From the Field" is written by a parent advocate portrayed in the film who is the parent of a child with multiple disabilities. She focuses on her son's progress since his inclusion within the district's general education program.

Chapter Five addresses one of the most troubling yet persistent issues in the field of education that continues to perplex educators: the overidentification of students of color in certain disability categories and their underrepresentation in programs for the gifted and talented. This chapter, written by researchers in this area, situates the occurrence of overrepresentation within a historical context, reviews possible explanations for its continued existence, and proposes various approaches (including culturally responsive instruction and response to intervention) to systematically address this issue. A director of psychological services from a large urban school district describes her perspective of this issue in "From the Field." She shares her understanding of overrepresentation based on her experiences and interaction with educational professionals and families in her district. She specifically responds to two approaches suggested by the chapter's authors to address this complex issue.

Chapter Six reviews the increased emphasis of early intervention and support for students considered at risk for special education identification over the past three decades. The primary author, a well-known researcher in early reading instruction, discusses the new emphasis on scientifically based research approaches to early intervention and response to intervention as a method of avoiding later special education identification.

"From the Field" is written by a school principal of a small urban school district with a large percentage of English learners and students from predominantly low-income backgrounds. She describes her school's initial efforts at implementing a response-to-intervention model calling attention to the realities many schools face when carrying out educational initiatives.

Chapter Seven reviews the development and practice of differentiated instruction as a method of addressing the academic needs of all learners, including students with disabilities, in general education classrooms. The chapter's four authors, experienced teacher-educators and researchers, discuss this student-centered pedagogical approach that promotes positive experiences and outcomes for all learners within inclusive environments. Through a case example, the authors explore two useful applications of differentiated instruction within an elementary and high school setting. "From the Field," written by a high school teacher, examines the benefits and challenges to successful implementation of differentiated instruction by general education classroom teachers.

Chapter Eight discusses an often overlooked yet critical area in the education of students with disabilities: transition from school to adult life centers on a systematic planning process involving the participation of families, teachers, educational professionals, significant peers, and the students themselves. This chapter, written by a university administrator and researcher in the area of transition, reviews the historical development of transition planning for students with disabilities and their families, current issues, and challenges related to transition. "From the Field" is written by a young advocate with a physical disability who describes her personal experience with transition from the world of education to the world of work and independence. She provides useful recommendations regarding this issue in order to better prepare youth with disabilities for the realities they will face as young adults.

Chapter Nine conludes the book by providing the personal accounts of three individuals with disabilities who experienced the law and its initial implementation in the schools. We felt it fitting to end with their statements describing how they navigated the system of general and special education at a time when mandated special education programs were in their infancy. Their contributions highlight issues addressed throughout the book related to understanding special education law, the importance of family, the inclusion of students with disabilities in general education programs, early intervention and identification of individuals with disabilities, and preparing students for competitive and fulfilling postsecondary experiences. The first author is a disability-rights advocate and college student with autism, who emphasizes the importance of recognizing the strengths and aspirations of students with disabilities and their families. The second author, an attorney, motivational speaker, and civil rights activist for the blind, describes his initial struggles interacting with nondisabled peers while calling attention to the need for the integration of students with special needs in general education programs and providing all students with instruction regarding the normalcy of disability. The third author, an educational rights attorney with a learning disability, brings attention to the importance of providing early supports for students who struggle with mainstream instructional practices and standardized curriculum. "From the Field" is written by an English teacher and codirector of a small learning community. Her reflection is based on how each statement exemplifies her school's educational philosophy of academics, leadership, and community.

The book's appendix includes questions for university faculty, district administrators, and educational trainers to discuss with students or group participants in order to promote dialogue on the issues raised in this book. These questions may also serve as prompts for student projects and written reflections related to the education of children and youth with disabilities. The questions address content from each chapter, including information presented within the "From the Field" essays. Discussion leaders may choose to select chapter questions based on the experience and knowledge-base of their individual students or participants.

# 1

# THE PROMISE AND PRACTICE OF THE INDIVIDUALS WITH DISABILITIES EDUCATION ACT

## Nancy E. Huerta

Disability is a natural part of the human experience and in no way diminishes the right of individuals to participate in or contribute to society. Improving the educational results for children with disabilities is an essential element of our national policy of ensuring equality of opportunity, full participation, independent living, and economic self-sufficiency for individuals with disabilities [Individuals with Disabilities Education Act, 20 U.S.C. Sec. 1400(c)(1)].

With these words, the U.S. Congress clearly mandates that education is the means for a person with a disability to participate and function as a self-sufficient member of society in the same manner as a person without a disability. As such, these words are the rightful introduction to the Individuals with Disabilities Education Improvement Act of 2004 (IDEA), the foremost piece of legislation on the rights and benefits of students with disabilities. These words also reflect how much national policy has changed over the past three decades regarding the treatment of children with disabilities.

This chapter traces the evolution of the philosophy of education for all in the context of special education law in several ways. First, these words will be placed in a historical context by reviewing previous incarnations of educational legislation. Then, using the Six Principles of IDEA developed by H. Rutherford Turnbull, cofounder and codirector of the Beach Center on Disability at the University of Kansas, the chapter explores how significant changes found in the new IDEA will affect the concept of education for all as we move forward.

## The History of IDEA

Before analyzing the impact of IDEA's newest reauthorization, we should reflect on how far special education law has come. As recently as the 1960s, national policy did not even address the fact that children with disabilities were routinely denied access to public schools. The reason was the belief that these children were uneducable and certainly not expected to lead independent, productive lives. As a result, many were hidden away in hospitals and institutions. As the 1960s moved on, however, political and social discourse became filled with words such as *discrimination, civil rights, equality*, and *segregation*, and soon disability rights activists began using those words to advocate for children with disabilities.

These activists also had the benefit of using one of the most important cases dealing with race and education: *Brown v. Board of Education of Topeka* (1954). Before *Brown*, local and state education agencies legally segregated students by race so the issue before the U.S. Supreme Court was whether this was constitutional. The Court analyzed the effect segregation had on the public education system and concluded that separating students on the basis of race generated feelings of inferiority and stigmatized those students far beyond the schoolyard. Thus, the Court held that segregation policies violated the separate-but-equal clause of the Fourteenth Amendment and altered the composition of school populations forever.

The application to children with disabilities is clear: if separate but equal is not allowed with regard to race, neither should it be allowed to segregate students with disabilities from participating in public school settings. Nor should individuals with disabilities continue to be warehoused in institutions without an opportunity to participate in society. What logically followed, then, were a large number of individuals being returned to local communities and local school districts. To help serve this population, Congress enacted the first generation of education laws relating to students with disabilities.

The first law was the Elementary and Secondary Education Act of 1965 (ESEA), which addressed the first concern: funding for these programs. ESEA established the first federal grants to the states to assist them in educating children with disabilities. Once the mechanics were in place by 1974, Congress was able to move beyond money to frame the beginnings of education policy with the goal of "full education opportunities for all children with disabilities."

In 1975, Congress went a step further and enacted the Education for All Handicapped Children Act (EAHCA). Known as the law that established the doctrine of free appropriate public education (FAPE), the EAHCA also set forth policy statements that were both simple and profound: to ensure students access to FAPE, protect parent and student rights, support state and local education agencies, and put in place a means for assessing the effectiveness of the state and local efforts.

The EAHCA was reauthorized every five years, so substantial changes were made to the law between 1978 and 1986. These reauthorizations expanded incentives for preschool special education, early intervention, and transition programs (1978); authorized the recovery of attorneys' fees by parents after a due process hearing (1983); and authorized infant and toddler provisions (Part C) (1986). In 1990, the EAHCA became the IDEA and formalized the concept we continue to work with today: children with disabilities were entitled to a free, appropriate public education with special education and related services designed to meet their unique needs.

All of these changes came with controversy, criticisms, and case law. IDEA 1997 responded to the intense debate surrounding discipline, parent participation, and appropriate programming by putting in place many of IDEA's procedures and compliance checklists. From a policy standpoint, Congress looked back to the four purposes of the EAHCA and confirmed that although there were successes in implementing IDEA at both the state and federal levels, special education still maintained low expectations for children with disabilities. There also was insufficient focus on research and methods of teaching special education students. Congress also acknowledged another serious problem: the overrepresentation of minority students in special education. Minority students were being placed into special education not because of a disability but because of inadequate instruction or limited English proficiency.

The solutions to these barriers are both student and parent focused and system focused. On the student side, Congress specifies that high expectations should be set for special education students. These students should have access to the general curriculum to the maximum extent possible with appropriate related services and supports. There also should be an increase in early intervention programs and whole school approaches to reduce the inappropriate labeling of students.

Parents are empowered through strengthened roles in the special education process. For the first time, parents and students were named as members of the individualized education program (IEP) team. The IEP team is responsible not just for evaluations but also for all programming and placement decisions, so team membership recognizes parents' unique perspectives, concerns, and right to participate in their child's education. IDEA 1997 also significantly expanded the rights of parents by providing for reimbursement of attorneys' fees if parents prevail in a due process hearing. This is an important issue for parents, since proceeding to due process is both costly and time-consuming. Without the right to seek reimbursement, many parents would be deprived from having legal counsel.

Systemically Congress encouraged high-quality, intensive professional development for all school personnel as well as a reduction of procedures that do not add to educational results.

More than any other prior reauthorization, IDEA 1997 spoke directly to the concept that "*all* means *all*" and that children with disabilities needed to be protected by established policies and procedures. This is best demonstrated in IDEA 1997's new discipline provisions. First, and most significant, IDEA 1997 states that a student with a disability cannot be expelled for more than ten days if the behavior was causally related to or a manifestation of the student's disability. Instead IDEA requires that a manifestation determination team consider three factors: whether the IEP services were appropriate and implemented, whether the disability prevented the student from understanding the impact and consequences of the behavior, and if the disability impaired the student's ability to control the behavior. If the answer to these is yes, the behavior is a manifestation of the disability and the child cannot be expelled. If the answer is no, the school can suspend the student for an extended period of time. If parents disagree with the manifestation determination, they can appeal the decision and the student is allowed to stay in the current placement until the dispute is resolved. A school can suspend a student with a disability for up to ten days, however, without triggering any such review. This is significant because it prevents schools from making unilateral placements and ensures that students receive interventions for behaviors resulting from their disability rather than being penalized for them. The concept of "all means all" can also be applied to the revised evaluation process. Evaluations were expanded to take into account the student's strengths and needs in all areas: cognitive, behavioral, physical, and developmental. This comprehensive approach helps to ensure that the IEP team collects sufficient information to identify all areas of need so an appropriate program can be developed.

## 2004 Reauthorization of IDEA

This brings us to the present: the 2004 reauthorization of IDEA and what topics and concerns are reflected in this latest incarnation of the law. Between 1997 and 2004, the debates about discipline and the measurements of success for children with disabilities continued. Districts argued that the discipline provisions of IDEA 1997 essentially gave special education students the means to avoid any type of "appropriate," behavioral consequences. They also argued that these provisions directly contradicted school policies designed to provide order and safety for all students.

There also were new laws and publications to consider, such as the No Child Left Behind Act of 2001 (NCLB), *Rethinking Special Education for a New Century* (Finn, Rotherham, & Hokanson, 2001), and the presidential commission report on improving special education (President's Commission on Excellence in Special Education, 2002). Both publications concluded that general and special education were ineffective in serving students with disabilities.

The President's Commission outlined numerous concerns about IDEA 1997, including how

- IDEA values process over outcomes and must be reformed to advance student achievement, reduce excessive paperwork, and ensure better outcomes for students with disabilities.
- Waiting for children to fail before starting any kind of intervention ignores the possibility that strong intervention based on research-based approaches could prevent many students from being categorized as special education.
- General and special education share the responsibility for educating children with disabilities. Just because a child is identified as special education does not waive the responsibility of general education.

- Parents do not feel empowered by the special education system, and in many situations, they have little or no recourse if their child fails to make progress.
- Extensive litigation has created a culture of compliance that diverts needed resources from actual programming.
- Students are misidentified because of outdated and invalid testing.
- Teachers are inadequately prepared to identify students' needs early and accurately.
- Research on special education is inadequate, and schools do not sufficiently apply evidence-based practices.
- The cultures of compliance and bureaucracy fail too many children and must be replaced by an emphasis on academic achievement, transition, and postsecondary outcomes (Turnbull, Stowe, & Huerta, 2007).

According to Finn, Rotherman, and Hokanson (2001), special education was also teaching students with disabilities that they were unable to participate in mainstream American life. Thus, they were entitled to be treated differently from other students (such as by having special discipline protections) and could expect a lifetime of support from the state and federal governments. Given this background, some of IDEA 2004's new provisions are not surprising.

In IDEA 2004 Congress affirms that U.S. national policy ensures equal opportunities, full participation, independent living, and economic self-sufficiency for children with disabilities. IDEA and special education are the avenues for ensuring this access. Congress acknowledged that students with access to FAPE and special education had demonstrated some progress and tangible results. However, low expectations and the lack of scientifically based research continue to impede these goals.

Accordingly, Congress provides eight solutions, some of which are repeats of solutions offered under IDEA 1997.

The first solution of having high expectations for special education students clearly responds to the continuing complaint that educators do not have high expectations for children with special education needs. High expectations, increased access to the general curriculum, and proper assessments to measure progress in that curriculum are essential components of preparing students to be independent and self-sufficient. The second solution attempts to address continuing parental concerns that despite the focus of IDEA 1997 to include them in the process, many parents still feel like marginalized participants. The third and fourth solutions emphasize that, along with higher expectations, special education should be an option only after all general education options have been exhausted. This means that any modifications available under special education, such as related services and supports, should be provided in the general education classroom. The fifth solution incorporates the concepts of highly qualified teachers and challenges schools to increase their capacity to serve children with disabilities. The sixth solution addresses the concerns discussed in IDEA 1997 about the overrepresentation of certain populations in special education. By providing incentives to schools to develop scientifically based early reading programs, positive behavioral supports, and early intervention services, Congress is hoping to reduce labeling students as disabled in order to provide services. The seventh solution addresses, once again, the idea of redirecting resources from paperwork and compliance documentation to teaching and learning. This appears to be a rather benign goal, but in practice, there are certain provisions designed to reduce paperwork such as allowing amendments to the IEP, which can have substantial effects on meeting participation, consent, and other principles under IDEA. Finally, Congress acknowledges that assistive technology devices and services are essential tools for maximizing accessibility for children with disabilities. These solutions clearly align IDEA with NCLB and NCLB's principles of accountability, highly qualified teachers, scientifically based interventions, local flexibility, safe schools, and parent participation and choice (Turnbull, Huerta, & Stowe, 2006).

But how do these solutions link with the overarching purposes of IDEA 2004? In order to implement the proposed solutions, Congress also declared six purposes, only half of which deal directly with children with disabilities and their parents. The first purpose reflects the four national goals of opportunity, full participation, independent living, and economic self-sufficiency by linking independent living with education. The second confirms that IDEA remains in place to protect the rights of children with disabilities and their parents. The fourth addresses the concern that early intervention services could help prevent the over-identification of children into special education, especially those who are linguistically and culturally diverse. But the rest deal with increasing the capacity development of educational agencies through research, technical assistance, and staff development to improve the overall delivery system of special education. This language addresses the concern that special education as a whole needs to be evaluated outside the specific language of IDEA to gauge results from the new changes. IDEA 2004 remains the template for ensuring that as we move forward, education for all—special education and general education—is raised to a higher standard.

## The Six Principles of IDEA

To truly evaluate the impact that IDEA has on the concept of education for all, IDEA needs to be broken into themes. In 1977, H. Rutherford Turnbull divided IDEA into six principles that together form a framework for analyzing IDEA: zero reject, nondiscriminatory evaluation, appropriate education, least restrictive environment, procedural due process, and parent participation (Turnbull, Stowe, & Huerta, 2007). The first four principles trace the steps that school districts must follow in order to provide a free and appropriate public education. The fifth outlines the procedures that parents and students can use to enforce the first four principles. Finally, the sixth principle summarizes all of the areas where parents participate in the special education process and become partners with the schools.

## Principle One: Zero Reject

Zero reject is at the heart of ensuring education for all children with disabilities and covers topics such as child find, private school services, and placement and discipline. *Zero reject* stands for the proposition that students with disabilities cannot be excluded, physically or functionally, from public education. In a phrase, "All means all." Thus, schools are responsible for enrolling and educating all children with disabilities regardless of the type or severity of their disabilities. This was not always the case.

Previously children with disabilities were segregated from nondisabled peers in school and in the community. Even if these children were allowed onto school grounds, many were prevented from having any meaningful access to the educational program. Thus, courts recognized that programs needed to be put into place to ensure children with disabilities the equal protection of the law (*Mills* v. *District of Columbia Board of Education*, 1972; *Pennsylvania Association for Retarded Children* v. *Commonwealth of Pennsylvania*, 1971). Congress agreed and adopted a zero reject policy by stating that IDEA is meant to ensure that all students with disabilities, from ages three to twenty-one, have a right to a free and appropriate public education (FAPE).

IDEA initially grants students access to school by requiring each school district to find, identify, and locate all children with disabilities in the district. These children include homeless children, wards of the state (in state foster care), and children attending private school. The 2006 regulations expand this list by adding children suspected of having a disability despite the fact they are progressing from grade to grade and highly mobile children with disabilities, including those of migrant workers.

Generally known as *child find*, this program establishes the method for determining if these children are currently receiving the special education and related services that they need. The significance of this provision is its comprehensiveness; by adding homeless, migrant, and foster children, IDEA acknowledges the problems of poverty and the changing social structure of today's families. These provisions help to ensure that children with limited English proficiency and other minority students do not fall through the cracks.

Similarly, the zero reject principle supports educational services for all children with disabilities without regard for educational setting. IDEA extends its coverage to public elementary and secondary schools, publicly operated residential facilities that provide education, students placed in charter schools, and students who are incarcerated.

Several significant provisions under IDEA 2004 also clarify that child find extends to children placed in private parochial schools and nonparochial private schools. As a result, special education and related services may be provided on the premises of religious schools with two exceptions: services cannot exceed constitutional limits, and they must be secular and nonideological. The inclusion of private parochial schools is significant because it allows parents of disabled children the option of supplementing a secular education with religious values without depriving their child of services.

This comprehensive coverage does not mean that IDEA extends all of its funds, rights, and benefits to students in private schools. In fact, the school district is required only to provide a proportionate amount of its Part B funds. So while parents can choose to place their children in private schools for various reasons, including religious ones, in reality they are forgoing that child's right to receive all of the specific special education and related services that the child would receive if he or she attended the public school. In addition, from a benefits and rights perspective, although IDEA requires the ESEA and local districts to offer students in private school an opportunity for an appropriate education at public expense, it does not require that education to be provided in the private school setting. If a free and appropriate public education is offered at the district level for these students and the choice is made for that student to attend the private school, the school district has met its obligation under IDEA.

Somewhere underneath the idea of education for all, though, is the division between IDEA as a concept and how IDEA works in practice. As a concept, children with disabilities are being physically included in school to learn through an appropriate education program. In practice, the concept of education for all does not ensure adequate programming or that parents and schools will agree as to whether a program is appropriate. That has led to one of the most litigated topic areas under IDEA: tuition reimbursement for private placements.

If parents believe that their district is not offering an appropriate education program, they can enroll their child in a private school or facility and seek tuition reimbursement from the district, usually through a due process hearing. A school district has to reimburse parents for tuition at a private placement if two factors are present: (1) the district did not provide an appropriate education program and (2) the private school was able to provide an appropriate education (*School Committee of the Town of Burlington* v. *Department of Education of Massachusetts*, 1985). This reimbursement can be reduced or denied. First, reimbursement can be reduced or denied if parents do not inform the IEP team that they are rejecting the proposed placement in order to enroll their child in a private school at public expense. This can be done at the last meeting, or parents can give notice ten business days before removing their child from public school. A hearing officer can also determine that tuition reimbursement can be reduced "upon judicial finding of unreasonableness with respect to actions taken by the parents" (20 U.S.C. Sec. 1412(a)(10)(c)).

The reason for these limitations is fairness. Before a district should have to pay for a private placement, it should have an opportunity to cure the deficiency by reviewing and adjusting the student's program. This can happen only if parents are required to give the district notice in advance. Fairness also works the other way: if the district prevents parents from providing the appropriate notice, if the parents were not informed that they even had to give notice, or if compliance with the notice requirement would "likely result in physical harm" to the child, reimbursement would not be reduced (20 U.S.C. Sec. 1412(a)(10)(c)(iv)). IDEA also recognizes that there are times when districts contract with private schools to educate some students. These students are beneficiaries of a contract between the private school and the district. All of the student's IEP rights follow him or her to the private placement. The district is still responsible for ensuring that the private school complies, at no cost to the parents, with all of the requirements of a free and appropriate education, such as providing special education and related services and following the IEP.

By providing provisions for parent placement in private schools and district placements in private schools, Congress was intending that the principle of zero reject apply to students in both situations. Either way, the state or the local district remains responsible for the education of these students, which reinforces that students with disabilities will continue to be educated.

Aside from physical locations of particular students, IDEA 2004 also clarifies that students cannot be excluded from programming on the basis of medication. Previously many educators were suggesting to parents that their child be put on medication or were making medications a condition of the child's attending school. Medication can no longer be a condition of school enrollment.

IDEA 2004 also preserves the discipline procedures of IDEA 1997, which established that students with disabilities have a right to a free and appropriate public education even if they have been suspended or expelled from school. The baseline rule is that districts can discipline students with disabilities in the same manner as students without disabilities. However, IDEA provides important protections for special education students: services cannot be discontinued while a student is being disciplined, districts must address reoccurring or serious behavior, and a student cannot be punished for behaviors that result as a manifestation of a student's disability. IDEA categorizes behavior in several ways: violations of student rules of conduct; violations that involve weapons, drugs, or serious bodily injury; behaviors that result in removals of fewer than ten days (short term); and behaviors that result in removals of more than ten days (long term). This comprehensive approach leaves little to a district's discretion, which helps to ensure that children with disabilities continue to be protected.

In practice, discipline is one of the most complex procedural areas, and there remain many gray areas. One area of potential abuse is when a district regularly suspends a student for fewer than ten days at a time. The 2006 regulations state that a change of placement occurs if the student has been subjected to a series of removals that constitute a pattern. However, increased discretion has been given to the district to determine on a case-by-case basis whether a pattern of removals constitutes a change of placement. If a parent disagrees, this determination is subject to review through due process and judicial proceedings, but the new standard will make establishing a pattern much more difficult.

One reason that districts prefer not to have removals total more than ten days is that those removals are considered long-term removals and a disciplinary change of placement. During a long-term removal, the district must provide services and, when appropriate, a functional behavior assessment and behavioral intervention services and modifications. A long-term removal may also trigger the manifestation determination exception.

The manifestation determination process is one of the strongest safeguards in place for children with disabilities under IDEA to ensure that "all means all." If the behavior is a manifestation of the student's disability, that student cannot be disciplined in the same manner as a student without the disability. To do so would essentially punish that student for having the disability, a clear violation of the zero reject principle. To be a manifestation, the team must determine if the behavior was caused by the student's disability, had a direct and substantial relationship to the student's disability, or was the direct result of the district's failure to implement the IEP. This language is substantially different from IDEA 1997, which focused on whether the student's ability to understand consequences of the behavior or control the behavior was impaired by the disability. Now, the language is narrower and requires a direct causal relationship for both the student and the district. Clearly this came about in response to the arguments that students with disabilities were avoiding discipline and thus accountability for their actions. Whether these stricter standards resolve this issue remains to be seen, but one of the strongest protections for students with disabilities has been weakened.

A second change affecting the idea of education for all is that the stay-put rule no longer has any real application with regard to discipline. Parents still have the right to appeal a manifestation determination or any decision regarding a disciplinary placement. However, during this appeal, the disciplinary placement ordered by the district is considered to be the stay-put placement during the hearing officer's review. In many cases, then, the student with the disability is removed from his or her current placement and will face the consequences of the transition and different setting even if it is later determined that the disability was the cause of the behavior.

A third change that potentially can result in the exclusion of students with disabilities for an extended period of time is the change from "calendar day" to "school day" for incidents involving weapons, drugs, or serious bodily injury (a new category). Currently, a district can remove a student for up to forty-five days to an "interim, alternative educational setting" (20 U.S.C.

Sec. 1415(k)(1)(G)). Changing the calculation to "school day" instead of "calendar day" effectively means that a student is out of school for nine weeks, almost a complete semester.

Zero reject is the principle at the heart of the concept of education for all. IDEA 2004 still supports the concept that students with disabilities are entitled to be found and educated through child find, appropriate programming, private school services, and placement. However, the new discipline provisions will be an area to watch as changed criteria, the loss of stay-put, and different timelines can result in special education students' spending more time outside their education programs.

## Principle Two: Nondiscriminatory Evaluation

Once a child is found under the principle of zero reject, the next step is for the district to determine whether the student has a disability and, if so, what must be done to develop an appropriate IEP. IDEA defines a child with a disability as a child with mental retardation, hearing impairments (including deafness), speech or language impairments, visual impairments (including blindness), serious emotional disturbance, orthopedic impairment, autism, traumatic brain injury, other health impairments, or specific learning disabilities and who, by reason of the disability, needs special education and related services. A multidisciplinary evaluation is the tool used to make this determination. An appropriate evaluation analyzes the student's existing levels of performance and related developmental needs and determines whether there need to be any additions or modifications to the student's program. An evaluation may not be biased because of race, culture, or language, and the instruments used by the team must be "validated" and "technically sound" (20 U.S.C. Sec. 1414(b)(3)). The team must use more than one instrument when conducting this evaluation and also needs to consider existing data and information from a multitude of sources. When done correctly, an evaluation will yield information on the four domains that affect a student's education: cognitive, behavioral, physical, and developmental.

By making the evaluation's purposes explicit and requiring them to be connected to program and placement, IDEA has added another step to ensure that children with disabilities are given an appropriate education.

The evaluation, then, determines eligibility, and for many parents, this is an area of confusion because having a medical diagnosis of a disability does not guarantee eligibility for special education. These evaluations are meant to determine the student's educational needs, not the family's needs or the student's needs outside his or her educational placement. If the disability does not interfere with the student's ability to learn in the general education setting, that student would not be considered eligible for special education.

The more obvious the disability, then, the easier it is to make that eligibility determination. One disability that is harder to observe or define is "specific learning disability," so IDEA 1997 regulations provided for a quantitative discrepancy standard to facilitate eligibility determinations. IDEA 2004, however, changes this standard by stating that a district is not required to take into account whether the student has a "severe discrepancy between achievement and intellectual ability" (20 U.S.C. Sec. 1313(b)(6)). Furthermore, the district may, but is not required to, use a "process that determines the child responds to scientific, research-based intervention and state-approved grade-level standards" (34 C.F.R. 300.309(a)(2)).

Clearly, IDEA is responding to the concerns of overrepresentation of minority students in special education by narrowly defining the category of specific learning disability. However, narrowing the definition while removing the one quantitative standard to determine eligibility could result in students' being excluded from services. Since a large number of children simply do not perform as well as others but do not have any other obvious disabilities, IDEA is now also requiring that these children receive appropriate, research-based instruction for a period of time before classification. However, during that time, they are not protected under the procedural safeguards of IDEA.

IDEA 2004 also clarifies that a reevaluation may not be done twice in one year unless the parents and the district agree. Districts and parents can also waive the three-year evaluation. This is one of those situations where IDEA is attempting to reduce the paperwork burden, but there could be unintentional effects on a student's education by not encouraging up-to-date evaluation information.

The evaluation process, then, is the second door that a student with a disability must pass through in order to benefit from special education. By requiring tests to be comprehensive and unbiased, IDEA gives educators the tools to educate special education students. As with any other process, however, there are students who have needs but do not fit a criterion exactly. So IDEA does somewhat expect parents and districts to work together to ensure that these students are still served within the spirit of education for all.

## Principle Three: Appropriate Education

After a school district finds and evaluates a student, the next step is to develop an appropriate education program for that student based on the evaluation data. Education for all means not only giving children with disabilities access to school but ensuring that the program confers some benefit.

The first special education decision from the U.S. Supreme Court, *Board of Education* v. *Rowley* (1982), remains the defining, two-pronged standard for what is an "appropriate" education. The first prong is a process standard: an appropriate education can result if all of IDEA's procedures are followed. These include conducting nondiscriminatory evaluations, developing IEPs, providing parents access to records, and convening due process hearings when necessary. The second prong is a benefit standard.

Since Congress did not intend to guarantee any particular level of educational benefit to students with disabilities, the only requirement is a basic level of opportunity. Thus, if the program provides the student with some educational benefit, the program is appropriate.

The mechanics for providing this education program are clear. The IEP is the universe for a student with a disability: if a service or goal is not in the IEP, it is not considered part of the program. Although there is no set format for an IEP from state to state or even district to district, there are basic components common to all. An IEP must contain the student's existing level of academic and functional performance, measurable annual goals, a means for reporting progress, a list of the special education and related services to be provided, a description of any accommodations needed for testing, transition services if applicable, and dates of service. The IEP also must account for why a student is removed from the general curriculum since Congress is clear that high expectations for students with disabilities means the option of being included with nondisabled peers.

Another critical part of the IEP that ensures that students with disabilities have the opportunity to remain in school is the section related to behavior and behavioral considerations. If a student exhibits behaviors that impede his or her learning or the learning of others, the district is obligated to use positive behavioral interventions and supports and other strategies to address that behavior. The hope is that this will help to control and modify negative behaviors, which will open up more inclusion possibilities for students in school and beyond.

The related services component also helps to ensure education for all by providing therapy services as well as nursing services when applicable. Such services even include catheterization and suctioning of a tracheotomy during the school day. Including related services as part of an IEP, then, supports placement in the least restrictive environment and helps to ensure that these children are not excluded on the basis of health or a district's unwillingness to provide these services. Note that IDEA 2004 clarifies that "related services" do not include implanted medical devices such as cochlear implants.

Transition services are also linked to outcomes and confirm that education for students with disabilities requires additional steps. Transition services under IDEA start at age sixteen and are meant to give students with disabilities the means to move from school to postschool activities, including postsecondary education, vocational education, integrated employment (including supported employment), continuing adult education, adult services, independent living, or community participation. IDEA 2004 has added more results-oriented language, which implies that districts will be held more accountable for this segment of its student population.

IDEA 2004 maintains the structure of the IEP team and ensures that parents remain participating members of both the IEP and evaluation teams. New provisions state, however, that an IEP team member is not required to attend all or even part of the IEP meetings if the parents and the district agree the member's presence is not necessary because the member's area of the curriculum or the related services will not be discussed. Furthermore, a team member may be excused from attending all or part of an IEP meeting even when the meeting involves a discussion or modification of the member's area. The parents and the district must consent to the excusal in writing, and the excused team member must submit a written report prior to the meeting. IDEA 2004 also allows parents and districts to agree not to convene an IEP meeting to amend or modify the existing IEP. Instead, they may opt to develop a written addendum.

Again, these new provisions reflect the congressional intent of paperwork reduction and reducing the administrative burdens on districts. However, parents will have to be extremely well informed to either agree or disagree with the excusals or agree to a change in services without convening an IEP team meeting. Since the IEP meeting is one of the few opportunities where the individuals responsible for providing services to that child come together, waiving this meeting could dramatically affect the resulting IEP since it is next to impossible to forecast all areas that might be discussed.

## Principle Four: Least Restrictive Environment

Least restrictive environment is the presumption that students with disabilities will be granted access to and educated in the general education curriculum and will participate in other general education activities. This presumption in favor of inclusion has always been part of IDEA. However, this is a rebuttable presumption. The amount of inclusion for a particular student is determined by each student's individual needs. This is done through the nondiscriminatory evaluation as well as the IEP development process, showing once again how IDEA links evaluation, appropriate education, and least restrictive environment to create a seamless approach for educating students. If inclusion is not appropriate for a student, more restrictive placements will be considered. However, IDEA requires the IEP team to justify any removal from the least restrictive environment during the IEP process. Since education for all started out as a means to end segregation of students with disabilities, the concept of least restrictive environment is the way toward achieving that goal. No one disputes that educating students with special needs is challenging and requires staff and resources. There also is the temptation to consolidate resources and programs. Even more challenging is finding the means to include these students with nondisabled peers. Least restrictive environment does not force inclusion, but it does make the team reflect on the possibility, which certainly can open opportunities for these students.

To briefly review, the first four principles of zero reject, nondiscriminatory evaluation, appropriate education, and least restrictive environment trace the evolution of education for all and how IDEA has opened the door physically and functionally for children with disabilities. The last two principles, procedural due process and parent participation, are the enforcement side of the equation.

## Principle Five: Procedural Due Process

Once rights are conferred, there needs to be a mechanism to enforce them. IDEA provides several means for parents and districts, including mediation, a special education administrative hearing run by a hearing officer known as a due process hearing, and appeals to state or federal court of those decisions. IDEA 2004 continues IDEA's prior protections, including notice, consent, access to records, and parent participation. However, Congress clearly acknowledges that although these safeguards are in place, the substantial increase of litigation since 1997 had an impact on its decision to provide expanded opportunities for parents and districts to resolve their disagreements in positive and constructive ways.

As a result, the thirty days preceding a due process hearing have become a resolution period, when parents and the district have several opportunities to express the problem and propose a solution. These opportunities include mediation and a new resolution session. The expectation is that parents will come prepared to discuss their complaint so the district will have an opportunity to resolve the complaint. Parents can also request mediation during the same time. Some states allow attorneys at both proceedings; others do not. IDEA provides for attorneys to attend resolution sessions only if both sides have counsel. Removing attorneys from the mix could create a less adversarial environment. However, once again, Congress is assuming that parents have access to the same level of information as the district. This is especially relevant when one considers that any agreement reached during these discussions is enforceable as a contract in court.

Ideally, the resolution period could bring parties together in another setting to discuss and resolve their issues prior to proceeding with a lengthy and costly due process. Practically, however, the mere fact that due process has been filed indicates that a breakdown in communication has already happened. Prior IEP meetings and efforts to work with a district have failed. Requiring parents to attend an additional meeting to reiterate their concerns simply gives the opposing party access to information and testimony outside the original complaint. This is critical, especially because anything said at a resolution session can be used later at a due process hearing.

If an agreement is not reached, the parties proceed to due process, which resembles any other court proceeding. The parties have the right to counsel, to examine witnesses, to exchange evidence, to receive written or electronic verbatim record of the hearing, and to receive a written or electronic findings of fact and decisions. The party who makes the complaint has the burden of proof, which means that, for example, if a parent is questioning the appropriateness of an IEP goal, the parent has to present evidence that the goal is not appropriate. Opponents of parents' having the burden of proof (since parents are usually the ones filing) stated that districts have greater access to information and experts and should be in a better position to defend their own program, but the Supreme Court ended the debate by ruling otherwise in 2005 (*Schaffer* v. *Weast*, 2005).

Finally, IDEA 2004 gives districts the new option of seeking to recover legal fees against the parents' attorney, the parents, or both if the complaint is found to be "frivolous, unreasonable, or without foundation" (20 U.S.C. Sec. 1415(i)(3)). Districts can also sue for fees against the parents or the parents' attorney if the complaint was brought to "harass, cause unnecessary delay, or to needlessly increase the cost of litigation" (20 U.S.C. Sec. 1415(i)(3)). Attorneys might recognize that the "frivolous" standard is a high standard to reach and does not mean simply that a parent loses the case, but parents generally do not understand. This translates to parents' being afraid to file for due process on the threat of having to pay the fees for the other side. This might properly deter some cases, but critics are questioning whether it will dampen legitimate litigation as well since parents are financially in much different positions than districts. This means that if a student's rights to an appropriate education are violated, thus negating the principle of education for all, there is a higher chance that the parents or the student will not pursue the issue in court.

## Sixth Principle: Parent Participation

The final principle, parent participation, is meant to encompass areas where parents and districts can become collaborators in making decisions about a student's education. The core of this principle is accountability: accountability for procedures and accountability for decisions. Parents are integral members of the evaluation, IEP, and manifestation determination teams. They have the right to place their children in private schools and seek recourse from the district for tuition if the district did not provide an appropriate placement. Under IDEA 2004, parents can waive the three-year evaluation and excuse IEP team members from attending meetings. Parents and the district can even make changes to an existing IEP without convening an IEP team meeting. Instead, they can develop an addendum to modify the IEP. These options place increased responsibility on parents and holds them accountable for their action, or inaction, with respect to their child's education.

These consequences are best seen in the seemingly benign procedure of consent. A district must obtain consent from a student's parents to conduct the initial and all subsequent evaluations. If a parent does not provide consent, the district can pursue mediation or due process to secure that evaluation. Thus, there remains the possibility that the district could still advocate for that child. However, if a parent does not consent to services after an evaluation, the district is not responsible for providing any special education or related services and cannot pursue due process to compensate for the lack of consent. Under those circumstances, the district is absolved from any obligations to provide a free and appropriate public education or develop an IEP for that student.

As a result, the implication under IDEA 2004 is that along with parent rights comes parent responsibility and accountability.

IDEA provides the opportunity for education for all, but parents must inform themselves about IDEA and its provisions in order to be knowledgeable advocates for their children. Parents who do not have a firm grasp of the law and the rights and responsibilities available under IDEA could mistakenly lose those same rights for themselves and their child.

## Final Thoughts

Taken as a whole, the evolution of special education cases and IDEA has made possible substantial progress toward the clear policy goal of educating these children so they can become independent, self-sufficient members of society. The philosophy of education for all is the heart of IDEA—whether one looks at access, evaluation, appropriate programming, least restrictive environment, procedural safeguards, or parent rights. IDEA 2004 raises the bar for parents with regard to what knowledge they need to make informed decisions, consent, and advocate for their child's rights. IDEA raises the bar for districts by requiring the use of scientifically based and research-validated interventions and the presence of highly qualified teachers to use these techniques. Most important, IDEA raises the expectations for special education students. Now that children with disabilities are in the classroom, the focus has to be on adequate programming.

IDEA 2004 continues to present many challenges and questions. Will the Rowley standard of "some educational benefit" be reconciled with the higher standards of the No Child Left Behind Act? Will the new resolution period prior to a due process hearing encourage issues to be settled before a hearing actually begins? Will the new emphasis on early intervention for children with learning disabilites and other developmental delays, especially for minority students, prior to eligibility result in these children incorrectly being left out of special education? Will the added responsibilites for parents, such as consent, result in parents inadvertently waiving their children's rights? Will the new discipline provisions increase suspensions and open the door for removing these children via the juvenile justice system?

IDEA has always been a source of dynamic change, and its new provisions will be used to both answer these questions and create more. But as long as questions such as these are asked, the legislature, the parents, the districts, and the practitioners will continue to make their mark on education to come.

## FROM THE FIELD: REFLECTING ON THE REALITIES OF IMPLEMENTING SPECIAL EDUCATION LAW

### Marlene Canter

I began my career in education as a special education teacher at Alta Loma Elementary School in Los Angeles, California, in the early 1970s. I spent the next eight years teaching at several schools throughout California working, often without an aide, with mostly elementary and middle school students. By requiring educators to better integrate children with special needs into our schools, Public Law 94–142 (adopted in 1975 and now called the Individuals with Disabilities Education Act, IDEA) codified many of the insights I learned early in my career. Indeed the individualized education program (IEP), which helped bridge communication gaps with all those involved in educating and caring for the student, was one of the seminal developments of the legislation. Most important, the IEP brought parents onto the team, helping them to understand their child's unique needs and empowering them to reinforce at home the work being done in school.

I have spent most of my adult life in education—first as a teacher, then as cofounder and co-CEO of a teacher training company, and now as a school board member for the Los Angeles Unified School District (LAUSD), the second largest school district in the nation. While I am now away from the classroom, I remain intimately involved in decisions important to classroom practices. As a policymaker required to deliver on the promises of IDEA, I use my firsthand experience in the classroom, my work with families, and expertise in supporting beginning and veteran teachers.

LAUSD has almost nine hundred K-12 schools and over 700,000 students. In the past thirty years, we have seen the number of students identified for special education services increase from 10,000 to over 80,000. The evolution of IDEA and the growing population of students with disabilities have created many challenges for LAUSD, especially since the district receives only a portion of the funding needed from the federal government. The role of a school in a child's life has also evolved over the past thirty years. More so now than ever before, schools are expected to provide services beyond instruction, including health screenings, assistive technology, community-based instruction, and psychological and counseling services. Nancy Huerta discusses in detail how Congress addressed some of these challenges when it reauthorized IDEA in 2004. Here I have chosen to focus on a few essential points that Huerta makes in her review related to professional development, due process procedures, maintaining high expectations, and the least restrictive environment (LRE).

## Professional Development

The 2004 reauthorization of IDEA prioritizes "supporting high-quality, intensive pre-service preparation and professional development for all personnel who work with children with disabilities" (20 U.S.C. sec. 1400(c)(5)(E)). Most veteran general education teachers in classrooms today received their training at a time when services for students with disabilities occurred in separate settings and instruction for these students was provided exclusively by trained specialists. Today general and special educators must navigate in a world where more students with disabilities are fully integrated in general education classrooms and schools increasingly favor collaboration, consultation, and coteaching models of instruction. Teachers, who often lack sufficient training, must learn to work effectively within these models, diversifying their skills as their roles and students' needs change.

Without question, school districts and school sites must continue to provide sufficient professional development and ongoing support to assist general educators in differentiating their instruction for struggling learners and those with identified disabilities. Districts must also depend on local institutions of higher education to provide adequate preservice and in-service training to the teaching force. When new teachers and teachers in training come to LAUSD, we find that many of them lack several essential skills. First, inexperienced teachers often over-refer students for special education evaluation simply because they appear disruptive in the classroom leading to an over-identification of students. Often these teachers do not have the skills to create the necessary structure, meaningful environment, and high expectations that students need in order to focus their energies on learning rather than participate in inappropriate behaviors. University training programs and districts must provide these teachers with assistance and training in how to appropriately manage a classroom. This was particularly important for me to learn during my first years in the classroom. It is essential that teachers have the skills needed to differentiate true learning needs from possible differences in culture, language, learning style, or a mismatch with the instructional environment, as well as appropriately manage their classrooms.

Second, classroom teachers need to know how to differentiate their instruction for students from diverse backgrounds. They have to be taught early in their career how to teach to the auditory, kinesthetic, and visual strengths of their students while integrating relevant familial, linguistic, and cultural experiences. Too often teachers' methods and style of instruction are driven by a teacher's personal style and past educational experiences rather than the unique needs of the children in the classroom. When teachers fail to differentiate their instruction to meet individual learning needs, they risk missing whole groups of students who may or may not have additional learning issues. The situation worsens as these students progress through the grades without proper support. University and district training must be sensitive to these issues.

Finally, the process of improving service delivery for students with disabilities requires additional training for teachers by local universities, districts, and teacher organizations. Educational professionals must recognize their strengths and share those with colleagues while acknowledging their weaknesses and pursue opportunities to address those weaknesses. In order to become better teachers, they must recognize the obstacles and inadequacies that may exist at their sites, reflect on their practices, seek additional learning opportunities, and work to become true change agents toward a more just educational system for all learners.

## Due Process Procedures

The law affords parents of children with disabilities particular rights and protections. When they perceive that those rights have been violated, we increasingly find ourselves in unfortunate and costly legal battles with parents and advocates, creating ongoing adversarial relationships between schools and families. In 2000, the LAUSD spent $880,000 in legal fees related to serving our special education population of just over eighty-three thousand students. In 2006 our legal fees grew to $3 million, more than a 300 percent increase, while our special education population remained unchanged. Most would agree these monies would be better spent directly

funding school programs for students with and without disabilities. The increase in litigation is symptomatic of a general
disconnect between parents' expectations and school implementation. Schools and parents must work together to
identify concerns at the earliest stage, not when an ongoing
lack of appropriate service delivery later requires more intensive and costly remediation. Furthermore, school districts
across the nation must continue to advocate for adequate
funding from the federal government to support the general
implementation of special education programs.

Ultimately it would be preferable to avoid litigation.
Huerta discusses the implementation of a new resolution
period written into IDEA 2004 when disagreements arise,
giving all parties the opportunity to discuss the issues and
propose solutions. Including such a mechanism within due
process procedures is an excellent suggestion. However, this
must be done in the spirit of resolution without the involvement of legal representation of either the district or the parents.
These discussions should keep the needs of the child at the
forefront and may require some level of compromise by both
districts and families alike.

Desperately missing from current IEP meetings are the
knowledge and practice of those skills necessary for educational professionals and families to work through disagreements. To my knowledge, teaching institutions and districts
do not provide adequate training to educational professionals in skills such as problem solving, negotiating, and active
listening, while respecting individual differences. Educational
professionals must understand the journey and responsibility
involved when a parent has a child with a disability. Teachers and administrators must demonstrate genuine empathy and
compassion for these families and the twenty-four-hour-a-day
care they provide. We must understand that parents, often
consumed by the emotional burden of navigating a frequently
confusing labyrinth of services and service providers, are

unable to articulate their questions and concerns. So too must families understand that educational professionals ultimately do care for their children and appreciate their vision for their child's future. In many instances, schools and families interact within a culture of mistrust and intimidation. This paradigm must change to one where partnerships are established and mutual respect exercised.

## Maintaining High Expectations and a Least Restrictive Environment

Prior to the reauthorization of IDEA 2004, Congress acknowledged the low expectations of many special education programs for students with disabilities and a lack of scientifically based instructional practices for these students. No one will argue the need to maintain high expectations and instructional standards for all students. However, I believe that when programs are coupled with the implementation of other legislative mandates, like No Child Left Behind, there can be some unintended consequences from these expectations. Some teachers and administrators may erroneously equate rigor with exclusive exposure to grade-level standards and curriculum at the expense of addressing individual student needs. Special education law is clear, as Huerta indicated, that access to general education and grade-level curriculum for students with disabilities is essential. The law is also clear that students' individualized education program must meet their unique learning needs.

The law also demonstrates high expectations for students with disabilities through its "presumption that students with disabilities be granted access to, and educated in, the general education curriculum when appropriate," according to Huerta. For some students, a general education program with support is the most appropriate placement; for other students, the least restrictive environment may constitute a separate classroom for a portion of their day. The law supports a continuum of placements if the multidisciplinary team determines that the general education classroom is inappropriate for a given student. In those instances, IEP teams should consider alternative placements.

Maintaining high expectations and providing more inclusive experiences will require that teachers have the time, support, skills, and resources to provide students with the instruction designed to satisfy these requirements under the law. Districts and institutions of higher education must assist beginning special and general educators to work, teach, and plan together. Specialists and general educators need access to necessary materials to teach essential academic skills while maintaining access to grade-level standards and the interests of the students they teach. The successful implementation of balanced special education programs and inclusive experiences for students with disabilities will depend on the leadership and expertise of school site administrators to create the necessary environment, advocate for teachers and staff, and truly understand and respect special education law. It will also require policymakers to recognize what is needed to deliver these services under the law.

## Final Thoughts

The reauthorization process is necessary to continually refine the law to address these issues and other challenges, including providing adequate early intervention for all learners, using response to intervention as a method of disability identification, conducting nondiscriminatory evaluation, reducing the overidentification of minorities in special education programs, and increasing parent participation. Parents, educational professionals, policymakers, and advocates must be committed to improving the law and creating a culture where the focus remains always on the individual needs of the child.

As Huerta highlighted, "Disability is a natural part of the human experience and in no way diminishes the right of individuals to participate in or contribute to society" (IDEA, 20 U.S.C. 1400(c)(1)). School districts, communities, parents, advocates, and lawyers must embed this truth in all that we do. We should ask ourselves, "To what end do my efforts and actions support IDEA and ultimately the child's right to participate in and contribute to society?" As we move forward in implementing IDEA and as society evolves, needs change, and resources adjust, we need to ensure that we are focused on the child's experience and remember the ideals that gave birth to the Education for All Handicapped Children Act of 1975. IDEA has been an important piece of legislation that has helped raise our awareness and responsibility we have to all children—prompting ongoing collaboration with colleagues and families. Children with special needs, no longer forgotten, challenge educators every day to refine and improve the ways we educate them.

# 2

# THE EVOLVING RELATIONSHIP BETWEEN FAMILIES OF CHILDREN WITH DISABILITIES AND PROFESSIONALS

## Elizabeth J. Erwin, Leslie C. Soodak

The year is 1966, and the Beatles, Bob Dylan, and James Brown have made their way to the top of the record charts. Many young men are serving overseas in an undeclared war that is claiming lives abroad and stirring controversy at home.

Jeremy Johnson has just decided to continue with his plans to enter the state college rather than join the military, despite his strong sense of patriotism. Both Jeremy and his wife, Rhonda, feel that their energies are best spent preparing for the birth of their first child.

For Rhonda and Jeremy, the birth of their son, Jeremy Jr., is the most exhausting and exhilarating experience in their lives. They are discussing how they will coordinate visits from excited grandparents when the obstetrician enters the hospital room. The doctor's voice is low, and his speech is deliberate. He uses words neither Rhonda nor Jeremy has heard before. *Mongolism. Retarded. Incurable. Institution.* As he speaks of a decision that is "better if made quickly," the nurse brings the baby to Rhonda. The doctor quietly points out "signs" of the disease. But Rhonda and Jeremy see only their tiny, much-loved, and long-awaited son.

Despite the advice of the doctors and Rhonda's parents, Jeremy is brought home from the hospital to his newly decorated room. Much goes as planned: the baby cries; the nights are long; the joys are many. But there is also the unexpected. Many of their friends seem to ignore the birth of their son. Had they forgotten? Why were some neighbors saying they were sorry? Why didn't other new mothers return Rhonda's calls?

As time goes on, the joys and challenges of parenting continue. Jeremy Jr. learns to grasp objects, walk, and say a few words, but these milestones come a bit later than Rhonda expects. Jeremy finishes college at night, so that Rhonda can stay home and prepare for their second child, who is to arrive shortly before Jeremy Jr.'s third birthday.

The next few years are particularly challenging for Rhonda and Jeremy. Jeremy Jr.'s delays seem more apparent and worrisome than ever before. Toilet training isn't going well, and his language is limited and difficult to understand. Over the next two years, Rhonda notices that with many skills, his younger sister, Amelia, is catching up with, and in some cases surpassing, her brother. Rhonda has few people to turn to for advice or understanding. When she approaches the local public school for guidance, she is told by the principal that there is a "multi-age" class in the district on the other side of town that they might be able to consider once Jeremy Jr. is fully toilet trained.

Jeremy Jr. is nearly six when Rhonda learns that a small group of families in the next town have begun a school for "handicapped" children. There is one multi-age class in the school that meets, rent free, in a church basement. The families share the cost of hiring a retired teacher, and each of the parents takes a turn helping out in the classroom. It's a stretch to pay for schooling, but Jeremy and Rhonda are pleased that Jeremy Jr. will be with other children and perhaps learn to take care of himself. Rhonda finds herself spending more and more time in Jeremy's school, speaking with other parents about everything from recipes to community resources for their children. She is particularly interested when one of the mothers tells her that a chapter of the National Association for Down Syndrome is starting up nearby. It is not long before she finds herself being an active member of this group, reaching out to other families in need of information and support.

The Johnsons' story is a reminder of the challenges that families faced prior to the Education for All Handicapped Children Act of 1975 (P.L. 94–142). From the late nineteenth century to the 1930s, some parents were actually blamed for causing their child's disability, particularly for youngsters with mental retardation and autism (Turnbull, Turnbull, Erwin, & Soodak, 2006). It did not take long, however, for parents to recognize the absence of educational services for their children with disabilities and bond together to address this critical unmet need. Parents were responsible for developing local and national organizations as well as creating specialized services that were aimed at educating or supporting their children with disabilities across the life span from the 1930s through the 1960s (Turnbull et al., 2006).

Since the passage of P.L. 94–142, there have been countless changes in the education of children with disabilities, and just as many changes in the nature of relationships between families and professionals. The roles that families have voluntarily played or have had assigned to them in the educational process have ranged from having to passively receive decisions made by professionals, to creating innovative programs for their children (as was the case for Rhonda and Jeremy), to participating as equal partners with professionals in all aspects of their children's education.

This chapter articulates the nature of the evolving relationship between families of children with disabilities and professionals since the passage of P.L. 94–142. We provide a historical context for understanding family-professional partnerships by reflecting on each decade from the 1970s through the early years of the new millennium. For each decade, we examine the nation's social and political climate, legislation related to education and disability, educational research and initiatives, and roles that families have traditionally assumed.

We use a chronological perspective to frame the review and explore what history has to teach us. Our intent is to provide snapshots of events in time that frame a particular experience and use this information to create new visions about the future. However, it is not our intention to oversimplify, minimize, or stereotype families' experiences given the diversity of perspectives and voices that have yet to be fully represented in our country's history or fully acknowledged in our educational and legal systems.

The major theme of this chapter is what can be learned from families through their experience and activism and what professionals still need to learn to achieve meaningful and individualized relationships with all families. The story that has been documented since the passage of P.L. 94–142 about families of children with disabilities has been primarily from a Caucasian middle- to upper-class perspective. The time has come for all voices to be heard and honored.

## The 1970s: The Decade of Promising New Beginnings

### Social and Political Climate

The early 1970s were characterized by activism and unrest, as many political institutions and social norms were publicly challenged. Antiwar protests and demonstrations advancing feminism and gay rights were staged locally and nationally. Individual rights were advanced through legislation (for example, Equal Education Opportunities Act of 1974) and Supreme Court rulings (for example, *Roe v. Wade*, 1973). However, the optimism and activism experienced early in the 1970s was tempered by the political and economic situation in the second half of the decade. On the heels of the U.S. withdrawal from Vietnam and President Nixon's resignation following the Watergate investigation, confidence in government waned. Education in the 1970s was shaped by growing interest in the nuclear family, liberalization of the school curriculum, and a continued focus on integration and affirmative action. Educators experimented with new formats for instructional delivery, such as open classrooms, and nontraditional areas of study, such as sex education.

Initially the education of students with disabilities was far less progressive. Prior to 1975, students with disabilities were educated at the discretion of local school districts, based on the determination as to whether a student was "educable." As a result, approximately 3.5 million children with disabilities were not receiving an education appropriate to their needs, and nearly 1 million children were receiving no education at all (U.S. Congress, 1973). However, due to the efforts of advocates for disability rights, and most notably the parents of individuals with disabilities, the schoolhouse doors were about to open.

## Federal Legislation

Public education became a legal right for all children with the passage of P.L. 94–142 in 1975. Two important legal cases brought forth by parents on behalf of their children, *Pennsylvania Association for Retarded Children (PARC) v. Commonwealth of Pennsylvania* (1971) and *Mills v. District of Columbia Board of Education* (1972), predated and had a direct effect on P.L. 94–142. The *PARC* and *Mills* rulings provided the legal basis for ensuring a free and appropriate education and ensured parents' rights to prior notice of proposed changes in their child's education, access to school records, and the right to appeal decisions made by the school district (Martin, Martin, & Terman, 1996). Each of these safeguards was included in P.L. 94–142. In addition, this legislation established the first parent and training information centers to help parents exercise their rights. The procedural safeguards afforded parents represented a historical milestone in that parents of children with disabilities for the first time were granted the right—and responsibility—to participate in decisions pertaining to the education of their children.

During this time, Congress also passed P.L. 93–112, the Rehabilitation Act of 1973, which added to the rights of individuals with disabilities by outlawing discrimination in publicly funded services. Section 504 of the Rehabilitation Act included the first statutory definition of discrimination toward people with disabilities. Section 504 of the Rehabilitation Act was aimed at eliminating barriers that exclude individuals with disabilities, whereas P.L. 94–142 was designed to ensure that individuals with disabilities are provided an appropriate education. Section 504 afforded parents the right to bring suit against those who discriminated against their children with disabilities in the provision of services, although most sought recourse during this time under P.L. 94–142 (Martin et al., 1996).

## Educational Initiatives

In 1972, *The Principle of Normalization in Human Services* was published in which Wolfensberger and his colleagues argued that deviancy was socially determined and all individuals should be enabled to lead lives like those of ordinary people. The principle of normalization had a profound effect on parents and other advocates as they fought for and developed community-based programs and schools. The belief that everyone has the right to as normal a life as possible, including the right to participate in communities and schools with their typical peers and neighbors, underlies the deinstitutionalization and mainstreaming inclusive education movements, both of which began in the 1970s.

Mainstreaming was the practice of placing children with disabilities who were being educated in segregated special education classes into general education classes for a portion of the school day. Mainstreaming quickly gained support as educators and parents sought placement options consistent with the mandate to educate students with disabilities in the "least restrictive environment" included in the newly passed P.L. 94–142. Mainstreaming was also supported by litigation and a growing body of evidence of the limited effects of segregated placements (Kavale, 1979).

Thus, the 1970s marked a critical milestone for students with disabilities and their families: for the first time, schools were mandated to educate students with disabilities and required to work in collaboration with each student's parents to ensure that the student's individual needs were considered as his or her individualized educational program was crafted and implemented.

## Parental Roles

Prior to P.L. 94–142, many parents were viewed as recipients of professionals' decisions about whether, where, and how their children would be educated (Turnbull et al., 2006). Textbooks used to prepare educators in the 1960s and early 1970s advised teachers to be directive and informative, for example, suggesting that "the child and the parents should be told that the child is being transferred into special education because the class is special. . . . The entire program should be explained so that the parents will understand what lies ahead . . . so they can support the efforts of the teachers" (Kolstoe, 1970, p. 42).

Once schools began implementing the procedures mandated by law to allow parent participation in decision making, particularly in the development of the individualized education program (IEP), the role of parents in educational decision making became more salient, although not necessarily more collaborative. Early research on the implementation of P.L. 94–142 indicated that parents were not readily accepted as partners in decision making (Brightman, & Sullivan, 1980; Salett & Henderson, 1980). In one case study, parents of a twelve year old described being "railroaded" into endorsing the IEP developed for their daughter ("Parents and the I.E.P.," 1979).

In order to ensure parental involvement in educational decisions, P.L. 94–142 mandated that parents be given written notice of their educational rights. In the early years of implementation, it was reported that many parents did not receive adequate notice of their rights (Yoshida, Fenton, Kaufman, & Maxwell, 1978). In addition, materials given to parents often had a readability level above the fourteenth-grade level (McLoughlin, Edge, Petrosko, & Strenecky, 1981). Although well intentioned, the law was not fully effective in involving parents in educational decisions pertaining to their children in the early years of its implementation.

During this period, parents were often expected to help their children achieve the goals identified by professionals. Fueled by a large body of evidence demonstrating that a child's environment influences his or her intellectual development (Bronfenbrenner, 1979), parents were encouraged to assume the role of their child's teacher in order to accelerate development. Evidence that parents could be effective teachers (Bricker & Bricker, 1976; Shearer & Shearer, 1977) served to justify this role. The popularity of parent training during the late 1970s and early 1980s prompted one researcher to identify a long list of competencies needed for parents to be effective "teachers" (Karnes & Teska, 1980) and another group of researchers to develop the Parent as Teacher Inventory to identify parents likely to be effective home instructors (Strom, Rees, Slaughter, & Wurster, 1980). The effect of parent training on the child's self-esteem as well as its impact on parents suggested that this role was not necessarily well suited to all and may in fact have been too strongly rooted within a professionally centered orientation to adequately support collaboration (Turnbull et al., 2006).

A third role that parents assumed during the 1970s, and one that continues to this day, is that of political advocate. Parent advocates were at the forefront of the disability rights movement, successfully demanding that their children be taken out of institutions and placed in schools where they would have the opportunity to engage in society like children who were not disabled. Parents brought right-to-education suits in every state and worked with the organizations they helped found (for example, the Association for Retarded Citizens) and professional groups (for example, the Council for Exceptional Children) to advocate for the federal legislation that was to become P.L. 94–142. Tom Gilhool, the attorney representing parents in the PARC lawsuit, credited parents for the significance of their accomplishments by stating that "the parent movement has reversed the course of history by insisting that segregated institutions cannot stand and must go" (Gilhool, 1997).

## The 1980s: A Shift
## to Family-Centered Approaches

### Social and Political Climate

The 1980s began with the election of President Reagan and the rise of conservatism and ended with a focus on international human rights issues in such events as the fall of the Berlin Wall and the Tiananmen Square massacre. The recession early in the decade resulted in high unemployment and poverty rates across the country. And while aerobics, personal computers, and arcade game graphics were introduced, deeper and highly charged issues, including gay rights and child abuse, were also now in the spotlight. The country was dealing with the AIDS pandemic, the *Challenger* disaster, and infamous terror attacks such as on the *Achille Lauro* ocean liner and the explosion of Pam Am Flight 103 over Lockerbie, Scotland.

During Reagan's presidency, special education was strongly influenced by political efforts to eliminate or restrict funds for social and educational programs. Lowell Weicker, a former Connecticut senator and parent of a child with Down syndrome, noted the Reagan administration's attempts in the mid-1980s to limit the government's responsibility for the education of children with disabilities: "It was assumed that in the rough and tumble world of politics [people with disabilities and their advocates] would not hold their own as a voting block or as advocates for their cause" (cited in Turnbull et al., 2006, p. 108).

In the budget and policy deliberations from 1981 to 1983, people with disabilities, families, and advocates were vocal and convincing as they stood their ground. Parents were forced to continue the fight to maintain and expand the educational rights for their children with disabilities that they had worked so hard to secure in the 1970s.

## Federal Legislation

Similar to the 1970s, the decade of the 1980s was marked by new landmark legislation that had a positive and profound impact on the lives of young children with disabilities and their families. Specifically, P.L. 99–457 extended the rights and provisions to young children from birth to age three that had been afforded to school-age children with disabilities in P.L. 94–142 (now known as the Individuals with Disabilities Education Act). P.L. 99–457 was shaped by the principles and practices of family-centered care (Association for the Care of Children's Health, 1989; Brown, Thurman & Pearl, 1993), which recognized that families are the stable and constant force in a young child's life and therefore play a critical role in the educational process. Furthermore, the concept of family-centered care as reflected in the legislation not only acknowledged the central role families have in the educational process but recognized that their priorities should drive the intervention process in concert with support and guidance from professional team members (Dunst, Trivette, & Deal, 1994).

In addition to P.L. 99–457, the 1980s saw the promulgation of the Regular Education Initiative (REI), which was supported and encouraged by the U.S. assistant secretary of education, Madeline Will. The initiative challenged the notion of the traditional and separate systems of educating children with and without disabilities and called for a major restructuring and merger of those systems. This initiative recognized that having dual systems of education (general education and special education) resulted in a fragmented and inadequate system for educating students with and without disabilities and proposed a shared responsibility for a unified system that would provide high-quality education for all children (Gartner & Lipsky, 1987; Stainback & Stainback, 1984).

The interest in establishing more inclusive educational opportunities for students with disabilities and the emergence of meaningful family participation in the 1980s resulted in numerous studies examining the perspectives of parents of children with and without disabilities on inclusive education, particularly in early childhood (Abramson, Willson, Yoshida, & Hagerty, 1983; Bailey & Winton, 1987; Green & Stoneman, 1989; Mlynek, Hannah, & Hamlin, 1982; Winton, Turnbull, Blacher, & Salkind, 1983). Before this decade, parent perspectives were seldom documented, particularly in the research literature. The trend toward more active parent involvement meant that parents were more visible than ever before in educational meetings and research investigations.

## Educational Initiatives

One of the most significant initiatives during this decade was the shared accountability for educating students with and without disabilities. Parents, professionals, and policymakers began to question the effectiveness, ethics, and feasibility of a dual system of general and special education. There were growing concerns among states about the existence of two separate systems of education and how to address such critical issues as overrepresentation of students of color in special education classes, the overuse of labeling so that students fit into the system (as opposed to the system meeting students' individual needs), and limited curricular and social opportunities afforded to students in segregated placements (Roach, 1995).

The 1980s was marked by an effort to establish more inclusive practices for both children with disabilities and their families. This decade was a critical time for continuing efforts aimed at securing legal rights, which ultimately led to greater protections for people with disabilities in the early 1990s (for example, the Americans with Disabilities Act and the reauthorization of the Education for All Handicapped Children's Act).

Overall the 1980s brought about important advances in establishing inclusive schools, which may have been shaped in part by the shift from a professional-centered system in education to a more family-centered one. Although more students with disabilities were being served in their neighborhood schools and there was an increase in the number of parents who participated in educational decision making, these options were not always widely available or accessible to most parents of children with disabilities. Erwin, Soodak, Winton, and Turnbull (2001, p. 13) noted, "When research results from across the entire decade of the 1980s are analyzed, we can soundly conclude that the concerns that parents [of young children with disabilities] expressed at the beginning of the decade were still being expressed at the end of the decade."

## Parental Roles

Legislation continued to play a major role in how parents were viewed and treated in the educational process. The focus on parental involvement included in P.L. 94–142 and on family-centered care that emerged following the passage of P.L.

99–457 was in stark contrast to the way that families had been previously perceived and treated in the educational process. The 1980s marked the shift in the field of special education from a perspective that was professionally centered to one that was more family centered (Turnbull et al., 2006). Although parents were more frequently assuming the role of decision maker in educational planning, many were still not meaningfully involved in their child's education (Turnbull et al., 2006). This may have been due to several factors, including limited opportunities by schools to facilitate parental participation and address cultural or language barriers, as well as lack of or absence of professional development for practitioners who were not adequately prepared or uninterested in involving parents. In addition, when parents offered their thoughts or asked questions, they were not always taken seriously or were treated as if they were the problem: "Whenever a parent disagrees or confronts the professional, that behavior can be dismissed as an expression of inadequate adjustment, frustration, displaced anger, or a host of psychological problems. Any interpretation is possible other than the parent is correct!" (Lipsky, 1985, p. 616).

Overall, the 1980s signaled a time of change, particularly in how and where children with disabilities were educated. And although more parents were involved in a more meaningful way in their child's education than ever before, not all parents' voices were being heard or were even represented at the table.

## The 1990s: Moving from Participant to Valued Member in Decision Making

### Social and Political Climate

Following the end of the cold war and the recession of the late 1980s, the 1990s began with a general sense of global unity and economic prosperity. It was a decade in which the United States was involved in few foreign conflicts and great strides were being made toward democracy, particularly in Europe and Latin America. The rapid rise in the use of personal computers and the Internet spurred the economy and revolutionized popular culture. The liberal ideals of the 1970s were resurging as concerns about social issues, such as racial equality and environmentalism, grew. Although President Clinton's domestic agenda included reforms in health care, social security, and gun control, policies related to each were left largely unchanged during his eight-year tenure. And although the continuing economic boom raised the country's spirits and spending, growing concern about terrorism abroad and violence at home left the country in an unsettled calm as the decade ended and the new millennium began.

## Federal Legislation

The decade began with the most sweeping disabilities rights legislation in history: the American with Disabilities Act (ADA), signed into law by President George H. W. Bush in 1990. This law brought full legal citizenship to Americans with disabilities by mandating that government-sponsored programs be accessible and businesses make reasonable accommodations for disabled workers and patrons. Also in 1990, P.L. 99–457 amended and revised the Education for All Handicapped Children Act (P.L. 94–142) to include people-first language, which resulted in its being renamed the Individuals with Disabilities Education Act (IDEA).

The Individuals with Disabilities Education Act was reauthorized again in 1997 with President Clinton's signing of P.L. 105–17. The amendments of 1997 included changes consistent with the emphasis on higher standards for all students that was occurring nationally by mandating that students with disabilities participate in the general education curriculum and statewide and district-wide assessment programs. This law further strengthened the role of parents in the education of their children with disabilities. Specifically, the 1997 amendments to IDEA increased parent participation in eligibility and placement decisions and established mediation as a primary process to be used in resolving conflicts between schools and the parents of children with disabilities. In addition, the amendments required more user-friendly language in delivering information to parents about their child's rights and required that parents be given access to all records relating to their child, not just records on the identification, evaluation, and educational placement of the child.

## Educational Initiatives

The 1990s was an important time of change in the education of students with disabilities and their families. Inclusive education—educating students with disabilities full time in general education classes alongside their nondisabled peers—emerged as an important new initiative. Inclusion, with its emphasis on full-time classroom membership and belonging, replaced mainstreaming as the least restrictive environment for children. Although the 1997 reauthorization of IDEA did not mandate inclusion, it did require students with disabilities to participate in the general education curriculum and accountability testing, thus making placement in the general education classroom a logical option for students with disabilities. The 1997 reauthorization of IDEA required states to begin collecting information about the race and ethnicity of students in special education in an effort to understand and remedy the apparent disproportionate representation of students from minority backgrounds receiving special education services. The persistent and alarming overrepresentation of children from minority backgrounds receiving special education overall and in more restrictive educational placements in general was of great concern to both policymakers and parents.

The 1997 reauthorization also spurred changes in the delivery of services by mandating that assistive technology be considered during the development of a student's individualized education program. *Assistive technology* refers to any device that may be used to increase or maintain the functional capabilities of a child with disabilities. The 1997 reauthorization further established new rules and procedural safeguards for disciplining students with disabilities, which, among other requirements, mandated the use of positive behavioral supports. Each of these changes was designed to enhance the equity and effectiveness of educational services for students with disabilities, and each assumed the full and meaningful participation of families. Clearly, by the year 2000, parents had moved from mere participants in decisions about their children with disabilities and were now striving to be valued and respected members of the decision-making team.

## Parental Roles

By the 1990s, the role of parents of children with disabilities as decision makers in their child's education had become standard practice, although the legacy of the past continued as educators struggled to implement family-centered policies and practices (Erwin et al., 2001). In fact, many of the issues that emerged in the 1980s regarding how parents were to collaborate with professionals in arriving at and implementing sound educational decisions for their children persisted.

Research suggested that although many parents were informed participants in their child's education, parent-professional relationships were not yet truly collaborative, and some parental voices were not being heard at all (Erwin & Soodak, 1995; Harry, Allen, & McLaughlin, 1995; Pruitt, Wandry, & Hollums, 1998). Echoing their concerns of the previous decade, some parents reported dissatisfaction with their own role in their child's education. Some parents of students with disabilities described feeling powerless when interacting with school personnel, leaving them to defer to "expert judgments" even when they disagreed with the decisions being made. A mother in one study commented that she "had absolutely no control over what schooling [her son] was getting" (Erwin & Soodak, 1995, p. 27). In another study, parents overwhelmingly spoke of their desire to be heard in their communication with professionals (Pruitt et al., 1998). For example, when asked how educators could be more sensitive to the needs of their family, one mother responded: "They need to listen and believe that the parents have input in their child's health and education. Some professionals believe that since they are the ones with the degree that they know everything and believe that the parents are inferior and don't know what they are talking about" (Pruitt et al., 1998, p. 162).

Although parents were considered members of the decision-making team in many school districts, the IEP meeting was reported to be particularly difficult for many parents (Erwin & Soodak, 1995; Pruitt, et al., 1998). Interactions during these meetings were consistent with what Biklen (1992) referred to as the "myth of clinical judgment" in which parents' options were limited by assumptions about the accuracy and importance of professional expertise. Of particular concern was the limited and passive role given to parents of children from culturally and linguistically diverse backgrounds, including those of African American and Latino descent and children of low-income families (Harry, 1992; Harry et al., 1995; Kalyanpur & Rao, 1991).

Parents were also concerned about the education their children were receiving. Research consistently indicated that most parents regarded social integration as a primary goal for their children (Green & Schinn, 1994; Gurlanick, 1994; Guralnick, Connor, & Hammond, 1995; Plunge & Kratochwill, 1995). However, parents did not feel that schools necessarily agreed that their children should "have the same opportunities that we've given everybody else" (Soodak & Erwin, 1995, p. 265). Some parents were concerned that special education was stigmatizing to their children. For example, one mother stated, "There was open lunch for the other high school kids [without disabilities]. The kids in special education class, though, stood and waited in line [for the rest room] .... What message does that give to the other professionals or the other students when you have to take a 17-, 18-, 19-year-old kid to the bathroom?" (Ryndak, Downing, Morrison, & Williams, 1996, p. 115).

Discrepant views about the goals for their children as well as their own lack of communication and trust with professionals contributed to the rising number of disputes between school districts and parents of children with disabilities (Lake & Billingsley, 2000).

During the 1990s, parents' desire for their child's social acceptance and learning that they could use to navigate in the real world as adults fueled their interest in and pursuit of inclusive education. While researchers continued to document parents' perspectives on the benefits and drawbacks of inclusive education (Bennett, Deluca, & Bruns, 1997; Diamond & LeFurgy, 1994; Green & Shinn, 1994; Guralnick, 1994; Guralnick et al., 1995; Ryndak, Downing, Jacqueline, & Morrison, 1995; Ryndak et al., 1996; York & Tundidor, 1995), some parents took on the role of advocate in the active pursuit of inclusive education for their own children (Erwin & Soodak, 1995; Ryndak et al., 1996). Once again, educational reform for students with disabilities was being led by the advocacy efforts of parents (Lipsky & Gartner, 1997; Turnbull et al., 2006).

## 2000 and Beyond: Partnerships and Positive Outcomes

### Social and Political Climate

The start of the millennium was marked by unprecedented events in U.S. history. In November 2000, one of the closest and most controversial presidential elections took place between Al Gore and George W. Bush. Less than a year later, on September 11, 2001, the country experienced devastating terrorist attacks. Terrorism was not a new phenomenon, and yet the world seemed to be suddenly plagued by escalating terrorist attacks, particularly bombings aimed at civilians, including the Bali nightclub tragedy, Madrid train massacre, and the London subway horror.

The beginning of the millennium was also marked by growing hostility and aggression around the world, including the conflict in the Middle East, the American occupation and civil unrest in Iraq, and the ongoing genocide in Darfur. These are just a few of the countless examples of the violence around the world at the start of the new century. There were also unprecedented natural disasters that left behind a trail of death and destruction, such as the tsunami that began in the Indian Ocean and Hurricane Katrina on American soil. Issues that were in the forefront of the consciousness of the United States at the beginning of this decade included homeland safety, increasing poverty among the middle class, global warming, immigration, technological advances, and resource depletion, particularly oil and natural gas.

## Federal Legislation

Four major themes important to education over the past fifty years continued to shape school reform: technological advances, low student achievement, the need for a competitive workforce, and civil rights (Turnbull et al., 2006). School reform continues to be at the forefront of educational debates and is now guided by new federal legislation, the No Child Left Behind Act (NCLB). When this law was signed in 2001, the intent was to benefit all children, including those with disabilities, from kindergarten through grade 12 by requiring states to hold school districts accountable for academic progress.

The focus of NCLB on family-professional partnerships is clear: schools must inform parents about the results of their child's academic progress and the overall performance of the school, as well as present data to demonstrate how their school compares with other schools locally and across the state. In addition, the school must provide options to families if it is not making steady progress each year. One principle of NCLB is parental choice, which encourages the involvement of parents in the educational process and provides them with information so they can make informed choices. Toward this end, NCLB provides funding for parental assistance information centers, which offer support and training to parents and organizations that work with families.

In 2004, IDEA was reauthorized with the signing of P.L. 108–446, the Individuals with Disabilities Education Improvement Act. Critical changes in this reauthorization included changes in due process, IEP procedures, and discipline provisions. Parent rights were affected by requiring parental consent prior to providing special education or related services specified in a child's IEP, specifying when notification of procedural safeguards is to be distributed, and, for the first time, allowing parents to request an initial evaluation to determine if their child has a disability. IEP procedures were changed by eliminating the requirement for short-term objectives and by making it possible, with parent approval, for IEP decisions to be made in the absence of all team members. The 2004 reauthorization also modified the definition of *parent* to include an adoptive or foster parent, guardian, or individual legally responsible for the child. In addition, the revised law provided expanded opportunities for early and less formal means of resolving disputes between parents and schools. The legislation early in the new millennium was guided by the principles that parents or other adults legally responsible for the child must be clearly informed and involved in the educational process.

## Educational Initiatives

Many trends are guiding practice in this new millennium, driven in part by NCLB. For example, there is increased interest in evidenced-based practices as well as how technology and alternative assessments can be individualized for students with disabilities. There is growing attention to school safety given the increased violence and publicized incidents such as the

Columbine massacre and Lancaster, Pennsylvania, shootings. A disturbing, although not surprising, trend is that the visible and growing aggression around the world, as well as the violence glorified in media, film, and video games aimed at children, is now reflected in growing aggression among school children. The American Academy of Pediatrics (2000), in collaboration with six major medical and mental health organizations, reported that children's viewing of media violence increases aggressive values and behaviors and that the impact of children's witnessing violence through entertainment sources such as the Internet, television, and video games is substantial and long lasting.

In general, trends in education suggest that educating children with and without disabilities together is more frequently being studied; however, access to and implementation of inclusive education is still challenging. In addition, despite the fact that some families are given more opportunities to have a role in educational planning meetings, the educational process is not always a positive one, as this mother shared: "In the beginning I was an insignificant member of this team. But as the years go on, I do find myself taking more leadership in this. But that bothers me because I don't want the leadership role, I want an equal partnership" (Soodak & Erwin, 2000, p. 37).

There are now more opportunities than in the past for families to be involved in their children's education, although they do not necessarily want to shoulder the entire responsibility of making decisions for their children in order for them to be successful in school.

Since the 1990s, increased attention has been given to ensuring that diverse and underrepresented families are included in the educational process. In addition, accessing information remains one of the greatest obstacles, particularly for culturally and linguistically diverse families (Park, Turnbull, & Park, 2001; Public Agenda, 2002; Zoints, Zoints, Harrison, & Bellinger, 2004). Consider this Latina mother's thoughts on obtaining knowledge about the educational system: "When a parent starts getting too smart and really learning the system then you little by little become a persona non grata wherever you go because you do know the system, you do know your rights and they like resent it" (Rueda, Monzo, Shapiro, Gomez & Blacher, 2005, p. 408).

The time has come for all families to feel that they are respected members of the educational process.

## Parental Roles

In the 1990s, the shift in the educational field from the term *parent* to *family* was emerging because of the understanding that just like parents, other family members such as grandparents or siblings, play an important role in the education of children with disabilities. Early in the twenty-first century, there also seems to be a new emphasis on the quality and nature of the relationship between families and professionals. As such, the notion of family-professional partnerships is becoming a new paradigm for promoting healthy and collaborative relationships between school and home (Turnbull et al., 2006).

Family-professional partnerships are built on the idea that there is a solid and coequal relationship that benefits both parties. In addition, these partnerships are rooted in trust as well as other essential principles, such as respect, communication, commitment, and equality, among others (Turnbull et al., 2006). Family-professional partnerships are defined "as relationships between families and professionals in which they mutually agree to defer to each other's judgment and expertise, as appropriate for the purpose of securing outcomes for the student, other family members, and the professionals" (Turnbull et al., 2006, p. 110).

In this way, a collaborative relationship occurs that is positive, meaningful, and individualized. Most important, it is beneficial for all stakeholders, and in particular, for the student with disabilities. Here is one parent's experience with family-professional partnerships:

It has been WONDERFUL. It has absolutely been the best thing. Not only have there been benefits and services that have come, but all of the people that we deal with have got to where there's a relationship there with everybody and there's this bonding and we're getting to where we're on the same page—nobody gets 100 percent of their way. It's everybody there, you put it in a pile and it's give and take [Wang, Mannan, Poston, Turnbull, & Summers, 2004, p. 151].

Since the passage of P.L. 94–142, parents have assumed a variety of roles, ranging from recipients of professional decisions to teachers, political advocates, and educational decision makers. It is long overdue for parents to be seen and treated as equal and welcomed partners in the educational system.

## An Eye to the Future

Early in the new century, family-professional partnerships have provided a meaningful context for creating healthy relationships between home and school. This mother articulated what family-professional partnerships look like: "It is a team effort, I think because myself, my husband, the grandparents, aunts and uncles, and the school are working together. It is like everybody is working for the best of Adam. They are all supportive of me and my husband. It makes such a difference" (Erwin et al., 2001, p. 142). With an eye to the future, this is the voice that so clearly articulates what family-professional partnerships should be like.

The themes of access to quality education, as well as equity in the school systems, have shaped this country's history and are evident in the experiences of families of children with disabilities. The story that has been told about families of children with disabilities over time has been primarily from an Anglo European lens. The absence of all voices in the collective experience of families of children receiving special education services is a major limitation to this review and the overall knowledge of families' experiences. In recent years, there has been an attempt to document the experiences and perspectives of families who have been traditionally underrepresented, such as families from non–Anglo European descent, those with gay or lesbian family members, families living in poverty, and single-parent families (Harry, 1992; Park et al., 2001; Park, Turnbull, & Turnbull, 2002; Rueda et al., 2005; Soodak & Erwin, 2000; Zoints et al., 2004). Looking toward the future, it seems the time has come to focus on *how* to maintain and strengthen partnerships between families and professionals, the implication being that partnerships are embraced for every family in every school.

Embracing the idea of partnership means moving beyond the recognition that families should be involved in the educational process and moving toward establishing relationships between families and professionals that are firmly rooted in the idea of an equal partnership. Turnbull et al. (2006) suggested that trust is the key to developing family-professional partnerships. They define trust as "having confidence in someone else's reliability, judgment, word, and action to care for and not harm the entrusted person" (p. 160).

When trust exists, there is an implicit understanding of safety and a shared perspective on children and schooling. One parent articulated her trust in the professional working with her child with severe disabilities: "I can trust her to do things the way I've asked her to do them. . . . She mirrors what we do" (Nelson, Summers, & Turnbull, 2004, p. 159). The following voice demonstrates the importance of trust in working with families from the perspective of a professional: "They trust me now, you know, and I can help them better if they trust me. . . . I build a lot of relationships through a lot of talking and giving them information and that's important to them" (Blue-Banning, Summers, Frankland, Nelson, & Beegle, 2004, p. 175).

Although trust is the sturdy foundation on which family-professional partnerships are constructed, other principles also facilitate the day-to-day interactions between families and professionals. These principles, which are firmly grounded in trust, include open and unrestricted communication, professional competence, mutual respect, a commitment to equality, and the willingness to advocate on behalf of children and their families (Turnbull et al., 2006). These principles collectively lay the groundwork for partnerships to occur. If trust is not present, a partnership will likely not survive. It becomes the shared responsibility of all stakeholders, including practitioners, administrators, policymakers, and university faculty, to ensure that partnerships with families are the standard across schools in America and that these family-professional partnerships not only are sustained but flourish. Imagine the following vignette becoming a reality for all families:

When their child was born, Rhonda and Jeremy would have experienced the jubilation that accompanies the birth of a child. Those assisting with the birth, perhaps a doctor or midwife, would have focused first on fostering the bond between parents and child. They would be available to talk to Rhonda and Jeremy about their son as they would with first-time parents of a typical child. The hospital or birthing center would provide the family with contact information for the early intervention team that is part of the unified early childhood intervention system in their state. In addition, Rhonda and Jeremy would be given information about the local parent-to-parent center so that they would be able to connect with other families if they chose to do so. The entire extended family, including grandparents, would be part of this process.

In the early months of parenting, the early intervention team would be available to Rhonda and Jeremy to help answer questions, provide information, and arrange services that Jeremy Jr. or his parents felt they needed. Recognizing delays in a way that a first-time parent might overlook, the speech and language therapist would have worked to increase Jeremy's communication and provide tips for Rhonda and Jeremy to use as they interacted with their son. The social worker on the team would listen to the family as they spoke of their joys and offer support and strategies when challenges emerged. When Rhonda and Jeremy needed time alone, particularly after Amelia was born, the strong network of their extended family as well as parents of children with and without disabilities that surrounded the family would help them arrange child care.

When Jeremy Jr. turned three and his parents decided it was time to enroll him in preschool, the professionals on the team would listen to Rhonda and Jeremy's desire for him to be in a setting with other children his age. The team would initiate contact with several local inclusive preschools whose open-door policies would provide the opportunity for the family to make the best choice for their son. Both parents would be fully involved in the transdisciplinary evaluation of their son; they would be asked to offer their thinking about the areas and methods of assessment and be given ample opportunity to provide information and guidance. The team would be particularly eager to learn about Jeremy Jr.'s likes and interests. The assessment would be used to develop a culturally responsive IEP that reflects the priorities, vision, and preferences of the family.

Because Rhonda and Jeremy would be treated with respect by all team members and their opinions would matter in decisions about their son, they would feel fully valued by the team. Jeremy Jr. would make a seamless transition to the public school when he reached the age of five, since the school-based team would take the time to meet the family far before he was to begin kindergarten. Rhonda and Jeremy would expect and be able to develop a strong and trusting partnership with this new team that would mirror their prior positive experiences with professionals. And to everyone's benefit, their expectations would be met.

This version of the Johnson family story demonstrates what is possible when the values inherent in the law governing special education are embraced and when family-professional partnerships are rooted in trust. There is much to be learned from the experiences of the past four decades that may help forge trusting partnerships between families and professionals. Families can and have assumed various roles in the education of their children with disabilities, from recipients of professional advice to political advocates. We know that the experiences of families are shaped within a social and political context. Perhaps most important, we recognize that although contexts and roles have changed over time, the desire for shared decision making, positive outcomes, and successful partnerships has not. Our hope is that as we move forward, parents and professionals will engage in partnerships that truly reflect the principles and spirit codified in IDEA.

## FROM THE FIELD: GABRIEL'S JOURNEY – NEVER QUITE FINISHED

### Virginia M. Victorín

Establishing and maintaining quality relationships between the professional community and families of children with disabilities takes patience, time, and extraordinary effort. These relationships can be frustrating, emotionally draining, confusing, non-committal, transitory, contentious, hostile, and litigious. And just as each professional is different, so are the families. Each family's ability to relate to the professionals involved with their

I thank Gabriel's teachers—Joy Burkhardt, Sherry Panganiban, Stewart Fordyce, and Deirdre Schaefer—who push Gabe to his limits. I thank Martha Saucedo, Gabriel's nanny since birth, and family. She was trained by our specialist in applied behavior analysis years ago. With the behavioral intervention team, Martha gives us great ideas when Gabe is having a hard time. Don Sykes, Gabriel's one-on-one aide since first grade, makes sure Gabriel understands what is being taught and provides him the guidance he needs to do well. I thank Washington Mutual for supporting employee volunteerism. Efforts like this deserve special acknowledgment.

child depends on the strength of their support system, how the day is going overall, the urgency of services needed, and their perception of the professional's competence, general nature, character, and philosophy of practice. It also depends on their lay understanding of medicine, science, education, and social service systems involved in the care of their affected child. The professional and the parent must realize that this is a shared journey. It is something they are in together. Elizabeth Erwin and Leslie Soodak walk us through this journey, and it is the relationship between families of children with disabilities and professionals that I wish to address here, speaking as the mother of a son with special needs.

In reflecting on the challenges in my family, I think of all the professionals we face. My son Gabriel's "crew" includes his pediatrician, pediatric neurologist, dentist, speech and language therapists, occupational therapist, neuropsychiatrist, geneticist, psychiatrists, podiatrist, pharmacist, dietician, attorney, three behavioral intervention specialists, their supervisors, his one-to-one aide, two public school teachers, school administrator for special education, school district field specialist, school district transportation supervisor, school nurse, day care staff during school breaks, his regional center case manager, and respite and specialized child care providers. Each one has individual proto-cols, rules of engagement, and purposes.

These professional relationships can range from paternalistic to collaborative, with a road that is long and where the gap is huge. It is important to understand the inherent power imbal-ance between professionals and the families they serve. This imbalance is linked to the difference in educational attainment, merit and entitlement, socioeconomic status, race, culture and ethnicity, and English-language proficiency, coupled with the limitations of our health care system and the education crisis gripping the country to adequately address the needs of all its citizens. In the enormity of what is expected of parents of special needs children in managing these professional relationships, the scheduling and the follow-up is the aspect of our work with Gabriel that continues to be the most daunting.

Although much has been done, public policies and laws historically serve as a framework for setting expectations, but they are not designed to govern standards of individual professional behavior. Graduate and professional schools are responsible for providing a theoretical framework for understanding best practices in law, business, teacher education and learning, social service provision, and other areas. How personal attitudes and knowledge of cultural differences and ethnic practices affect the relationship with families under their care and the menu of treatment options offered is critical to understanding effective partnership and collaboration. A professional who treats families with respect and dignity, communicates with compassion and a willingness to listen, asks probing questions, and responds with clarity about next steps effectively neutralizes this power imbalance and creates the environment necessary for establishing trust and a collaborative partnership in the quest to address the whole child.

The journey for any parent is to obtain the resources necessary for his or her children to thrive now and in the future. However, the political debate is still about whether our children with special needs have real value as contributing citizens and whether the financial investment in their care and their education is justified in an environment of strong competing interests and limited resources. As parents can tell you, this subliminal undercurrent plays out best behind closed doors of IEP meetings in the local school, or in case management meetings with service providers who are pressured by limited resources to act as if this is a game of twenty questions, where if you know what to ask for, maybe your child will get it. The most effective parent negotiators and system navigators have developed strong advocacy skills with keen English-language skills and full knowledge of the American educational system and processes. So what happens to families who are new to the

United States, are non-English speaking, and have no under-standing of our complex society and structures?

It is important to know that not everyone's experience in seeking and receiving special education services is similar. Family-professional relationships by nature are complex. Most of the books written come from a traditional Anglo perspective and point of view. For people of color, speaking up about our journey provides a unique opportunity to identify others in similar circumstances. It offers a safe place to share through common ground. It also teaches those not familiar with our culture or traditions about what really matters to our family and how differently the system works for us. It also serves to set best practice standards on how to better design programs and ser-vices, outreach, and education campaigns that more effectively reach us. And it contributes positively to the current body of research and makes substantive change possible.

It is through the lens of my family's path that I share with you our story. Given Elizabeth Erwin and Leslie Soodak's obser-vation that all voices are not represented in the literature base because it is viewed through a predominantly Anglo European lens, we hope that through our account, professionals better understand what we really want and need from them. For other parents who can relate, our message is of mutual love and respect and of motivation to push through the most difficult of times, with energy, will, and vigor to celebrate the small vic-tories and maintain the resolve to act.

Our journey started when Gabriel was sixteen months old. Working out downstairs on my stationary bicycle one very early morning, I heard what sounded like heavy pounding on the door. Headphones in place, I moved the blinds and saw nothing outside. Then I heard another even bigger bang. Jumping off, I ran toward the stairs. To my horror, Gabriel had fallen down one flight of stairs, with my husband close behind. We were concerned because Gabriel had received the mumps, measles, and rubella vaccination the day before and had run a fever. He had climbed up and down the stairs before. Why was this time any different? This incident is marked forever for me as the beginning of our journey.

Although Gabriel looked fine, we took him to his pediatrician (who shall remain nameless) as soon as possible. We noticed that after the fall, Gabriel's head would repeatedly hit his high chair table, causing him to cry and then fall asleep. We told the doctor of our concerns—violent body jerks that started within a day after the fall and the lack of language progress. To our shock, the doctor looked at me squarely and said, "Your son doesn't talk because he does not have to. All you fat Latina moms ever do is feed them when they cry. What incentive does Gabriel have to speak if all you do when he cries is stuff a bottle down his throat?"

As a professional woman of color, I recognized these racist comments all too well. My concern was for Gabriel. The doctor continued with his ridiculousness, reassuringly telling us that the jerking motion was nothing more than a stiff neck, with memories of the fall fresh in his mind. My husband and I walked away in shock and confusion. The jerkiness and sleep episodes lasted another month before divine intervention helped us find the path. My elderly mother-in-law had regular appointments with her neurologist. In broken English and Spanish, she told her doctor about the episodes that Gabriel was having, and the neurologist immediately asked us to come in so that she could see Gabriel herself. I remember noticing that drinking from his bottle would sometimes trigger an episode. So as she held Gabriel, I gave him the bottle, and within minutes he had an episode. The doctor exclaimed, "See! Look at his face; it's as pale white as his lips. This is a seizure. He has epilepsy. Who is his doctor? I am going to call him right away."

The good neurologist shamed the pediatrician into quick action. The health maintenance organization we found had absolutely no capacity to serve Gabriel. Referred to Children's Hospital Los Angeles, which had a five-month waiting list for magnetic resonance imaging (MRI), my husband, Andres, and I instantly became advocates. With Gabriel in my arms and the electroencephalogram (EEG) in hand and without an appointment, we headed to Children's. Rejected by the gate-keeper staff, we refused to leave until a resident read the EEG. Gabriel was kept for three days, poked and prodded, and we felt a sense of relief that comes with clarity. We had to provide Gabriel injections of steroid-based clinical trial drugs. Nothing worked. His infantile spasms (seizures) came in clusters of ten to fifty, three to five times a day. After several failed pharmaceutical attempts, the neurologist succeeded, and the seizures stopped. Gabriel's regressions were significant. The seizures caused loss in motor-skill development, and his ability to learn was severely compromised.

Our initiation into this unfamiliar territory was a severe blow to our initial expectations for our only child. As older first-time parents, we had huge dreams like everybody else of having our son go to college, like his proud parents—hopefully, a "future" UCLA alum like his mom. Coming from a rather traditional Mexican family, we expected large gatherings to be the norm for our family. Yet we noticed how difficult it was for Gabriel to enjoy more than a few minutes with his cousins before asking to go home. It was all too much for him. And, frankly, after we learned that Gabriel not only suffered from epilepsy but that he was in the moderate range of the autistic spectrum—the lack of proper language development, the lack of affect, that is, no smiles or tears, and even after visibly harming himself, the social detachment and refusal to be embraced—we knew our life would be very different. How different, we could never imagine.

After twelve years of advocating for Gabriel, my husband and I have learned that parents and professionals have a shared responsibility not to get stuck in what does not work. We must build on what works together. It is incumbent that we as parents listen very carefully to what is being said about our child's current level of performance, any achievement gaps that may exist, and strategies for addressing these. Professionals must offer parents a comfortable, nonthreatening environment that fosters open dialogue and exchange of ideas for improving outcomes.

We must also acknowledge that our child may behave differently in school than at home. There are very good and caring teachers, administrators, and classified staff who bring rigor and high expectations into the classroom experience. Teachers need to share what they experience in the classroom in terms of what works and does not work with parents, so that parents can try new ways of supporting their children's learning at home.

Parents need to know what questions to ask at different stages of the educational process and when. They should not hesitate to ask seemingly dumb questions because there are none. This is not to say that I have not been reduced to tears by the insensitivity of the process, the ease with which services are reduced or cut out completely, and the manner in which educational and service decisions are made prior to meeting with parents in anticipation of a scheduled IEP meeting while pretending that this is a "team" effort. Here is where working with a family advocate and support group can help parents learn what their role and responsibilities are and what questions they should be asking as they move through the educational process.

Fiesta Educativa, a local parent organization, provided our family the family-centered approach we needed. Located in the Lincoln Heights community of East Los Angeles, Fiesta took me by the hand and walked me through very difficult moments as I looked for hope and courage. Their love, information, and guidance gave us a new sense of hope and a better understanding of what to expect moving forward. This organization exists because parents of special needs families, lawyers, and advocates saw the need to provide monolingual and bilingual Spanish-speaking families support almost thirty years ago. They later offered me the opportunity to learn to advocate for the rights of others. Since my introduction to Fiesta, I have been working wherever I am needed as a presenter, an advocate, a fundraiser, a hell-raiser, and friend to other monolingual and bilingual Spanish-speaking families across the country. It was my work with Fiesta that led me to pursue political office.

With a new mayor of Los Angeles, the first Latino in more than a hundred years, I decided the time was right for me to help the disability community in a different way. Appointed by Mayor Antonio Villaraigosa and confirmed by the city council in 2006, I am one of the newest members of the Commission on Disabilities for the City of Los Angeles, where along with my fellow commissioners, we take on issues in the areas of education, health and HIV/AIDS, seniors, and parks and recreation. We tackle infrastructure problems, transportation, access, and inclusion.

Our journey with Gabriel and his team and my volunteer work with Fiesta and the Commission on Disabilities have led me to believe that parents who work closely with teachers and other professionals are more engaged in the welfare of the whole school and of the community at large because they have a stake in the outcome. As educators and advocates, we know that one of the most important predictors of a child's success in school is the role of the parent. This is especially true for parents of special needs children. Families take the first step in learning how to engage the professional community during the early identification and early intervention process. It is here that knowing where to start and who to go to can seem insurmountable when a family is in crisis. It is here where advocacy and family-centered support systems play a vital role. More efforts to promptly connect families in crisis to appropriate and culturally, linguistically relevant services pay the most dividends.

Family-professional partnerships are built on the idea that there is a solid and coequal mutually beneficial stake in a positive outcome. Because accessing information is still one of our biggest barriers to success, particularly for families unfamiliar with our system of service delivery, who may come from different ethnic and cultural backgrounds and may have limited command of the English language, these partnerships act as a bridge.

Gabriel has made remarkable progress over the past twelve years. He attends a public middle school day class for autistic children. He has a great teacher who has taught him video techniques for his own TV show on campus. Gabriel has learned how to read, write, and do multiplication using a calculator and is a certified computer geek. In 2005, he was awarded the Presidential Award for Academic Achievement during his fifth-grade graduation ceremony. His extraordinary effort to get it right stems from wanting the praise that comes from his hard work, even with his significant limitations. He has the challenges that other children like him have when there are lots of people, or it is too loud, or he is doing something outside his routine.

It is our hope that Gabriel grows up in a country that defines him not by his quirks but rather by his fun-loving nature and unconditional love and that he has a safe and affordable place to live and is able to be anything he wants to be. Our hopes ultimately rest on the shoulders of those partnerships we have established with professionals over the years in Gabriel's schools and within our community. We continue to work and hope that these shoulders remain strong.

Although our journey with Gabriel is incomplete, our life is blessed. My husband and I truly believe that the question is not to dwell on the "Why me?" or "Why us?" but instead on the "Who better?" Through our sorrows and frustrations, Gabriel and his crew of loving and caring professionals have taught us about unconditional love, persistence, and perseverance, joy, and success in the little things that really matter. The pursuit of happiness rests on what we envision individually and together as a community, not only for Gabriel's sake but for all the children and families like ours.

# 3

# INCLUSION OF STUDENTS WITH DISABILITIES IN GENERAL EDUCATION

## Holly Menzies, Mary A. Falvey

The structure of special education was formed by its political and research histories. The struggle to obtain services for students who were once denied entry to school or were poorly served when admitted created a system that relies on a well-defined turf to safeguard student rights. The influence of educational psychology on special education has also contributed to a system that sets itself apart from general education. It claims a knowledge and use of educational techniques specifically designed for special learners (Keough & MacMillan, 1996). This history of separateness from general education, combined with a constant yet contradictory pressure to avoid labeling and segregated placement, makes inclusive schooling a contentious issue within special education.

Inclusive schooling, or the education of students with disabilities with their nondisabled peers, has its origins in the movement to include individuals with disabilities in the mainstream of society. This movement, based on the principle of normalization (Wolfensberger, 1972), was first championed in Scandinavia and then in the United States in the early 1970s. The goal was to make life for those with disabilities as culturally normative as possible. The resulting trend was one of gradual enlightenment, moving slowly from ignorance and fear of the disabled to increasing acceptance and understanding. This same trend is currently reflected in our educational system, most notably through the landmark legislation, Education for All Handicapped Children Act (P.L. 94–142, 1975), which guaranteed a free and appropriate public education for all students regardless of their disability, in the least restrictive environment. However, a closer look at the educational experiences of students with disabilities, and the manner in which schooling is organized for them, says much about our perceptions of the significance of having a disability.

Special education in the United States is predominately structured as a dual system (Stainback & Stainback, 1984) with minimal collaboration or communication between general education and special education. As such, it emphasizes disability rather than normalizing it. Current special education legislation conceptualizes special education as a service, not a placement, and views services to students in terms of the intensity of support necessary; however, for many reasons, these services are most often offered by setting. Special classes for students with disabilities have the advantage of offering a lower teacher-pupil ratio, a teacher with specialized training, and a setting where it is easier to focus on the distinctive needs of students whose goals may not match the curriculum for general education students. Yet despite the fact that the vast majority of students with disabilities spend at least half their school day or more in general education classes, once they are identified for services with a qualifying disability, they are still viewed as "belonging" to special education. To a large extent, their relationship to the school is then seen through the lens of their disability status.

Inclusive schooling is an attempt to normalize disability by eliminating the divide between special and general education. It is an extension of the normalization principle and part of the trend advocated by some constituents of the special education community to change the cultural view of how we interpret the meaning of disability. Within the special education community is considerable debate about the benefits and possible outcomes of inclusive schooling, and a sharp political division between those who advocate for a total integration of general and special education and those who caution against such radical reform (Fuchs & Fuchs, 1994). The debate, which has been characterized as a struggle between the anointed and the benighted (Kavale & Forness, 2000a), reflects the many forces that shape the context of the discussion, including beliefs about social policy, educational practice, research agendas, and political ideologies. Yet it is the manner in which each group conceptualizes disability that drives the argument for a particular delivery of services (Andrews et al., 2000).

One perspective is based on the medical model that views disability as a within-child phenomenon. In this case, disability is something to be treated with special procedures, which are sometimes best implemented in separate placements, in order to remediate the deficit or impairment. The other perspective looks at disability as a social construction that is minimized or exacerbated by the student's environment. Varenne and McDermott's writings (1999) have demonstrated the power of schools and culture to create disability in some settings and eliminate it in others. While the nature of disability lies somewhere between residing within the individual and as a construct of society, special education demonstrates what Pugach (1995) refers to as a failure of imagination. It is impeded by the medical model emphasis on disability as a manifestation of the individual and for the most part is unable to capitalize on the possibilities that arise when the focus is shifted to context.

This chapter addresses the issue of inclusive educational experiences for students with disabilities in the United States. It starts by looking at special education's beginnings and then examines the least restrictive environment mandate and its relationship to inclusive schooling. It discusses the research findings in regard to inclusive practices and provides model cases to illustrate what inclusive schooling might look like at the elementary, middle, and secondary levels. The chapter concludes by noting current issues that are likely to have an impact on the future of inclusive schooling.

## History of Inclusive Policy and Practices

Federal legislation has been instrumental in providing the legal basis for inclusive practices. Interpretation of the law through court cases has strengthened a student's right to receive services in inclusive settings.

### Public Law 94-142

Public Law 94–142 was carried in on the high tide of the civil rights movement of the 1950s, 1960s, and 1970s. Advocates for students with special needs used the same ideological arguments and political strategies as civil rights leaders—court challenges, enlisting popular political support, and legislation—to ensure all children access to a free and appropriate public education.

Before the law's passage, many students with disabilities were either excluded from school or were not provided with services that allowed them to participate fully. Over 1 million children were denied access to an education on the basis of their disability. Ninety percent of children with developmental disabilities were served in state institutions rather than neighborhood schools (Gartner & Lipsky, 1987).

This legislation has guaranteed students their educational rights for more than thirty years with subsequent reauthorizations of P.L. 94–142, the Individuals with Disabilities Education Act (IDEA; 1990, 2006) and its amendments (1986, 1997), and has expanded its scope by focusing on improved academic and social outcomes for students with disabilities and adding new categories of eligibility. This expansion also included an emphasis on collaboration between special and general education to make general education a more viable choice as the least restrictive environment.

## Mandate for a Least Restrictive Environment

The inclusion movement grew out of the legislated requirement that students with disabilities be educated in the least restrictive environment (LRE). The intent of this provision is to ensure that special education is not a place where students go but instead is a service provided to guarantee equal access to education. Federal regulations require that children with disabilities be educated with their nondisabled peers to the maximum extent possible. They also require that special placements occur only when education in a regular class cannot be satisfactorily achieved with the use of supplemental aids and services (IDEA, 2004). IDEA mandates that schools provide a continuum of placements. Local education agencies are obligated to choose the least restrictive setting in which an appropriate educational plan can be delivered. Therefore, depending on the severity of a student's disability, the least restrictive environment can be any of several settings: a general education class, a resource pull-out program, a special day class, or a special school.

A number of court cases have affirmed that the least restrictive environment can be a variety of placements. The paramount consideration is that the needs of the student are appropriately met (Katsiyannis, Yell, & Bradley, 2001). For example, in *Daniel R.R. v. State Board of Education* (1989), the court determined that a school must ask two questions: (1) Can education in the regular class be satisfactorily provided with supplementary aides and services? and (2) If a child is placed in a more restrictive setting, is he or she integrated to the maximum extent possible?

General education is presumed to be the least restrictive environment, and schools must show good-faith efforts to provide services in it. Yet the courts made clear in *Roncker v. Walter* (1983) that although the general class is considered the least restrictive environment, inclusion is not required when a student with a disability will not benefit from placement in general education, or the marginal benefits would be significantly outweighed by benefits that could feasibly be accomplished in a separate setting.

*Mainstreaming.* The first effort to provide the least restrictive environment for students with disabilities was called mainstreaming, and the term is still used to describe the placement of students with disabilities in the regular school program for any part of their day. As P.L. 94–142 was implemented in the 1970s, schools established programs to provide services for the new population of students. Social pressures that emphasized normalization principles, as well as the mandate to educate students in the least restrictive environment, made it necessary to devise ways to accommodate students in general education. These part-time placements in general education became the forerunner of inclusive practices.

The most common model of mainstreaming is the use of the resource room, where the child attends a special class for a small portion of the school day (perhaps one to two hours) led by a special education teacher who works with individual children or small groups, but the student's primary placement is in general education. At the middle and high school levels, a student attends at least one or two classes in a separate special education room, but other classes are in general education (MacMillan, 1982). Mainstreaming also refers to cases where a student's primary placement is in a self-contained special education classroom, but the student may attend activities or other events, such as art, music, or physical education, in the general education setting.

Initially enthusiasm for mainstreaming was high, but questions began to emerge about the effectiveness of serving students with special needs in general education. Concerns about academic achievement, peer acceptance, students' self-concept, and the preparation of general education teachers to accommodate students with disabilities tempered the response to mainstreaming.

Flawed efficacy studies and widespread attempts at mainstreaming under less than ideal conditions made it difficult to ascertain the effectiveness of mainstreaming practices, but neither was it clear that separate special education placements resulted in significantly better outcomes (MacMillan, 1982). Special education was also under increased scrutiny for over-identification of minority students and for use of an identification process some considered stigmatizing (Gartner & Lipsky, 1987). These conditions led to disagreement as to the best service delivery model and laid the groundwork for the debate over inclusive schooling. While issues about identification, efficacy, and stigmatization were primarily concerns of special education, reform movements in general education were examining how to improve outcomes for low-achieving students. This created an opportunity to bridge the two systems by increasing collaboration between them.

**The Regular Education Initiative.** In 1985 Madeline Will, assistant secretary for the U.S. Office of Special Education and Rehabilitative Services, suggested that both special and general education be reorganized with the goal of forming a partnership that would provide effective instruction for all students and thereby eliminate the duplications of the dual system. Her ideas were in agreement with researchers and advocates who wanted to increase the capacity of general education to accommodate students with mild and moderate disabilities. This was the birth of the Regular Education Initiative (REI), which had three major goals for the transformation of special education: (1) merge general and special education into one inclusive system, eliminating the need for the eligibility process; (2) mainstream most students with mild and moderate disabilities in general education; and (3) improve the academic achievement of students with mild and moderate disabilities (Fuchs & Fuchs, 1994).

The hope was that special education and the compensatory programs of regular education, coupled with new instructional arrangements from special education researchers such as the adaptive learning environment model (ALEM; Wang & Birch, 1984), would work in tandem to offer instruction that could improve the academic outcomes for both at-risk students and those with mild to moderate disabilities. ALEM, developed by Margaret Wang and her colleagues at Temple University in the early 1980s as a comprehensive approach to meeting the needs of diverse learners in the general education setting, was designed to improve academic and social outcomes through the systematic use of effective instructional practice and attention to classroom management.

In addition, REI would eliminate the stigma of labeling students for services and avoid the problems associated with overidentification of African American and Latino students. The intent of those who supported REI was not to dismantle the continuum of services but to restructure it. They proposed that students who were served in residential and day schools would move to their neighborhood schools and be placed in special day classes. Students with mild and moderate disabilities served in resource and pull-out programs would be mainstreamed in general education classes.

## Inclusive Schools Movement

Proponents of the inclusive schools movement advocated a far more radical approach to special education reform (Gartner & Lipsky, 1987; Thousand & Villa, 1990) than did supporters of the REI. They viewed special education as the reason that general education was unable to accommodate students with disabilities (Stainback & Stainback, 1984). In their view, special education gave general educators permission to ignore students whose behavior and academic abilities made them more challenging to teach. It made disability solely a within-child phenomenon and absolved teachers of the responsibility to make accommodations in order to educate these students.

Inclusive schools' advocates claimed that all students with disabilities, even those with severe cognitive impairments or emotional and behavioral disorders, should be served in general education (Stainback & Stainback, 1984). They used the term *full inclusion* to describe the placement of all students with disabilities in general education. The inclusive schools movement began an intensive campaign to move beyond Will's proposal for increased collaboration between general and special education, calling for a complete reorganization of special education that would eliminate the need for separate placements. All students, regardless of the severity of their disability, would be served in the general education class. It was to be a reconceptualization of both special and general education.

Many in the special education community worried that services would be inadequate or nonexistent if placement in a self-contained classroom was not retained as an option (Kaufman, 1993; Lieberman, 1996). They sought to preserve a continuum of placements for students whose disabilities require intensive treatment that is best delivered in a separate setting (Borthwick-Duffy, Palmer, & Lane, 1996). While it was accepted that it might be feasible to meet the needs of students with mild to moderate disabilities in general education, it was doubted that it could be an appropriate placement for students with severe disabilities (Palmer, Borthwick-Duffy, & Widaman, 1998) or behavior disorders (Braaten, Kauffman, Braaten, Polsgrove, & Nelson, 1988). Requiring these students to be served in general education would in fact be a more restrictive environment if their needs could not be adequately and appropriately met.

The debate about inclusion and the changes it has engendered has been productive because, as Pugach states, it is really a debate over "the degree of optimism various stakeholders have regarding the capacity for the educational system, which includes special and general education alike, to recreate itself with inclusion as a basic premise and achievement as a tangible goal" (1995, p. 213). Since the late 1980s, inclusive models of educating students with disabilities alongside their nondisabled peers have expanded in the United States. We now have considerable empirical knowledge about how to provide supports and services in an integrated approach that can appropriately meet the needs of learners with special needs.

## Inclusive Research and Resulting Practices

The first generation of research to examine inclusive schooling practices in the 1980s and early 1990s focused heavily on teacher perceptions of inclusion (Scruggs & Mastropieri, 1996), the efficacy of general education teachers in meeting the needs of students with disabilities (Scott, Vitale, & Masten, 1998), and academic and social outcomes for students with severe disabilities (Hunt & Goetz, 1997) and mild disabilities (Manset & Semmel, 1997). Although much of the research reported mixed findings, there were some general trends: (1) a majority of teachers were in favor of the concept but not necessarily the practice of inclusive schooling; (2) most teachers felt they did not have adequate time, training, or expertise to meet the needs of exceptional learners; and (3) although a majority of teachers saw the usefulness of adaptations and accommodations, they did not use them in a sustained way. Other studies (Baker & Zigmond, 1990) brought to the light the challenges inherent in the task and painted a dismal portrait of early inclusion efforts.

These early programs nevertheless heralded a policy shift that emphasized an increased focus on general education as the LRE. This shift was codified in the 1997 amendments to IDEA that called for increased collaboration between general and special educators, expanded access to services, and improved academic outcomes for students with disabilities. For example, the 1997 legislation required that the individualized education program (IEP) indicate how a student would participate in the general curriculum and justify the extent to which a student was not educated with his or her nondisabled peers. This was a distinct change from the 1990 reauthorization of IDEA, which required justification for the amount of time spent only in special education. The onus was now on schools to explain why a student's needs cannot be met in general education. Studies conducted after this policy shift provide insight into the most recent generation of inclusive schooling.

Recent literature provides empirical evidence that inclusive schools can support high outcomes for students with disabilities. For example, Rea, McLaughlin, and Walther-Thomas (2002) compared academic and behavior outcomes for students with disabilities in a school that used an inclusive delivery of services to one that used a pull-out or resource model and found that students in the inclusive setting performed significantly better on a number of indicators. Those in the inclusive program achieved higher scores on the Iowa Test of Basic Skills in language and mathematics and had comparable scores in reading, science, and social studies. Students in the inclusive program also had comparable scores on the state proficiency exams in reading, writing, and mathematics. They earned higher course grades in language arts, mathematics, science, and social studies. Inclusive and resource students had no significant differences in the number of suspensions, but inclusive students had better rates of attendance.

Students in the inclusive program also had the benefit of receiving more individualized attention and more rigorous IEP goals than those in the traditional resource model. Special education teachers at the inclusive school used a coteaching model and cotaught in each of the general education content classes that students with disabilities attended. The resource model students received services only during a study skills period they attended in lieu of an elective class. They had no individualized support in their content classes. A difference in the quality and number of IEP goals between the two schools was also evident. The IEPs in the inclusive school emphasized instruction, as opposed to behavior, and focused on the general education curriculum rather than a remedial curriculum. In addition, the overall number of goals was higher for inclusive students. For example, a typical goal at the inclusive school stated that the "student will master vocabulary definitions" as opposed to a resource goal of "student will master short vowel sounds." The expectations for included students appeared to be similar to those held for students without disabilities. This is an important finding given that one of the purposes of educating students in general education classes is to move away from the remediation model and provide access to the core curriculum. An overemphasis on skill building deprives students of opportunities to experience the content to which their peers have access.

These findings are related to those of Wallace, Anderson, Bartholomay, and Hupp (2002), who used an ecobehavioral assessment to examine teacher behaviors, student responses, and classroom ecologies in four inclusive high schools from different geographical regions in the United States. (Ecobehavioral assessment is a quantitative approach to analyzing the interaction of teachers and students within the context of the school environment.) The study found high rates of engagement for both teachers and students in these schools. Teachers were observed spending 75 percent of their time interacting, instructing, and managing students in their classrooms and a small percentage of their time disciplining students (1.37 percent) or not responding to students (10 percent). In addition, 44 percent of their time was focused on a group of students that included a student with disabilities. These rates of teacher activity are higher than those typically reported in general education classrooms. The authors hypothesize that perhaps effective instructional strategies are now more widely in use in inclusive classrooms, compared to findings from the mid-1980s. Rates of student engagement on academic tasks (45 percent) for students educated in inclusive settings were also higher than the 34 to 39 percent reported in the literature for noninclusive settings.

Research on inclusive schooling has also added to the knowledge base about the contextual factors that promote, or impede, the success of inclusive models. Fisher, Sax, and Grove (2000) and Zollers, Ramanthan, and Yu (1999) note that the success of the inclusive schools they studied was due in large part to the shared leadership at the school site. Although the programs were instituted because of partnerships between local universities and school districts, the site principals fostered participatory leadership and gave teachers a voice in the decision making. As one teacher said, "We created it, and we like it the way it is" (Fisher et al., 2000, p. 220). The programs became an integral part of the school, and in fact came to define the schools as unique and visionary.

Interestingly, the term *inclusion* took on a new meaning to school staff as it was viewed as a way to offer help to any student who needed it and was not just a description of the service delivery model for special education students. For example, one school's Title I and bilingual personnel worked with resource specialists to provide comprehensive support to all students who required more intensive help. *Inclusion* was defined as a classroom comprising students with a range of abilities, not just the addition of students with disabilities.

Inclusion was also seen as a way to respect the diversity of the school community. Initially it was a new model for delivery of services, but it came to mean the establishment of a climate of "openness, respect, and shared power" (Zollers et al., 1999, p. 11). Each school created a culture of inclusion that delivered unexpected benefits. For example, the positive manner in which students were perceived and the culture that supported these perceptions were also manifested in relationships with parents and the way in which teachers collaborated. Both schools had high parent satisfaction levels after implementing an inclusive model, as evidenced by one school's dramatically increased attendance rates and the other's need to establish a waiting list for students who wanted to transfer to their site. Parents viewed these schools as desirable educational environments for their children.

However, other studies offer a warning that lack of leadership and a top-down approach to implementing an inclusive program can lead to negative outcomes. Mamlin (1999) describes an elementary school where the principal subverted efforts of teachers and a restructuring facilitator to include students with mild to moderate disabilities in general education classes while ostensibly promoting the program. By the end of the first year of implementation, most students were served in separate, not inclusive, settings and, ironically, in some instances were separated to a greater extent than before "inclusion." General and special education staff did not collaborate and rarely even communicated with one another. The external pressures that introduced the program to the site—directives from the district and assistance from the university—were not enough to create an organizational change where inclusive practices could take hold and grow. Without leadership to mobilize and involve staff in crafting a program that was adapted to the needs of their site, there was no inclusion.

Fox and Ysseldyke (1997) also describe a purported inclusion program that was inclusive in name only. Students were pulled out of general education classes when the special education teacher felt the material was too difficult for them. General education teachers did not change instructional strategies to accommodate their needs, and seventh- and eighth-grade students with disabilities attended science class not in general education but in a resource room. Although there was increased time in general education compared to the school's previous program, the site lacked a stable, comprehensive delivery of inclusive services; as a result, students' placements in general education were tenuous.

# Inclusive Models

The studies previously reviewed demonstrate that inclusive schooling can be successful if implemented with close attention to each school's unique context. Given inclusion's strong association with individual beliefs or values about how schools should be organized, it requires strong leadership to establish and support a common set of expectations for all stakeholders in the school's educational community. School leadership must develop and promote a vision of inclusion that guides the staff while they plan for and implement their chosen model (Halvorsen & Neary, 2001; Villa & Thousand, 2005). Attitudes toward inclusive practices can also have an impact on the quality of educational services and the climate a teacher establishes in the classroom (Falvey, 1995). In addition, district-level commitment is vital because that is where decisions are made about funding for staff and instructional materials; where staff development in areas such as curriculum differentiation, collaboration, and IEP planning is supported; and where the resources to provide supplementary services are managed. Sustained attention to all of these factors is critical to the success of an inclusive school; without leadership, support, and shared commitment, a school is unlikely to be successful (Sindelar, Shearer, Yendol-Hoppey, & Liebert, 2006).

We look at three examples of how schools can include their students with disabilities in general education classrooms within a high school, middle school, and elementary school setting (Menzies, 2005). Other configurations are possible, but the key to success in implementing these models is that each school creates a system sensitive to the needs and values of its own educational community.

## Dewey High School

Dewey High School is located in an urban area of southern California. Many parents move to its neighborhood due to its reputation as a high-quality school. It serves approximately fifteen hundred students, and the racial and ethnic mix of its student body is 3 percent African American, 17 percent Hispanic, 34 percent white, and 37 percent Asian. Six percent of students qualify for special education services.

Dewey uses a three-tier model that offers graduated support with an emphasis on providing services in general education. The level of support a student receives depends on the intensity of his or her needs. In the first tier, a special educator consults with the general education teachers to determine which students need only minimal support to be successful. These students (mostly with mild or moderate disabilities) attend all of their classes in general education. The special educator works with the general education teachers to modify curriculum, facilitate communication between home and school, and identify resources. She also checks on student progress at least once every two weeks.

Students in the second tier attend the learning lab one period a day to receive more intensive support with study skills, organization, and homework assignments. The learning lab teachers maintain a daily list of lessons and assignments from the general education classes so that they can help students manage their work. Students may also attend another period of intensive skill development in either mathematics or reading.

Dewey High School serves very few students in its third tier. At this level of support, students attend all academic classes in the learning lab with a special educator and are included in general education only for electives and physical education. Students in the third tier receive instruction in functional life skills as well as skill development in reading, writing, and basic math.

Dewey's program means that special educators must be both knowledgeable and organized. They must truly be specialists. As an example, Mrs. Samuels, Dewey's special education teacher, has a caseload of forty students who are served in all levels of the three-tier model. She is responsible for monitoring the progress of twenty-six students who are served in the first tier. In addition, eleven of her students attend the learning lab for study skills and mathematics, and three receive third-tier support. Mrs. Samuels teaches two periods of mathematics (a prealgebra class and a math skills class), two periods of study skills, and one period devoted to consultation with general educators. The remaining period is her preparation time. Clearly she has a demanding schedule that requires a high level of expertise.

## Florence Nightingale Middle School

Florence Nightingale Middle School is located in a suburban area of southern California and serves fifteen hundred sixth-, seventh-, and eighth-grade students. The student body is 8 percent Asian, 9 percent African American, 25 percent Hispanic, and 55 percent white. Approximately 7 percent of its students qualify for special education services. The school has won several awards for academic excellence and is a model demonstration site for its inclusion program.

All students with mild and moderate disabilities are fully included in general education classes. The special education staff uses a mix of coteaching and collaborative consultation to provide services for these students. In the coteaching model, a general and special educator work together to provide instruction and share responsibility for all students in the class. They rely on each other's expertise to deliver the core curriculum while providing specialized accommodations for those who require them. The collaborative consultation model requires the special educator to meet regularly with the general educator to assist with lesson planning, providing appropriate accommodations, and adapting curriculum. The special educator may work with individual children, but the main focus of his job is to provide resources to general education teachers that allow them to deliver appropriate instruction to their students with special needs.

Mrs. Sandoval, the general education algebra teacher, and Mr. Maio, the special educator, coteach a fifth-period algebra class and often meet during their common conference time to plan. Mrs. Sandoval lays out the overall lesson, while Mr. Maio provides strategies or accommodations that align with the lesson's objectives. They find that discussing the lesson together helps them troubleshoot possible problems or devise more effective teaching techniques.

Florence Nightingale Middle School also relies on a teaming model to create an enhanced learning environment for its students. Teachers from each of the academic content areas form a team. The team shares the same group of 150 students, which enables them to monitor student progress more efficiently. Every week the history, science, language arts, elective, mathematics, and special education teachers meet in their teams to discuss their students. They identify any students who require additional support and then create an action plan to assist them. The action plan consists of a host of strategies to be implemented by the general educators, the special educator, the parents, and the student. After a plan is formulated, the student and his or her parents are invited to meet with the team to discuss their recommendations. Nightingale's philosophy is that the concerns of both parents and the student must be valued in order to develop an effective plan. The Nightingale teachers find that this model makes it possible to offer social and academic support that improves student outcomes.

Students with severe emotional or behavioral disorders and those with low incidence disabilities such as more severe retardation or autism attend nonacademic general education classes such as physical education and some elective classes in combination with specialized classes depending on their individual needs and goals. The multidisciplinary team determines the appropriate classes, with an emphasis on promoting success in the general education classroom to the fullest extent possible. In addition, all students share a common lunch period and attend schoolwide events together. Nightingale has established a "buddies" club that pairs students with severe disabilities with nondisabled peers to integrate them more fully into the social fabric of the school.

## Nelly Bly Elementary School

Nelly Bly Elementary School is located in a midsized city in southern California. It is the smallest of the district's thirty-seven elementary schools and has 330 students from kindergarten through sixth grade. Eight percent of students are African American, 27 percent are white, and 62 percent are Hispanic. Nelly Bly has an unusually high percentage of students (19 percent) designated to receive special education services due to parent interest in its inclusive model.

Nelly Bly School uses an inclusive model of instruction for its students with mild and moderate disabilities and, much like Florence Nightingale Middle School, offers a combination of general education and special education classes to serve students who require more intensive support. However, these students belong to a general education class and spend some portion of every day there.

The special educators provide all students with direct support during language arts instruction. Every general education teacher plans forty-five minutes of small group instruction in language arts. During this time, students are grouped according to their instructional need and meet with their classroom teacher, a paraprofessional, or the special education teacher. All students benefit from this model because it lowers the teacher-student ratio and allows highly individualized instruction based on each student's academic needs. Although the teachers are responsible for different groups, they work together to plan instruction. This helps the specialist become more familiar with the grade-level curriculum and helps the general educator implement specific modifications or accommodations to support students who have special needs or are at risk for school failure.

Ms. Moreno, a special education teacher at Nelly Bly, has eleven students on her caseload. She spends the majority of her time in each of the classrooms during language arts instruction and then collaborates with teachers to provide these students with indirect support for mathematics. During the collaborative consultation over mathematics, Ms. Moreno assists teachers in assessing student progress toward their IEP goals, helps teachers use manipulatives to teach for conceptual understanding, and plans lessons for remediation. She has a good working relationship with all the teachers on campus and is often called on when teachers are looking for effective strategies to support their struggling learners.

All of the teachers at the school feel comfortable asking for Ms. Moreno's assistance. For example, Mr. Cervantes, a second-year teacher, often consults with Ms. Moreno when making decisions about mathematics instruction. She helped him support his students' conceptual understanding of multiplication using materials such as Unifix cubes and games such as Circles and Stars. This was a critical change in his practice as it made him aware of the need to move more slowly from concrete to abstract reasoning for all his students.

## Promoting Success

These brief descriptions offer a few examples of how schools can increase access to the general education curriculum. Of course, any model must be adapted to ensure a good fit with a school's local context. The school site principal is instrumental in promoting the success of an inclusive model. As both the site administrator and instructional leader, the principal must have an understanding of how the various components of effective practice fit together organizationally and be able to create a site-specific plan for a comprehensive approach to inclusion. The principal must also attend to the school's ability to provide inclusive education by building consensus and anticipating possible problems. Promoting an inclusive vision, scheduling, staffing, encouraging collaboration, providing staff development, and welcoming parental involvement are necessary components of school leadership that promote effective inclusive practices.

## Future Perspectives

Models of inclusive schooling and empirical knowledge of effective practices are readily available to guide schools in creating successful programs to serve their students with disabilities in inclusive settings. However, the reauthorized Elementary and Secondary Act (2001; No Child Left Behind [NCLB]) has the power to have a substantial effect on inclusive schooling, and it is not yet clear whether the results will be positive, negative, or, as is most likely, some of both.

NCLB calls for increased accountability through standardized test scores. This has raised questions about how students will be affected in terms of access to general education, quality of instruction, and promotion and graduation policies (Ysseldyke et al., 2004). It is possible that increased accountability will promote inclusive practices as schools search for effective methods to increase all students' test scores, particularly for populations that have had limited success in this area. However, it is also possible that measuring educational quality through the use of standardized tests will result in negative consequences for students with disabilities, such as an increase in both dropout rates and placements in more restrictive settings. Another concern is that the focus on standardized testing may promote remediation at the expense of a high-level and engaging curriculum, particularly for students with disabilities.

An important question is whether students with disabilities receive the accommodations necessary to ensure that their disability does not interfere with the accurate assessment of their performance on high-stakes tests. Some evidence suggests that not all students receive appropriate or useful accommodations, that needed accommodations are not always documented in the IEP, and that some students receive testing accommodations that they have not had experience with during instruction (Shriner & Destefano, 2003; Ysseldyke et al., 2001).

In addition, new provisions in the most recent reauthorization of IDEA may substantially change how general and special educators work together over the issue of literacy. IDEA now allows use of an additional method to identify students for special education services. The response-to-intervention model is intended to provide effective instruction for all students who may be at risk for early reading difficulties. It eliminates the need to formally identify a student with a disability in order to provide initial support. The model has the potential to ameliorate or prevent reading difficulties from becoming more severe and to promote collaboration between general and special education professionals. It is a design well suited to schools seeking to provide an inclusive education for their students. However, researchers caution that we need to carefully implement and monitor its use. A host of issues still need to be addressed, including (1) the use of valid, reliable, and common assessment measures to identify nonresponders to intervention (Fuchs & Fuchs, 2006a); (2) problems related to scaling up and sensitivity to local context (Gersten & Dimino, 2006); (3) concerns related to culturally responsive literacy instruction (Klingner & Edwards, 2006); and (4) the implications of using different perspectives to conceptualize reading difficulty (McEneaney, Lose, & Schwartz, 2006).

Encouraging schools to use inclusive models of education is more difficult when they are negotiating multiple reforms simultaneously. Nevertheless, it may be possible to leverage an inclusive service delivery model to more effectively reach their goals. Explicit attention to the possible unintended consequences is especially critical because of the complexities that each of these reforms entails.

## Conclusion

Schools are complicated organizations, and
to change the status quo do not happen quic.
of students with disabilities in general educatio..
goal, but it is possible to minimize disability by educat..
with their peers in general education while providing appro,
supports and services. It is our opinion that effective inclusive
schooling is still the exception to the rule, and too often schools
emphasize a student's disability through separate placements.
However, it is important to remember the substantial progress
made over the past thirty years and the history of special education
has been one of greater inclusiveness as we work to redefine what
it means to have a disability.

With the collective power of P.L. 94–142 and its subsequent
amendments and reauthorizations, court decisions, and the REI
movement, we confidently believe that the least restrictive environment for students with mild disabilities is a general education
classroom in their neighborhood school. We also expect students
with moderate to severe disabilities to be fully integrated in the
social fabric of their neighborhood school, as well as placed in the
least restrictive academic setting that meets their needs. These
are critical standards that hold schools and districts accountable
for providing inclusive placements.

The advocacy work of those who pressed for greater participation in general education has been critical in changing how
students with disabilities are perceived. In addition, the research
community has created an extensive knowledge base about effective teaching practices for students with disabilities, as well as an
understanding of the organizational structures that support inclusive schooling. This is an indispensable resource for designing
and implementing inclusive schools. With a continued focus on
the necessity of implementing inclusive practices in all schools,
we look to the next generation of research to richly inform policy
and practice in inclusive education.

# FROM THE FIELD: A PERSONAL AND PROFESSIONAL JOURNEY WITH INCLUSION

## Robert W. Farran

The legal mandates are well documented regarding the rights of students with disabilities to be included in general education and the positive benefits of such inclusion. Holly Menzies and Mary Falvey have discussed in detail the definition of and history and research on inclusion and examples of practice.

The journey to this place is filled with a history of separation, advocacy, and emotion that mirrors my own experiences over the past half-century as a child, beginning teacher, principal, and, now, a special education local plan area (SELPA) director. My journey is as an observer, a bystander, and, later, a working professional in the field of special education. The journey of parents of children with disabilities is the more significant journey. The pioneering spirit of these families created the very laws that protect the rights of individuals with disabilities today. The journey results in an inevitable change in one's awareness based on the experience of raising a child with a disability or knowing or teaching such a child.

I grew up in rural Nebraska on a family farm and had an incomplete understanding of what was happening to children with disabilities and their families. When farm neighbors a few miles away gave birth to a child with Down syndrome, hushed whispers from farm ladies and other adults attempted to keep their children from knowing. With the support of doctors and other professionals, these parents, like those of others with children with disabilities, placed the child in the state hospital. No consideration of other options existed, including educating him in the local public school. Education, in fact, was not considered. Medical care was reduced to custodial care, as no real medical issues existed. Given the large number of similar children residing in these hospitals across the country, society made this option the norm. This approach of treating disability as a medical condition within the child is referenced in the literature as the medical model.

On a high school field trip to the state hospital arranged by a caring teacher bent on expanding the awareness of young minds, I remember being struck by the similarities of the residents to my own experiences. The programs at the hospital mirrored life in rural America, with chores, tending gardens, manual labor, and working with others in a group. It was ironic to have separated these individuals from the communities when their lives seemed parallel to the lives of those living outside their walls.

Forty years later, this hospital finally closed its doors, and the neighbor's child I had never met came home to the farm. Farm life was and still is filled with manual labor, opportunities for endless outdoor activities, and hard work respected and valued by the community—tasks this individual easily handled. So why did forty years have to elapse to achieve community-level inclusion?

The attitudes of people today, including professionals, continue to be shaped by our history as a nation. The civil rights movement of the 1950s and 1960s leading up to the significant legislative changes of the 1970s started a process that challenged the way we thought about educating and including individuals with disabilities, unlike the medical approach. Regardless of these initial efforts and the changing view of disability as possibly a response to social norms and the environment, progress toward more inclusive practices has been all too slow.

In the years before the enactment of P.L. 94–142, I started my teaching career in California in a special day classroom on a general education school campus. I was young, full of ideas, and loved my group of young children, who exhibited language and developmental delays as well as autistic-like behaviors. My colleague next door, another young first-year teacher, and I were stunned by the notice from the principal that we needed our own recess, our own lunch period, and our own bus drop-off point away from the front of the school. No support existed for changes. It was up to us to win over the staff. Our attempts at advocacy to foster collaboration included trays of cookies for the teachers' lounge and holiday parties inviting other teachers and students to visit our rooms. Our attempts were met with mixed reviews. The parents, however, were grateful to be on campus and grateful for our enthusiasm, even though we were two distant systems operating in the same school. When the law changed in 1975 and for years later, little change occurred. Even today, this entrenched notion of separation permeates our schools. In hindsight, we were too complacent.

Later, in the 1980s, I had the opportunity to serve as a special education principal assigned to the Lanterman State Hospital in southern California, with the task of dismantling the on-grounds school and bringing the students to a segregated school in the community. Like my neighbor on the farm in Nebraska, many of these students had been placed at Lanterman at birth by parents encouraged to do so by so-called well-meaning professionals. My heart still hurts when I reflect on the broken bonds between parents and their children brought about by the medical model, an ignorant society, and professionals unaware of the impact of such recommendations. The resistance of the hospital staff and many teachers was a major barrier. When the large yellow school bus picked up the more than twenty students from Lanterman State Hospital and headed down the freeway toward Pomona and El Camino School where I was the new acting principal, these students' lives were changed forever. Think about the levels of excitement these students, who had never been on a bus before or traveled at the speed limit on a bumpy road, experienced: fears, joys, and new sensations, sounds, smells, and sights. It was a journey brought about solely by a change in the law in America and brave parents and advocates who insisted that the law apply to everyone. It was a major move, but still miles away from a seat in a general education classroom.

In the 1990s, the mothers who approached me to support them in seeking inclusion for their children changed how I thought about the process forever. I learned that no prerequisites apply for inclusion. I learned that creative solutions can be found for any problem. I learned to value each experience and each story of new friendships, of full access, of participation. One brave parent who pushed the system for her daughter and countless others called me the day her daughter "ditched" school with the other students and got in trouble. This too was a success story for inclusion—not because of the situation but because this student had become a member of an adoptive peer group, in on the plan and loyal to this adolescent cause. Peer group status is a clear success indicator for inclusion. Inclusion became a more available option for families when family support systems started to evolve.

When early intervention was expanded to include infants in California as part of Early Start legislation in 1993, parent support and parent needs, priorities, and resources were legislated as part of the process. This movement was the catalyst for the development of a host of parent support systems, family resource centers, and access to information at the community level. With this new knowledge, families now had support and information to seek increased inclusion opportunities.

For all of these years since the laws were passed in the 1970s, the most significant barrier to inclusion, other than attitudes of individuals about disability, is enforcement. The law is clear, but achieving compliance has been a challenge. It appeared for many years that since the state and federal government knew the mandate was underfunded, compliance monitoring would be at a low standard. Thus, the only option that parents were often left with was filing a formal complaint (due process). Once they filed, their relationship with the school and district seldom improved and often deteriorated. With new knowledge and later armed with the research discussed in this chapter, parents have prevailed, and systems have learned to adapt.

This spawned both a well-meaning advocacy and legal community along with some interests that used this approach to exploit systems, students, and the law. What was and is still needed is clear understanding of the mandate, creative approaches to addressing each child's unique needs, consistent monitoring, and enforcement.

In my current position as regional director of special education programs in the southwest area of Los Angeles, more has happened to move toward inclusion. In the 1990s, we trained special education teachers, created basic support systems, and identified general education teachers willing to work collaboratively as partners. Progress was always best achieved when the parent pushed enough to make inclusion part of the IEP and when the school identified willing partners. When the teachers were less willing, or administrators less supportive, or the parent more demanding, we typically saw staff working to a point, but resisting real change. With a special day class just down the hall, staff often felt less responsible since options were available.

In the last few years under the banner of "response to intervention," some well-informed districts have moved away from special classes and opened up a wide range of learning centers and other interactive settings where both students with disabilities and students who just need some extra help seek support. These new settings have not solved our problems or typically included pupils with more severe disabilities, yet they are a positive outcome, bringing truth to the notion that special education is more about services than placements. These new models also are small steps toward schoolwide intervention for all students. It has been a long time in coming, and we need to observe and collect the data necessary to determine the benefit of these new settings on individual student outcomes. Regardless of the approach to inclusion, the research discussed in this chapter points to the opportunity for a new kind of strong, ethical leadership that supports high expectations for staff and students and with a view that all children belong and all can benefit from inclusive education.

Today the journey continues. The progress has been far too slow. I, like others, never thought that we would still be at the awareness level thirty years or so after the law was passed. Today schools seem to want an award for including students with mild learning disabilities into the general education classroom—groups I believe were never intended to be pulled out of general education in the first place. It appears that society still needs firsthand experience with an individual with a disability to understand: that is, to see the child as a whole, happy, complete human being, capable of great joy and love and success, with disability only a feature of his or her character like hair color and other individual differences.

We must move beyond the notion of less able and think about civil rights for individuals with disabilities in a proactive way. It is not just the responsibility of driven parents to seek a place in general education for children with disabilities. It is the system's responsibility to ensure that such a seat exists, as well as the necessary supports and services to assist children in learning. We already know that equal education is not the mandate, but the appropriate education called for in the mandate must be reasonably calculated in order to result in educational benefit. This is what the law provides, a law that speaks well of us as Americans. It is time we make inclusion a reality.

# 4

# GAINING ACCESS TO THE SCHOOLHOUSE

## Richard Cohen
### with Terese C. Jiménez

The Los Angeles Unified School District was
accused of systematically violating the civil rights of
its 65,000 special education students in a class
action lawsuit filed in 1993. Individualized education programs were not being followed or even
created. Special education services were not being
provided in a timely manner nor were children being identified for these services. Student files
were lost. Parents found themselves ignored by the
schools, their concerns dismissed. Many students
with disabilities were warehoused in a district
described as deeply entrenched in a culture of
segregation. The board of education accepted
liability for these civil rights violations and entered
into the Chanda Smith Consent Decree, a court
supervised agreement promising to bring the
nation's second largest school district into compliance with federal and state laws.

—*Richard Cohen,*
*Going to School—Ir a la Escuela (2001)*

On April 15, 1996, Judge Laughlin Waters ordered the Chanda
Smith Consent Decree as the result of a negotiated settlement to
*Chanda Smith* v. *Los Angeles Unified School District*, a class action
lawsuit. (A consent decree is a court-supervised agreement to

oversee a district's compliance with federal and state laws.) The district admitted serious problems in its delivery of special education services and was found to be out of compliance with both special education and civil rights laws.

Following the beginning of the consent decree and over several years, the district began to carefully and purposefully overhaul its services for students with disabilities. In order to facilitate the process of educating teachers, parents, and staff about the needs and realities of students with disabilities, the Class Member Review Committee of the Chanda Smith Consent Decree commissioned Richard Cohen, an independent filmmaker, to produce two short scripted educational videos, one in English and one in Spanish. Cohen and the committee were dedicated to producing an honest documentary that would move audiences, challenge stereotypes of children with disabilities, share the experiences of parents, and bring viewers closer to a common humanity. Months of painstaking research resulted in the film *Going to School—Ir a la Escuela.*

The film primarily chronicles the experiences of Latino families—their struggles, dreams, and hopes for their children. Cohen interviews several administrators, teachers, and parent advocates, inquiring about their perceptions regarding the difficult process of enforcing inclusive practices within the large district. He follows students with disabilities, documenting their experiences on school playgrounds, in their classrooms, during therapy sessions, and in their homes. *Going to School* addresses such issues as inclusion, advocacy, parental involvement, and disability rights, among others, from the unique perspectives of adults in the district and the students under their care and supervision. Although the film focuses its attention on one district, it raises themes of educational inequity that apply nationally and internationally.

This chapter poses a series of questions to Richard Cohen where he discusses his experiences in making the film and his thoughts regarding the inclusion of students with disabilities. The documentary filmmaker talks about how the film portrays the role of parents, students, teachers, administrators, and the media itself toward facilitating more inclusive practices for students with disabilities within the educational system. Throughout the chapter, Cohen uses the terms *inclusion* and *inclusive practices* to represent the education of students with disabilities on general school campuses within general education classrooms rather than segregated special education settings. Inclusive practices may involve providing unique services such as occupational or speech therapy for students outside a general education classroom only briefly and as needed.

Since the film's release in late 2001, *Going to School—Ir a la Escuela* has been used in departments of education, social work, psychology, disability studies, pediatrics, nursing, physical therapy, service-learning, and sociology. Thousands of copies of the film have been obtained by parents, school districts, and parent groups throughout the country. Approximately five hundred universities and colleges across the United States have obtained the film, and that number continues to grow. Given its widespread influence, the chapter discusses this filmmaker's journey making the film and its power on the educational community.

*The film explores the implementation and climate around the inclusion of students with disabilities on integrated school campuses and in general education classrooms. What were your general impressions regarding the district's move toward more inclusive rather than segregated practices?*

When the project began, there was an influential movement within the district to integrate the school campuses and remedy the ways in which the district had been violating the civil rights of children with disabilities and their families. This was a period of hope and optimism. Two consent decree administrators were hired to identify the problems and were in the process of creating plans to bring the district into compliance with the law. My own initial contacts with both the consent decree committee members and the school district administrators were very positive; this continued from before I was commissioned to make the film and later as I conducted months of research in preparation for production.

When I was originally asked to submit a proposal to a subcommittee of the consent decree, it wasn't clear to me that I wanted to make this film, so I attended a meeting of a committee of volunteers working on the decree. This was one of several committees of volunteers, mostly parents of children with disabilities, but also teachers, psychologists, administrators—really, a fair representation of the educational community. Their purpose, as I recall, was to advise and assist the two consent decree administrators in formulating plans to bring the school district into compliance with IDEA [Individuals with Disabilities Education Act] and federal civil rights laws. The committees worked on plans to remedy essential components of special education programs including individualized education programs [IEPs], behavioral intervention, expulsion, accessible buildings and grounds, and least restrictive environment, perhaps the most controversial aspect of their work. Least restrictive environment is the educational setting where children with disabilities are educated alongside their same-age, nondisabled peers to the maximum extent possible.

That first committee meeting was enough to convince me that this project was extremely important and I really wanted to be part of it. Fortunately, the subcommittee commissioning the film selected me for the project. This committee was composed of four mothers of children with disabilities, pioneers of inclusion in the district. I spent a day with each one during my first week of research, and their personal stories prepared me for the work that was to come.

Once I moved away from this nucleus of hands-on social justice work and out into the vast school district, at times it seemed to me that the mere mention of the words *inclusion* or *Chanda Smith* was taken like "fighting words." It was difficult to predict where a person stood on those issues. I found many gradations of resistance to inclusion, at least in schools that I visited and in the various administrative and legal meetings I attended as part of my preproduction research. Resistance did not necessarily mean opposition: inclusion was something new, and that's always hard. I think this is why I was eventually selected to make *Going to School*—to bring a meaningful video to the entire educational community, one that would inspire understanding and dialogue.

For an inclusive experience to work in schools, there has to be a willingness to view the needs of children with disabilities not as special, but as normal needs just as you would view the needs of any other child. In fact, I would do away with terms like *special needs* or *exceptional needs* or *special child*. If special education is not a place but a service, then it certainly is not a special child. The term *special needs student* takes away self-respect, a sentiment some of the students in the film often shared with me. This may not be true for many people, but I think that in our world, these words have created one more barrier for children with disabilities to overcome. Children are separated in school when they must reunite later in life, whether as consumers in shopping malls, or as professionals in banking or legal practices, or as teachers, scientists, short-order cooks, street sweepers, or filmmakers.

When we made *Going to School*, there were seventeen segregated special education campuses in Los Angeles. It occurs to me that by maintaining separate campuses, we are saying that segregation of children with severe disabilities must be done. As a society, we can't have the weakest children in our midst. These kids are indeed part of all children who are being educated. The more that schools implement inclusive practices, the more quickly society will change—just like racial integration. If you integrate the schools, you integrate society, and that's how a generation grows up making change. I believe this is the case for the generations growing up with inclusive practices now.

Before Public Law 94–142 [Education for All Handicapped Children Act] was passed in 1975, many children who were labeled as retarded or referred to as "nature's misfits" or "hopeless ones" were institutionalized. We built state mental hospitals to protect the vulnerable from the evils of society, and for more than a century we often brutalized institutionalized patients. Even the question of killing young children deemed as "nature's misfits" was debated in professional journals and at organized conference meetings [Kennedy, 1942], though no eugenics policy like this was adapted. It hasn't been too many years since this kind of thinking was deemed inhumane and this treatment outlawed. As the pendulum swings away from such historical injustices, perhaps we're still living with the mind-set that produced and tolerated segregated and abusive settings. There is always a need for vigilance, even in the face of well-intentioned people and their actions. Does society not owe children who have been segregated compensation, adjustments for past and present injustices? Does society not owe them, in effect, a better chance?

*A driving force behind this film is family advocacy. You describe families' ongoing journey as they attempt to navigate the school system and advocate for their children with or without the skills to do so. What did you learn about the parents in the film?*

It was really an eye-opener for me. So many parents of children with disabilities work harder at school, at home, and at their jobs in order to be decent parents. They devote much more of their lives to their children's interest and con- tribute more to the school than most other parents when given a chance to be part of the parent community. Many parents understand the importance of education because they see how important it is for their children's future.

Some parents in the film struggled with personal and profes- sional responsibilities in order to meet the added demands of raising a child with disabilities. The family of Cynthia Delgado, a student with muscular dystrophy, planned to get her a larger wheelchair, much like the way parents think about larger shoes or clothes as their children grow up; Cynthia's parents were also planning to move out of their small apartment into a home with wider hallways for their daughter to maneuver. Mr. Delgado was already working two jobs to support his family. Similarly, the family of Sally Sewell, a student with cerebral palsy, had to plan for the enormous cost of buying a van with a lift. These brief examples hint at the kind of additional expenses parents have to consider for their children with disabilities.

David Bruck was another example of this type of dedication. David, whose son Aaron has autism and was in the second grade at the time of filming, was originally a professional accountant. David cut his workload and operated out of his home in order to attend to Aaron's needs and expressed this in the film: "I was a corporate employee . . . [and] department head. I gave up . . . that world. I became a freelancer [and] make less money but I have a much more fulfilling life. I know I've made a difference in [Aaron's] existence." David took care of Aaron, driving him to and from school, and participated regularly as a school volunteer. His ongoing presence on campus made Aaron's dad extremely visible and respected.

The parents of children with disabilities must also demonstrate confidence and determination even when professionals around them begin to lose hope in their children. In one scene, David Bruck recalls a doctor's pessimistic outlook regarding Aaron's future.

[Aaron] had a condition . . . his eyes were pointed outward. They were not in alignment. And we took him to this specialist who did eye surgeries. And [the specialist] looked at Aaron [who] was all of nine months old and he said, "Don't bother with the operation. This kid is so damaged . . . it won't make any difference. Even if you correct his vision he's got so many other problems he'll never make it."

[David, looking straight into the camera and smiling broadly] So, you were wrong! He did make it!

When David turns to the camera and laughs, the audience gets it, and we laugh with him. The scene reflects the kind of courageous decisions parents must make to ensure a future with dignity for their children. We understand the humanity of the moment of not abandoning your child, of defying the arrogance and prejudice that would so easily condemn his boy to whatever bleak fate was imagined for him. This is how change occurs. This was the moment when David and his wife, Helen, decided that their faith and hope in Aaron was stronger than the art of one man's medicine.

Since filming in 2001, Aaron has developed his talents in music and currently excels as a pianist in a jazz combo while attending an arts magnet middle school in the district. Even before Aaron moved out of elementary school, David brought him to visit the arts school. This preparation made it easier for Aaron as well as the school personnel to embrace the transition. Each term David talks with Aaron's classmates about his son's condition and continues to invest a lot of energy in facilitating change in the schools.

The film also underscores the efforts of Sandra Rentería, whose son, Richard, was the first fully included student in his middle school. Richard was born with multiple disabilities, including cerebral palsy and severe hearing loss. Sandra was a highly visible person and really an incredible subject for the kind of documentary filmmaking I most enjoy making. In one scene, Sandra lifts Richard out of the car and into his wheelchair, and that's how her day begins. Sandra often brought her son to school and picked him up after school. By filming this scene, we understand the emotional interaction between a mother and her son. In that moment, we know and feel what Sandra has to do every morning before she goes to work, and we know how Richard's day begins.

I met Sandra before the production when I observed her during an IEP meeting for Richard. Sandra brought along a law book and was prepared to quote from it in order to justify what she wanted for her son. Because of her know-how, she commanded respect from the rest of the team, whether they agreed with her or not. In the film, she shares that it should not be a fight for parents of children with disabilities to get what other children receive naturally: "My interest is my child and I'm not willing to negotiate my child's education. Why should I have to do that if other parents are not being asked to do that who have typical children? Why should I have to sit at a table and negotiate what my son should receive or not? Why can't he receive what he needs. . .and that's it?"

Like David Bruck, Sandra spoke to students in Richard's classes and with his teachers about inclusion and disability. Sandra brings a spirit that invigorates other parents and the educational community. She rallied parents, offering them support and instruction on how to stand up for their children and get the best education for them. Through her continued advocacy, other parents saw that it was possible to get more for their children. It seems to me that Sandra possesses an evolved consciousness about the normalcy of disability beyond many parents and teachers I've met. She is not confined by the limitations of her experiences or by the disabilities of her own child. She put faith in God and took the necessary actions to make change. She was enthusiastic about making the film, seeing its potential for spreading the word about parent advocacy and inclusion.

Another exemplary parental advocate in the film is Teresa Vasquez, the mother of Ruben Rodriguez, a seventh grader with cerebral palsy. There were days when Ruben became so ill that Ms. Vasquez had to interrupt whatever was going on in order to drive to school and take him home. In the film, rather than proceed with a previously scheduled IEP, Ms. Vasquez requests the team to reschedule the meeting given the absence of her son's teacher. However, she does not miss this opportunity to voice some concerns about her son's welfare to the school nurse and counselor, half the IEP team. Ruben's mother may not have carried a law book into her IEP meetings, but as you can see in the film, she stands her ground.

Near the end of the film shoot, I visited the Vasquez home to get an image release that I had previously overlooked. Ms. Vasquez read the image release to Ruben and held it up for him to review. She asked him if it was okay for her to sign the release. Ruben smiled while nodding yes. His mother's actions and attitude gave Ruben the ability to participate in a decision that would directly affect him.

Parents of children with disabilities often feel isolated and stigmatized by their experiences with the school district and other parents. In order to better support these parents, the school district, as a result of the consent decree, established the Parent Resource Network (PRN), a center for families to obtain necessary information regarding their rights and responsibilities as parents of children with disabilities. The advocates hired for the center were parents themselves. The film includes a powerful scene of a woman who had just walked off the street and into the center. Discouraged by the school's lack of support for her almost nonverbal daughter, the mother receives assistance from Sandra Rentería, one of the center's parent advocates, to prepare for her daughter's IEP scheduled for the following day. The woman sobs almost uncontrollably as she recounts her story of frustration:

*Ver ahora a mi hija que está como un animal allí arrinconada. No es justo. Y... yo pedía a la escuela que yo quería justicia porque es mi hija. La escuela a mi... no me quiere escuchar. Y yo por ser madre tengo que ir a muchos lugares. Y por eso estoy aquí.* [To see my daughter like an animal there in the corner. It's not fair. And I asked the school that I wanted justice because she's my daughter. The school doesn't want to listen to me. And because I'm a mother I have to go to many places. And that's why I'm here.]

When this woman originally walked in off the street, her face told the story. I asked if it was okay for us to film, and she consented. Actually, we went to the PRN office that day to film moments that would reflect a typical day. These are the kinds of scenes that Baird Bryant, my long-time cinematographer and friend, has earned his reputation for as a master of the hand-held camera. We were talking recently about this particular scene and about how it sheds light on the filmmaking process. Bryant said, "There is so much pain and suffering going on for the parents and children, but [as a cinematographer] you are insulated by looking through the camera. At the same time, enormous compassion is generated, and you hope this is what will carry through to the audience because in that way, what you do makes a difference."

In this scene it is amazing to see how one parent understands the feelings of another, how the parent advocate acts compassionately and imparts a sense that the other woman's child will be treated justly. The Parent Resource Network has been instrumental in educating thousands of parents how to be confident in IEP meetings and to get the most for their children. Advocates at the PRN travel into the community, present workshops at schools, bring parents together for support, and communicate over the phone in several languages. Parents are finally learning how to navigate the system. The PRN was a major positive outcome of the consent decree.

Over the past few years, the Office of the Independent Monitor overseeing the consent decree has conducted annual public hearings to help evaluate the school district's work. In 2005, I attended one of these events. It was remarkable for me to witness parents and other family members finding the courage and the will to express their outrage publicly and honestly. Their testimony showed the continued widespread violation of the laws in the schools and their great dissatisfaction with the progress that had been made. Mother after mother after father after sister after grandparent testified about delays in IEPs, failure to provide special education services, misinformation provided by school officials to parents, emotional abuse at the hands of administrators, and teachers' stonewalling. The experience was shocking, tragic, and bewildering. Still, it must be gratifying for the many parents who once volunteered and those who continue to work on the consent decree to know that more and more families continue pressing for reform.

Even if parents were not fully informed about their rights, I became aware, in making the film, of a tremendous devotion, love, and commitment of time pouring from families to benefit their children. The parents of children with disabilities may recognize one day their collective strength by making themselves visible in the community. Nationwide, in public schools these families comprise up to 14 percent of the population [U.S. Department of Education, 2005]. Ultimately if it takes a community to educate a child, then a community acting with the dedication of the parents of children with disabilities would leave no child behind. If there are failures, the community is accountable.

*Various students with disabilities appear throughout the film. They share their opinions and their dreams. How important do you feel it was to include students' experiences and voices as part of the film?*

The student voice is the heart of my film. While the committee may have hired me to put forward the experiences of the parents, my own life experience drew me to the children. I was hospitalized with polio for nearly a year when I was six and walked with crutches for most of the time that I attended grade school. I don't recall words like *mainstreaming* or *inclusion* being used back then or even *special education*, although special education schools existed. I attended my neighborhood schools, and that was the way it was. My experiences weren't always perfect and ideal, but they weren't always unpleasant either. There were bullies, and there were friends. There were inspiring teachers, and there were some who were not so inspiring. My elementary school principal must have been an enlightened woman because she made accommodations for me. For instance, instead of taking gym class for a couple of years,

I was encouraged to pursue my interest in theater and was allowed to form a small ensemble company; we wrote and performed plays for the school.

While my early educational experiences nurtured my pursuit of the arts, junior high school was a more troubling and isolating time in my life. For example, the alternative to gym class was sitting alone in someone else's homeroom period, often feeling more like detention. Reflecting back on those junior high years, I see the absence of other children with disabilities in my life. In this regard my experiences were very different from those of the students in *Going to School—Ir a la Escuela*. This created a curiosity for me, and the film is their story. What impressed me most about these kids was an unquestioning sense of belonging at each of their schools, even as their district and society were tangled in a legal and political civil rights struggle. This was very powerful for me to observe. These students were motivated and independent. They maintained friendships, were proud of their loving families, and displayed an incredible amount of self-confidence.

Some time after the film was completed, Cynthia Delgado, a seventh grader in the film, told me during a visit about the unexpected death of her close high school friend during a surgery. After the film was released, I visited with Ana Uribe, a seventh grader in the film, who was preparing herself for another in a series of corrective surgeries. These moments reawakened me to the fact that children with disabilities often experience substantial issues and in some instances confront their mortality at an early age. This point is illustrated in the film when Ana Uribe, injured as a young child from a grenade attack in El Salvador, recounts in one scene the incident with amazing calmness and clarity:

> They had a war over there. And we lived [in] something like this [Ana looks around her yard] with my mom and grandma and some other people. And there were soldiers [revolutionaries] around [the neighborhood] and they wouldn't let anybody in or

out. The police to...get them out...started throwing bombs. But that didn't work. And one of the bombs, I think they were grenades...went down and the little pieces of metal went into my back and made a hole. And it hurt my spinal cord and I lost a lot of blood.

The day we filmed that interview, we rode home with Ana in the school bus. She was greeted by several joyful children living in the area. We filmed the interview at the front door of their small one-room unit where Ana and her mother lived. In the next scene, Ana's mother relives the emotional trauma of what happened a lifetime ago when she carried Ana for three days in her arms to the nearest hospital:

*Como estuvo en el hospital como un mes y medio y yo estuve con ella. Lo que se puso fue muy mal de los nervios. Porque tenía miedo que la...inyectaran y todo eso. Tantas inyecciones y suero. Tanta cosa que le pusieron. Entonces ya después como que salió muy nerviosa porque en las noches gritaba. Despertaba llorando y asustada.* [Since she was in the hospital like a month and a half and I was with her. She became very nervous. Because she was afraid that they would inject her and all of that. So many injections and plasma. So many things they put in her. And she would wake up screaming and frightened.]

For Ana's mother, memories of the ordeal will never be forgotten. For Ana, suffering at an early age may have shaped her steadfast confidence. When we spoke not long ago, she made it clear that disability is not part of her fundamental identity. She knows her limitations, and she continues to maintain her long-range dream of going to college. But for now, her immediate goal after graduating from high school is to ease the burden on her mother by supporting herself financially.

Several students in the film also talk about their dreams after finishing school. The film creates a clear sense that other students like Ana did not perceive their disability as an obstacle to their future plans. In one scene, Nhien "Le" Doan, an eighth-grade student, freely describes her intention to advocate for others in the future.

> I want to go to [a] four-year university.... And...I really wish to be a lawyer and I could fight for the people right. I would like things changed. I would like to see the kids start going out to regular class[es] and not to stay in one building all day long and see the same people and I think they should have the same right to learn as much as the other kids do.

In this scene, it is easy to share with Le the injustice of seeing students segregated in a single special education building on a regular campus. We hear from her that it is wrong, and we believe her when she matter-of-factly tells us that she will fight for the civil rights of students with disabilities. How amazing for a girl that young to know her future so clearly. Le graduated from high school and did go on to college.

The students did not only dream of fighting for their rights, but actively found ways to advocate for themselves and their peers. While I was editing the film, one student told me a story about how she was often late to class on the second floor of the school building because it was necessary for her to go to the nurse's office and get someone to walk down the hall and unlock the elevator for her. She and another student went to the principal and asked him for their own elevator key. He thought it was a good idea but told them to speak with the vice principal, also a head counselor. Together the girls approached the vice principal with their request. After the vice principal responded by telling them it was sweet, she told them no. The administrator then made the mistake of "petting" one of the girls on the head. This petting on the head was taken as an insult, a condescending action because the student was seated in a wheelchair. The girls protested to the principal both the decision and the woman's behavior and eventually were given a key. What these girls did was fantastic! They took matters into their own hands. They were empowered to transcend IEPs and demanded that their needs be met so that they could achieve a meaningful education. That's an example of the school's positive response. More important, it's a reflection of the girls' self-confidence, a reflection of the loving support given to them by their parents.

Several of the students in the film, including Cynthia, Le, and others, graduated high school and went on to attend college. Across the country, an increasing number of students with disabilities are enrolling in universities and colleges—post P.L. 94–142 [Horn & Berktold, 1999], where at least 11 percent of undergraduates report having a disability [Horn & Nevill, 2006]. This means more people with a disability rights perspective and an understanding of the system will return to the public schools as teachers, parents, and activists. They will change things for the better from the inside. Cynthia plans to teach at the elementary school she attended. Having Cynthia teaching in any public school will shake up the status quo. She is a quiet, thoughtful powerhouse who speaks her mind when it matters. She sees what is right and what is wrong.

*Special educators are critical members of any school staff in supporting the education of students with disabilities. In the film, you specifically highlight Greg Laskowski. Could you describe why his work with his students and their families was so significant?*

Greg Laskowski, the special education teacher featured in the film, was a fearless advocate. The first time I approached Greg, he was racing to the football field where the school's class photograph was being taken. The previous year, his students who used wheelchairs were excluded from the picture, pushed aside. That year it wasn't going to happen again.

Greg took a lot of heat for his determination to protect the rights of his students and for encouraging them to find their rightful place in the world. Parents turned to him for advice on their IEPs, whether he was a team member or not. His outspokenness and his actions often put his job on the line.

Greg welcomed our crew into his class, and this led to some very memorable moments in the film. For example, in one scene, he stands in the classroom within earshot of his students and speaks freely of significant issues: how the school administration had ignored his requests to build a ramp at the main entrance so that all students could enter through the front door: "I'm waiting for the front of the school to get ramped. So I'm waiting. I'm patiently waiting to see if that will ever come to pass. Sometimes I hear that there is not enough room to have the stairs and the ramp. Well ... so maybe everybody can walk up the ramp." The middle school had a large number of physically disabled students, yet at the time it wouldn't build a ramp at the front entrance. Greg also spoke of how important it was for students to attend their neighborhood schools, so they could grow up with their siblings and neighbors and share those memories:

> To have the kids go to the neighborhood school ... because they live in the neighborhood of that school and that's where all the other students are going to school. All their friends, all their neighbors, their brothers and sisters are all going to that school. And if they go to that school too that is the experience that I think almost all of us grew up with. When you take the child and bus them into a situation and then he's bused back into his neighborhood he never gets the chance to become as social as you and I [were] when we were in school.

When I talked with Cynthia Delgado as she was about to graduate from high school in 2005, she mentioned Greg as the teacher who most influenced her. You can see in the film how Greg encourages his students to think about their futures, to realize that they have futures. In each of the locations I visited, there were teachers and staff who fully believed in inclusion and equal education. These people were doing everything in their power to integrate inclusive practices into the educational system, much like Greg Laskowski.

*In the film, you interview several district administrators and specialists. Could you discuss how you believe these individuals facilitate the process of change toward more inclusive educational experiences for students with disabilities?*

Ultimately I believe the superintendent makes a difference in how reform is implemented and enforced. If the superintendent is courageous and proactive in making change, voices tolerance and equality for all children, then the employees and teachers in his or her district will be encouraged to act to achieve the ideal educational environment and to speak their minds without fear of retribution. From open dialogue comes a better society.

There is a scene in the film that I like very much. Superintendent Ramon Cortines talks with parents of the Class Member Review Committee. He condemns the segregation of students in special education day classes: "There is integration in a classroom and integration in a school.... I'm trying to set a new culture...of inclusion...of a deep understanding of what it all means.... I think we've talked a lot in most districts, not just this district, about all children but it's been more rhetoric than practice."

While Mr. Cortines was acting superintendent, I noticed a spirit of cooperation in consent decree committee meetings I attended. There existed hope that years of effort by the lawyers, consent decree administrators, and the many devoted volunteers (including parents, teachers, and representatives of the educational community) to bring justice and reform to the school district would soon succeed. I think after Mr. Cortines left the district, the effort to genuinely follow through with the consent decree faltered. This is clearly evidenced by remarks made in the annual reports given to the school board by the independent consent decree monitors and their predecessors [*http://www.oimla.com*]. That's not to say there weren't administrators who did their best to discourage inclusion under Mr. Cortines. For example, while we were filming Richard Martinez learning to maneuver his wheelchair around the school playground, a vice principal approached me and told me off camera that inclusion was a "big waste of money," referring to Richard's placement in the school. These kids can't learn, and there's no benefit to having them there. In the film, I share this incident with Cathy Henig, a special education facilitator, who said, "There are those feelings and I'm sure there will always be those feelings. Well, we don't know what Richard's capable of doing. Richard can live a full and good life, and he can learn a lot of things, and I'll reiterate what I said before: I think a society is measured by what we do for those who are most in need."

This administrator highlighted the need for advocates to work at the district level—advocates like Cathy Henig and her supervisor, Nancy Franklin, who is also interviewed in the film. Nancy trained the district's inclusion facilitators, some of whom were parents of children with disabilities. If someone believes in his or her heart in inclusion and respect for all children and rises to a position of authority, that message will be conveyed clearly to everyone working under him or her. In the film, Nancy Franklin reflects on the divisive growth of two separate worlds: special education and general education: "Some of it has to do with the development of these two kingdoms of special ed and general ed. Once we start...on this road...where these are two separate groups, then you lose the things that are the most important. You lose belonging. You lose that sense that this child can demonstrate mastery in different ways." Nancy's words describe the longstanding culture of segregation existing within many educational programs and its negative consequences on children and teachers. This climate of segregation most certainly explains why it remains difficult to implement the practice of inclusion in schools.

Another administrator who impressed me was Gloria Sierra, who was the principal at Eagle Rock High School in the early

1990s when the district began an inclusion program. In the film, Ms. Sierra recounts how she was approached by an administrator outside a district principal's meeting and told quite apologetically that she would be receiving the first inclusion student at her school. This attitude has not entirely disappeared. In the film, Gloria Sierra greatly contrasts these sentiments as she describes the need for inclusion. She becomes emotional when telling a story about the mother of her first inclusion student:

I love this story a mother told. She was shopping at the local supermarket. For years and years that she had lived in that community and shopped in that supermarket and taken her son to shop, walking down the aisles, he had no peer group. And she was invisible, she and her son were invisible. But for the first time [after being included in a regular school] she'd go shopping and students that saw Ralph in class would say, "Hi, Ralph." And the way she expressed it . . . almost makes me emotional right now . . . . It is a civilized way of dealing with other human beings in our society . . . . The child learns, the child learns that he or she . . . is valuable . . . is not expendable.

It was only by chance that we met Gloria Sierra during the production, and she consented to this interview on the spot. It was moving for me to hear her talk, and suddenly I realized that the mother she was describing was Barbara Marbach, one of the four women who had commissioned me to make the film. This shows how the remarkable determination of parents like Barbara and the three other women affects educators and administrators, who in turn take that experience with them to different schools, and that's how change happens.

*Film has the power of bringing awareness to important issues in a very different way from other mediums. Could you discuss how you feel the film facilitates change regarding the inclusion of students with disabilities?*

I think it's important for schools and families to bring together the entire educational community in dialogue over issues regarding special education services, inclusion, accessibility, IEPs, and disability rights. It shouldn't be left to administrators and the courts to bring about compliance with the law. *Going to School—Ir a la Escuela* was produced so that it would facilitate a dialogue of change among parents as well as among the educational community outside special education such as administrators, teachers, students, janitors, cooks, bus drivers, family members, and so on. A good vehicle for accomplishing this is a documentary. If *Going to School* were screened at local PTA meetings, rotary clubs, city councils, boards of education, and places where civic-minded people get together, I think we would begin to see more support from the general community.

The dialogue has to move beyond special education and disability interests and into the broader community so that *inclusion* itself becomes an obsolete term in a world of equality. Over 34 percent of adults with disabilities live in extreme poverty with an annual income of fifteen thousand dollars or less [O'Neil, 2005]. How else is this going to change? If the district had shown the film at every school or for staff trainings or to all parents, it would have started the discussion. I'm sure it would get them talking today. They would hear different points of view and how schools were accomplishing inclusive educational practices. Negative experiences could become lessons. Breaking down these barriers would make people less fearful and diminish stigma and suffering. That is a way of using media in the schools and within the community as a first step.

Mostly what I want for viewers is to feel the humanity of the students, parents, and teachers. If a viewer can laugh with Le Doan when she expresses her desire to be a lawyer, or feel her anger at the unfair isolation of children with disabilities within the school, limiting their chances to learn, then I think the film is working. There are images I hope viewers will remember: the expression of curiosity on the face of Richard Martinez when he gets a chance to look through a microscope in his general education science class, the strong manner and humor of special education teacher Greg Laskowski standing tall in his classroom, speaking his mind in front of his students. It shows the respect he has for them. I want viewers to walk away remembering Greg's main lesson to his students: to feel that they can go anywhere in the world and be welcomed. It's important to see Ruben Rodriguez eating lunch through a tube into his stomach in class—to not turn away but to appreciate the nuance of his expressions, subtly revealing of his life experience: choosing a flavored beverage to be poured down the tube, nodding his objection to the arm restraints, and smiling when another student, Ellie, wheels over to him and asks if he is full after eating lunch. These are important moments in the film.

In part, this was the purpose for making *Going to School—Ir a la Escuela*: to create a film that would emotionally reach a wide audience of viewers of different ages and backgrounds while showing how everyone is affected by the inclusion of children with disabilities.

The film can inspire other students or teachers to say there is something of value here. That's what a film can do. I can't necessarily change people who are dead set against inclusion or who have their reasons or are prejudiced. But the stories of these children and their families and teachers can inspire people who are receptive. Film can catalyze in people some kind of awakening, break down the stigma that exists, and fortify self-confidence in people who are otherwise oppressed. It can expose people in a meaningful way to the issues of inclusion, special education, and disability rights. It stirs discussion in classrooms and accomplishes what we set out to do in the making of the film. It inspires parents of children with disabilities to struggle on for their rights. A film can bring Sandra Rentería to a school. It can bring her charisma and her story, and it can inspire other people like her to be like her. I believe that the consciousness of the society will change the more that truthful images of children and persons with disabilities are visible.

## Postscript

Since its release, *Going to School—Ir a la Escuela* has been broadcast on television in California through KQED and KCET. In 2004, National Video Resources in New York included the film in its Human Rights Video Program funded by the MacArthur Foundation. The program distributed the documentary to 350 public libraries around the country. The documentary has been screened at the Dallas Video Festival, East Lansing Film Festival, Vermont International Film Festival, and, most notable, the first Disability Rights Film Festival in Moscow, Russia: Breaking Down Barriers. After that screening, disability rights activists translated the film into Russian and screened it in Moscow schools. In spring 2007, Cohen was invited to the Second International Forum on the Human Rights of Children with Disabilities, in Doha, Qatar. After the screening of *Going to School*, Cohen was asked for permission to add subtitles and voice-over in Arabic to the film. It will be used to help introduce the idea of inclusion to communities in Qatar. Cohen is currently working on a new documentary exploring the lives of several of the students in the film who have gone on to college. (*Going to School* is currently distributed by Richard Cohen Films: *www.RichardCohenFilms.com.*)

Since 1996, the Los Angeles Unified School District has met five of its eighteen outcomes designed to assist the district in reaching compliance with special education law [J. Hernandez, personal communication, March 23, 2007]. For information regarding the district's progress, refer to the Office of

---

Terese C. Jiménez assisted Richard Cohen in developing and writing the current chapter. The chapter's content, ideas and opinions entirely reflect Mr. Cohen's experiences and perspectives regarding the topics discussed.

the Independent Monitor through its Web site, *http://www.oimla*
*.com/index.html.*

## FROM THE FIELD: ACCESSING THE SCHOOLHOUSE FOR RICHARD

### Sandra Rentería

I am the mother of Richard Martinez. Richard Cohen filmed my
son and me for the documentary *Going to School*. Richard was
born premature and weighed one pound, twelve ounces, and had
multiple disabilities, including cerebral palsy and severe hearing
loss. After reading Cohen's account of the film, I began to realize
how far my son and our family have come since that time in our
lives. The interview took me back to where we were at the time,
to all our hard work and struggles. Since 2001, Richard has made
incredible progress on many of his goals, including his full inclusion in the general education setting, training toward future
employment, and improvements in communication, mobility,
and strength.

The year Cohen filmed *Going to School* was the first time we
fully included Richard in all general education classes. Previously in elementary school, Richard attended special education
classes for the deaf and hard of hearing and mainstreamed
into a general education English class five days a week. In junior
high school, we began the fight for Richard's full inclusion in
all general education classes. Richard's full inclusion in the
middle school as an equal participant would require an incredible amount of effort and collaboration on everyone's part. It
would not be sufficient for Richard to simply take up space in
the back of a classroom hoping to gain the attention of a teacher
and the recognition of his peers.

During this transition, the problem often was not with the
students in his classes; it was with the adults and their resistance.
Everything had to be explained as to why it was important for
Richard to be fully included. Resistance came from teachers who
did not know how to make the necessary accommodations and

modifications but did know that it would require work on their part to make it happen. During IEP meetings, I would provide teachers with a folder including Richard's picture and an action plan identifying his strengths and weaknesses and our goals. Once they saw Richard making progress, teacher buy-in became much easier. Ultimately our goal was for his peers and teachers to acknowledge Richard as an equal participant, a member of the student body. By the time he graduated from middle school and began high school, Richard had met this goal.

Cohen provides several examples of students expressing their hopes and dreams, including Ana Uribe, Le Doan, and Cynthia Delgado. Although my son was not verbal and could not express himself in a way typical students communicate their thoughts and desires, he did have dreams and the expectations to actively engage in his education. A major test of these expectations came when Richard's government class traveled to Washington, D.C., with the Close-Up Foundation, a nonprofit agency whose purpose is to inform participants of the democratic process through educational programs. Richard attended the field trip with his interpreter and one-on-one aide for the entire week, his first time away from home and his mother. The experience and the growth he made as a result of the trip made us see that Richard needed to be involved more with hands-on, meaningful activities. Once back home, Richard chose to participate in student government and work as a representative on the student council. Like the other students described in the chapter, Richard wanted to advocate for other students with disabilities on campus. Typical students became more considerate, compassionate, and accepting of students with disabilities as members of the student body as a direct result of Richard's visibility. He advocated for all students' inclusion in planned activities and reminded the school of its responsibilities to make necessary accommodations and modifications.

As Richard's mother, my goal was to ensure equal access to education and promote his inclusion by visiting his classes and talking to his peers and teachers about Richard. Cohen describes my efforts in his interview. I had hoped other students would begin to accept Richard for who he really is and not for who they perceived him to be. I wanted to remind them that there is a person behind the disability, that he is Richard first. This approach, I believe, facilitated Richard's purposeful inclusion in activities and experiences available to all students throughout the year, including serving as a prince on the homecoming court. In high school, Richard continued working in student government and participated in school dances, football games, and school theater.

Another major goal for Richard involved ensuring he would meet all of his credits toward graduation. Little did we know at the time that the graduation rate was so dismal for students with and without disabilities. I'm certain that many viewers of the film least expected Richard to be one of those graduates. At the time, we made sure that even though Richard had accommodations and modifications, he would obtain the necessary credits expected for a high school senior. That was a goal I had for my daughter, who is a typical child in general education.

Along with this goal was our expectation that Richard would acquire skills he could use after high school for future employment. As the mother of a child with severe disabilities, you always ask yourself, "What will your child do once he graduates? Will he have a job, or will he just sit at home and forever rely on those around him to access the world?" Richard loves working with children, and so with this in mind, we made sure he took the appropriate courses toward postsecondary employment, much like many of his peers without disabilities.

Richard began taking courses at school including child development classes, providing him the opportunity to work with children. Richard has since worked as a teacher's assistant in a local general education preschool program. He assists children with coloring, working with numbers, and practicing the letters of the alphabet. In the classroom, Richard has his own table and works with three to four students at a time, directing them through his interpreter. His students refer to him as Teacher Richard and respect him as another educator in the classroom. Overall this has been an amazing experience for him. Richard knows he has a lot of responsibility and has handled it extremely well. The teachers adore Richard; they appreciate his work with the children and welcome him to the class. Having Richard in the classroom and working with these children exemplifies Cohen's point in the chapter that we need to have individuals like my son within educational settings to motivate students with and without disabilities to embrace diversity and advocate for change.

Since middle school, we have had other goals for Richard involving overall improvements in communication and mobility. During the film, Richard had only limited communication skills. He was not truly able to communicate voluntarily without prompting. He knew some sign language but needed a lot of assistance from his interpreter to communicate with others. During that time, Richard was not able to tell me how his day was or initiate a conversation about what happened at school. Through sign language, he is now able to communicate his needs; he is no longer dependent on someone else to facilitate for him. Today he comes home and tells me where he went, what he did, who was at school, and whom he likes and dislikes. Finally, as a parent, I am at peace because I know that if something happens to him, he can come home and actually tell me. No one really expects children with severe disabilities to have this capability.

At the time of the film, Richard used a strider walker, but mostly he moved around the school campus and in classrooms using a wheelchair. Ultimately we wanted Richard to be physically capable of walking with crutches in order to provide him with more freedom and flexibility. Getting Richard to get up out of his chair and go to therapy five days a week was completely draining. Today Richard can walk up to 250 feet in fifteen minutes while wearing his leg braces and using his crutches for added assistance.

Meeting each of these goals required an incredible amount of dedication and hard work on behalf of Richard and those supporting him along the way. Richard had an excellent inclusion facilitator, Marisa Delong, who had compassion and respect for Richard and our goals for him. She allowed Richard to maintain his dignity, acknowledging him always as an equal participant in the decision-making process. She trusted that what I wanted for Richard was what anyone would want for their child. We've achieved this progress as a result of the ongoing support and consistency of all his service providers, including his interpreter, Corina Lujan, and his one-to-one aide, Edward Acosta. Richard has had an ideal team since junior high school. They respect not only our yearly goals, but our daily, monthly, and long-term goals. They allow me to dream for my child, to imagine the possibility of seeing Richard as an independent and contributing member of the community.

Ultimately, in order for parents to see their dreams fulfilled, they need not only the support of dedicated service providers but also the attention of teachers and administrators genuinely listening to them. Cohen highlights the efforts of special education teacher Greg Laskowski and acting superintendent Ramon Cortines and other administrators who saw the importance of breaking down the divide between general and special education and listening to the parents and students themselves. The administrator is the primary individual who sets the tone for parents as well as teachers. If administrators at any level bring with them attitudes of divisiveness and absolute inflexibility, parents will only logically fight against this treatment. In my case, rather than being recognized as the "mother from hell," why was I not viewed as an expert of my child's history and needs and treated as such? My initial reaction to this treatment was matching hostility with hostility. Educational professionals must learn to build trust in their relationships with families. When everyone can exercise mutual trust and respect while acknowledging parents as equal participants, true collaboration and sharing can begin.

Today in my work as a parent advocate, I continue to see parents in distress because they cannot access appropriate services for their children. Cohen shares this emotion while describing one of the public hearing meetings he attended where parents testified their concerns. Schools still fail to acknowledge parental input regarding the needs of their child. Although most parents continue to face ongoing struggles, the district is providing parents and schools with more training, resulting in a higher level of awareness. Accountability, however, is still missing. I tell parents they need to understand their child's disability in order to know how best to represent their child's interests. Parents must also remember that they do not need to know the law in detail but should understand they are chief implementers of the law as their child's most important advocates.

The message of the film calling for advocacy and understanding on the part of parents, educators, and students themselves was extremely powerful; the images were even more powerful. It is meaningful for parents and educators to see the problems and the possibilities—to see my son struggle from his wheelchair to his desk, to see him look through a microscope and glance at a pretty girl, and later participate with peers on a classroom assignment. Through these images, they see that there are more options for their children. No one truly understands what parents go through when they have a child with a disability. Film can bring those realities to the general public in a genuine and compassionate way, raising awareness while inspiring us into action.

Today Richard presents at local conferences regarding his work as an advocate for individuals with disabilities. He loves to be around family and looks forward to vacation and fun getaways, including camping on the beach. He has attended a local college, is the godfather of one of his friend's daughters, and has his own ATM and California identification card. Through his transition workability program, Richard earns a monthly pay-check for his work as an assistant at the preschool. In 2007 Richard was awarded the Si Se Puede ("Yes, we can!") award through Fiesta Educativa, a parent advocacy group for families who have children with special needs. The award is given to an individual with a disability who is judged to be the most inspir-ing and positive model in the disability community while demonstrating personal and educational growth, job success, and leadership qualities.

# 5

# REDUCING DISPROPORTIONATE REPRESENTATION IN SPECIAL EDUCATION

## Overview, Explanations, and Solutions

## Robert Rueda, Janette Klingner, Nicole Sager, Alejandra Velasco

Special education was institutionalized in the American educational system with a noble goal: to provide educational services to students with disabilities who would otherwise be excluded. It was through Public Law 94–142 (Education for All Handicapped Children Act) that students with disabilities who previously had been denied access to public schooling gained the legal right to receive a free and appropriate education. Many students have benefited and continue to benefit from special education services, but the promised benefits have sometimes been diminished by issues related to equal access, appropriate educational services, and others. At times the courts and legal system have had to intervene because of the contentious nature of the debate.

One persistent problem has been the overrepresentation of culturally and linguistically diverse students in special education. This has been particularly acute for select groups (African American and Latino) and in select categories (mild mental retardation, learning disabilities, emotional disturbance, and speech and language). Although it is the intention of special education programs to meet the needs of students with disabilities and help them achieve to their potential, there is consensus in both general and special education that general education programs are ultimately the least restrictive environment in which students can obtain the greatest access to high expectations and challenging curriculum, without labels. The overrepresentation of students of color means that they have limited access to general education experiences and the opportunities those experiences provide. In this chapter, we provide a brief background on the issue of overrepresentation, discuss various perspectives on the causes of the problem, and then review some considerations for addressing it.

## Historical Perspectives on Disproportionate Representation

No characterization of the history of public schooling in the United States would be complete without considering the dynamics of race and education. For over fifty years, Americans have fought for equal rights within both general and special education (Bullivant, 1993). Although much progress has been made since the beginning of the civil rights movement of the 1960s, it is generally recognized that the educational system has not succeeded in ensuring educational access, equity, and social mobility for all (Kozol, 1991, 2005; Glazer, 1997; Kincheloe & Steinberg, 1997). The design, content, and assumptions on which American schooling are based continue to validate the goals of white Americans, sometimes at a cost to students of color. In this section, we present a brief discussion of how students of color have been affected by various movements in education and society over the past two centuries.

## Challenges Prior to the 1954 *Brown v. Board of Education* Decision

Native-born Americans of color as well as immigrants have faced many challenges in their efforts to obtain an equitable education for their children. African American children were largely excluded from schooling in the nineteenth century, particularly in the South before the Civil War. For example, Alabama enforced statutes prohibiting slaves from learning how to read until 1856 (Bond, 1969). For the next hundred years, schools for African Americans and other students of color in many states were segregated. Beliefs about white superiority were well entrenched.

Around the early 1900s, with a fresh influx of immigrants to America, the educational system's potential as a tool for the indoctrination of America's youth was realized. Schools forbade the use of languages other than English and emphasized the principles of the U.S. Constitution. Tyack and Hansot (1982) and Tyack (1993) tracked U.S. immigration policies and goals as they changed from the early 1800s to the years after World War II. They clearly showed how these policies reflected the nation's values and needs at different times. Through its educational system, the country was able to instill at an early age the values of capitalism, Protestantism, and individualism and create a populace well suited for the industrial age.

The experiences of white immigrants and immigrants of color drastically differed. For immigrants considered white, such as ethnic immigrants from eastern and southern Europe, schooling was required. The focus of schools was to rid them of their foreign languages and cultures and Americanize them as soon as possible. Chinese, Japanese, Mexican, and other immigrants of color, as well as native-born African Americans, had to struggle to gain access to any education at all. Some communities took matters into their own hands, constructing and staffing their own schools. Tyack (1993) suggested that this dichotomy stemmed from entrenched feelings of white supremacy, which "defined people of color as nonassimilatable, ineradicably different, and therefore not full citizens" (p. 20).

Special education has its own history of inequities. Prior to existing federal special education legislation, individuals with disabilities often were sterilized or even euthanized, sent to residential centers, or simply denied access to public instruction (Owen et al., 2003). The extent to which services were considered educational rather than custodial varied according to time and place. Children with obvious mental retardation, such as those with Down syndrome, were frequently institutionalized at birth (Smith & Polloway, 1993). Even individuals with an IQ score between 70 and 85, who today would be considered in the low-normal range of intelligence, were often subjected to involuntary sterilization.[1] Students of color were more likely to be considered mentally deficient.

By the turn of the twentieth century, beliefs regarding the racial inferiority of nonwhite individuals and immigrants were well entrenched in society. These beliefs played out in significant ways in special education identification, which relied heavily on assessment and targeted students of color unfairly. Mental testing soon became a national obsession (Fass, 1980; Gould, 1981). For example, the psychologist Henry Goddard was hired by the U.S. Public Health Service to help screen immigrants as they arrived at Ellis Island. He concluded that 83 percent of Jews, 87 percent of Russians, and 79 percent of Italians were "morons" (Rogoff, 2003). Mental testing was widely used to implement a program of exclusion of both racial minorities and white ethnic immigrants from the mainstream of the educational system. It was also a driving force behind the eugenics movement, of which Goddard was a leading proponent.

Eugenics flourished in the first half of the twentieth century. Individuals with mental retardation were considered to be burdens on society and to have inferior genes. Indiana was the first state to pass eugenics laws, in 1914, and other states soon followed. These laws resulted in forced sterilization, incarceration, and occasionally even euthanasia of the mentally retarded, as well as ethnic minorities, and particularly people of mixed racial heritage (Medterms, 2006; Selden, 1999). The number of sterilizations increased steadily per year, up to 21,539 in 1935. Perhaps the most egregious example of this program, supported by the U.S. government, the medical community, and the local government of Puerto Rico, was the sterilization of approximately one-third of Puerto Rican women from the 1930s to 1965 (Rogers & Bowman, 2003). The women targeted for this program were the uneducated and those living in poverty, not necessarily those considered to have disabilities.

## Brown v. *Board of Education* and Special Education

*Brown* v. *Board of Education* and the subsequent civil rights movement of the 1960s and 1970s, with its values of equality, helped advance the implementation of universal schooling for children regardless of ethnicity or handicapping condition. The drive to promote equal access to education for students of color is generally considered to complement efforts to provide special education services to students with unique educational needs (Zirkel, 2005). However, in some ways these movements ended up working at cross purposes, with a disproportionate percentage of students of color targeted for separate services (Harry & Klingner, 2006).

Even after the 1954 decision in *Brown*, change was slow and arduous. Although the decision represented increased access to schools for African American students, it also meant a loss of local control. Students who previously had been taught by teachers they knew from their churches and in their communities found themselves taught by teachers with very different perspectives and sympathies (Foster, 1993). They no longer could count on being educated by teachers with high expectations who taught in culturally compatible ways. Instead, many African American children in desegregated schools were viewed as deficient and faced rejection by their teachers. At the same time, many African American teachers and administrators lost their jobs, and African American parents lost the leadership roles and easy access to their children's schools they had experienced under the segregated system (Delpit, 2003; Morris & Morris, 2000). Also, this period coincided with an increase in the numbers and percentages of African American and other students of color identified as disabled, particularly as mentally retarded, which allowed their continued segregation under the guise of providing them with special services.

With various states hesitating to comply with the *Brown* ruling came accusations that special education served as a means to secretly perpetuate racial segregation. *Johnson v. San Francisco Unified School District* (1971) was the first legal suit filed that charged a school district with erroneously placing African American children in classes for the "mildly retarded." Another case of great importance was *Larry P. v. Riles* (1972), which claimed that due to the bias inherent in IQ tests, African American students were overrepresented in programs for those with mental retardation. At the time, 28.5 percent of students were African Americans, yet 66 percent of all students in classes for mental retardation were African American. The courts ruled that IQ tests were in fact biased against African American children, and their use led to discrimination in the form of overrepresentation in programs for students with mild mental retardation. Subsequently the courts issued an order to ban the use of IQ tests with African American students and eradicate the overrepresentation of African American students in programs for the mentally retarded. Nevertheless, in the class action case of *Parents in Action in Special Education v. Hannon* (1980), the judge stated he could find little evidence of bias in test items for African American students. This case established that standardized intelligence tests are valid when used as part of multifaceted, multidisciplinary evaluations (Meyen & Skrtic, 1995).

African Americans were not the only group facing such struggles. Two pivotal cases related to the language used for testing were filed. *Diana v. California State Board of Education* (1970) argued that Latino children who spoke only Spanish should not be evaluated with tests in English. A similar case involving Latino and Native American students was filed in Arizona, *Guadalupe Organization v. Tempe Elementary School District* (1972). These two key cases in which the rulings were in favor of the plaintiffs led to the mandate for nondiscriminatory assessment procedures in the civil rights legislation of section 504 of the Rehabilitation Act of 1973. This in turn established the groundwork for the mandated procedures of nondiscriminatory testing and the due process safeguards against misclassification in the passage of the Education for All Handicapped Children Act (P.L. 94–142; Jacob-Timm & Hartshorne, 1998).

This history regarding the education of students of color and those with disabilities provides a backdrop to their overrepresentation in disability categories and special education programs. Although P.L. 94–142 attempted to ameliorate the injustices of the past, the unfair education of students of color within special education continues.

## Overrepresentation: A Current View and Possible Explanations

Few aspects of the issue of overrepresentation are characterized by widespread agreement, including how it is defined. A very general definition is that *overrepresentation* refers to "unequal proportions of culturally diverse students in special education programs" (Artiles & Trent, 2000, p. 514). A common way of specifying overrepresentation is to calculate a target group's representation in general education or special education in reference to the representation of a comparison group, most often white students. There are different indicators, however, including a risk index, composition indices, odds ratios, and even percentage variation, that provide different lenses on the scope of the problem. Because each indicator gives a different perspective on the issue, there is controversy about the best indicators.[2] Agreement about the procedures and formulas used to determine overrepresentation is not widespread (see Reschly, 1997, for a discussion of the strength and limitations of these formulas).

Table 5.1 provides some recent data on the issue of overrepresentation. Although there may be controversy over the best ways of assessing overrepresentation, two things are less controversial. First, overrepresentation continues to be a problem (although the severity and patterns vary across groups). Second, the most common disability categories involved are mild mental retardation (MMR), emotional/behavioral disorders (E/BD), and specific learning disabilities (SLD), and the most frequently affected groups are African American, Chicano/Latino, American Indian, and a few subgroups of Asian American students (see Artiles & Trent, 2000, and Artiles, Harry, Reschly, & Chinn, 2002, for a comprehensive overview of overrepresentation).

A lingering question is what causes persisting problems in overrepresentation. When one begins to unpack overrepresentation as some have suggested, the possibility arises that overrepresentation may be a more complex phenomenon than intuition might suggest. For example, Artiles and Trent (1994) noted:

1. The larger the minority student population is in the school district, the greater the representation of students in special education classes.

2. The bigger the educational program, the larger the disproportion of minority students.

3. Variability in overrepresentation data has been found as a function of the specific disability condition and the ethnic group under scrutiny.

### Table 5.1   Overall Risk Ratios for Students Ages Six Through Twenty-One, by Race/Ethnicity for Selected Disability Categories: 2001-2002

| Disability | American Indian/Alaska Native | Asian/ Pacific Islander | Black (not Hispanic) | Hispanic | White (not Hispanic) |
|---|---|---|---|---|---|
| Specific learning disabilities | 1.50 | 0.39 | 1.31 | 1.07 | 0.88 |
| Speech or language impairments | 1.21 | 0.65 | 1.07 | 0.82 | 1.13 |
| Mental retardation | 1.09 | 0.44 | 2.99 | 0.58 | 0.63 |
| Emotional disturbance | 1.25 | 0.29 | 2.21 | 0.52 | 0.87 |
| Multiple disabilities | 1.33 | 0.57 | 1.40 | 0.76 | 1.00 |
| Hearing impairments | 1.25 | 1.20 | 1.11 | 1.19 | 0.81 |
| Orthopedic impairments | 0.89 | 0.70 | 0.96 | 0.90 | 1.15 |
| Other health impairments | 1.07 | 0.36 | 0.99 | 0.44 | 1.69 |
| Visual impairments | 1.19 | 0.94 | 1.21 | 0.89 | 0.96 |
| Autism | 0.64 | 1.22 | 1.17 | 0.52 | 1.22 |
| Deaf-blindness | 1.94 | 0.93 | 0.90 | 0.96 | 1.05 |
| Traumatic brain injury | 1.25 | 0.56 | 1.27 | 0.62 | 1.18 |
| Developmental delay | 1.98 | 0.64 | 1.65 | 0.44 | 1.06 |
| All disabilities | 1.33 | 0.47 | 1.45 | 0.86 | 0.93 |

Note: Overall risk ratios were calculated by dividing the risk index for the racial/ethnic group by the risk index for all other students. Risk was calculated by dividing the number of children with disabilities in the racial/ethnic group by the total number of children in the racial/ethnic group.

Source: U.S. Department of Education, Office of Special Education Programs, Data Analysis System (DANS), Tables AA15 in vol. 2. Data are for the fifty states, Washington, D.C., Puerto Rico, and the outlying areas. Population data are July 1 estimates for 2001 released October 2003. The multiracial category of the census was apportioned into each of the five single race/ethnicity categories in proportion to each category's relative size. The estimates are based on the 2000 decennial census and come from the Population Estimates Program, Census Bureau, Population Division.

Others have suggested that overrepresentation may differ depending on socioeconomic levels in the school (Oswald, Coutinho, & Best, 2000; Oswald, Coutinho, Singh, & Best, 1998), as well as on factors like students' level of English proficiency in both their native language and English (Artiles, Rueda, Salazar, & Higareda, 2002, 2005). The explanations for overrepresentation have been quite varied, and these have not been divorced from paradigmatic differences that have characterized the larger field of special education (Andrews et al., 2000; Artiles, 2003).

In general, the explanations have tended to range across a variety of factors. Some have focused exclusively on within-child deficits: deficiencies in basic cognitive and linguistic abilities, either inherent or due to less-than-optimal home and family circumstances related to poverty or other factors. Others have focused on external social and institutional causes, including biased referral and assessment, impoverished instruction, racism, and unequal distribution of educational and other resources. A complete review of all of the possible factors contributing to overrepresentation is beyond the scope of this chapter. Nevertheless, we briefly review some of the most commonly referenced aspects.

One highly visible source that examined this issue in some detail was the National Research Council's report (Donovan & Cross, 2002) on the overrepresentation of minority students in special education. For heuristic purposes, it is useful to examine how the panel addressed the problem. That panel considered a range of explanations surrounding this issue, and this report is worth considering because it encompasses several different perspectives. The panel drew on a wide-ranging conceptual model (see Figure 5.1) that includes overlapping circles of teacher, child, and classroom with student achievement at the center of the overlapping circles. Within each circle is a description of key factors. For example, under the child circle, factors include biology (genetic endowment, environmental influences), family context (income, education, culture), and community

## Figure 5.1   A Contextual Model of Student Achievement

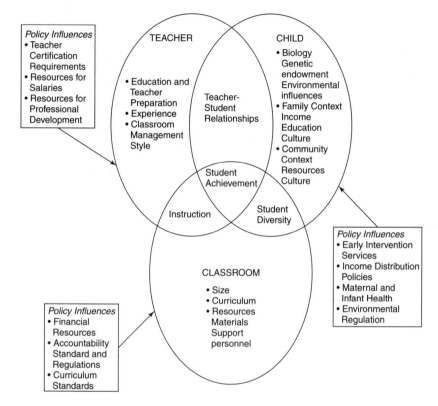

*Source:* Donovan & Cross (2002).

(resources, culture). Finally, external policy factors for each circle are listed. In the child circle are listed early intervention services, income distribution policies, maternal and infant health, and environmental regulation. Within this framework, the panel considered the general areas in the following paragraphs as possible causes of overrepresentation.

## Poverty and Its Secondary Effects on Development

One of these explanations was focused on the secondary effects of biological, social, or contextual factors in development. This included specific influences such as poverty, and the report noted elevated rates of poverty among families of color as well as possible secondary effects, such as higher rates of exposure to harmful toxins, including lead, alcohol, and tobacco, in early stages of development. Other secondary factors in this area include low birthweight, poor nutrition, and home and child care environments that are less supportive of early cognitive and emotional development than would be typically found for children in higher-socioeconomic-status (SES) groups. In essence, this explanation argues that pervasive poverty creates risk factors that in turn jeopardize development and later school achievement.

## Effects of School Factors

A second general explanation that the panel considered was whether schooling and school experiences provide independent influences on the incidence of overrepresentation. The panel found reason to believe that schools with higher concentrations of low-income, minority children are more likely to have teachers who are less experienced and less well trained. Moreover, the panel found evidence that per pupil expenditures in schools attended by low-SES students of color are lower, and these schools are less likely to offer advanced courses and other supplemental services for their students. Thus, the opportunity to learn afforded by schools is less for students of color who come from low-SES backgrounds, potentially contributing to elevated rates of special education referral and placement.

## Bias in the Referral and Assessment Process

The NRC panel considered the issue of bias in the referral and assessment process in terms of race or ethnicity. Most of the referrals for special education come from teachers, and therefore teacher bias might be an important factor in elevated rates of special education for some students. In terms of the referral process, although the panel considered the possibility of bias, it found some weaknesses in the research base. Specifically, the experimental studies with hypothetical cases suggesting that bias is an important factor in referral may not reflect what teachers actually do in the presence of students in real classroom situations.

Of course, once students are referred for special education, they must be assessed as eligible or ineligible within the system and legal requirements. The panel noted the significant amount of controversy that has revolved around this issue for several decades (Reschly, 1997b). The panel did note that research shows that context, including familiarity with test taking and the norms and expectations of school, may be important to the scores of students whose experiences prepare them less well for the demands of classrooms and standardized tests in particular.

As a related question, the panel considered whether the assessment process identifies the right students—that is, students who need and can benefit from those programs. The panel determined that the subjectivity of the referral process allows for students with significant learning problems to be overlooked for referral, and the conceptual and procedural shortcomings of the assessment process for learning disabilities and emotional disturbance give little confidence that student need has been appropriately identified. It was also determined that the process results in placements later in the educational process than is most effective or efficient, thus further handicapping students who are not well served by the existing system.

Rueda and Windmueller (2006) summarized these positions as focusing on two basic explanations: a systematic bias hypothesis (that is, bias at some level of the system leads to disproportionate identification and placement rates for some groups) or an achievement difference hypothesis (that is, students who demonstrate greater need are in fact those who get placed). Drawing on a sociocultural framework, it was proposed that there is another possibility: the misalignment or imbalance of the multiple levels of the teaching-learning system according to the features and demands of the local context. These levels are described in the following paragraphs, along with discussion about how an imbalance might serve to exacerbate the overrepresentation problem.

This position is based on recent extensions of sociocultural theory that conceptualize learning and development as a function of one's transformation of participation in multiple interacting levels of influence, or planes of development (Rogoff, 2003). These planes of development are the individual, the interpersonal, and the community-institutional focus of analysis (see Figure 5.2). Factors at the individual level include cognitive, motivational, and other learning-related characteristics that have typically been the central focus of special education research and intervention efforts. Specific aspects include cognitive skills, learning strategies, metacognitive and executive

### Figure 5.2 The Multiple Planes of Learning and Development

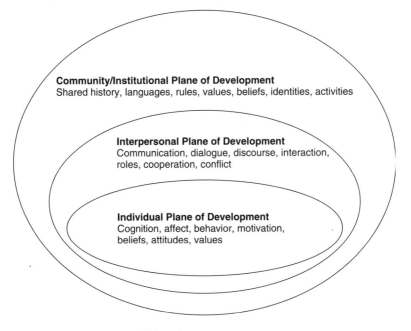

Community/Institutional Plane of Development
Shared history, languages, rules, values, beliefs, identities, activities

Interpersonal Plane of Development
Communication, dialogue, discourse, interaction, roles, cooperation, conflict

Individual Plane of Development
Cognition, affect, behavior, motivation, beliefs, attitudes, values

*Source:* Adapted from Rogoff (2003).

factors, and motivation-related variables such as self-efficacy and attributions for failure and success.

At the next level of this nested system is what are loosely called interactional factors. These include interpersonal relationships, social interactions, and the social organizational and discourse features of the specific settings where people interact—for example, the classroom or testing situation. Finally, the outermost level includes institutional and community factors, particularly home and family, community, and larger sociopolitical considerations such as policy debates over issues like bilingual education, immigration, and the distribution and allocation of economic resources. This plane of development, often overlooked in behavioral science, focuses on factors such as current and past power relationships among various groups, how these become embedded in social institutions and practices, and how these are experienced by individual groups and communities. From this perspective of multiple levels, the causes of student achievement and overrepresentation are within neither the child nor the larger social and institutional system; rather, they are within the interaction of these multiple layers. Thus, if only a given level is targeted, it is likely that overrepresentation issues will not be addressed. For example, special education has traditionally focused primarily on individual-level factors, with relatively much less attention to the other levels.

As a simple example of how this might be problematic, consider the integration of a student with disabilities into a regular classroom. Special tutoring and instructional accommodations might be made to ensure the smooth integration of this student into the classroom, but it is possible that he or she might be rejected and treated poorly by one or more students in the new setting because of limited English ability. Thus, attending solely to the individual-level factors and ignoring the social interactional factors will likely not be sufficient to ensure a successful transition. As another example, focusing on teaching cognitive strategies to a student who is a poor reader will not negate the inequality of distribution of resources that contributed to impoverished opportunity to learn for that student. Importantly, even when attention is paid to factors at the community or institutional plane of development, which is often neglected, there is no guarantee of positive student outcomes unless it is done with consideration for the other levels. For example, attempts to increase the economic or political well-being of families and communities will not necessarily improve the cognitive strategies or motivational beliefs needed to succeed in complex academic tasks. One implication of this view is that overrepresentation can be seen as a symptom of underlying problems, not as an outcome. That is, the underlying multiple causes of numerical overrepresentation need to be addressed systemically and comprehensively. The argument is that all dimensions of the issue must be considered systematically in a balanced fashion.

## Summary

Overrepresentation has most often been studied as an outcome, but the suggestion here is that it should be studied as an indicator. Thus, a simple effort to reduce the numbers of students in certain categories does not ensure remediation of underlying causes or other important short- and long-term student outcomes. Different hypotheses for overrepresentation have appeared to characterize differing approaches to solving the problem, and it has been argued that the special education system is embedded within different analytical levels. Thus, comprehensive solutions need to address each of these levels in a coordinated and aligned approach.

## Addressing the Challenge of Overrepresentation

Thus far, we have discussed the history and background of the issue of overrepresentation, and discussed alternative perspectives on the causes. We now turn to considerations relevant to addressing the problem. In particular, we consider two frequently mentioned alternatives to reducing overrepresentation: culturally responsive instructional practices and response-to-intervention (RTI) approaches to assessment and early intervening services. In addition, we address two broader concerns that we argue merit consideration in implementing specific remedies: framing overrepresentation as a multiple-level problem, thus taking into account multiple-level solutions, and taking into account the influence of context-specific factors in implementing solutions. We consider first the most commonly mentioned remedies (culturally responsive instruction and early intervening services, RTI), and then address the mediating factors related to a multiple-level approach and the influence of contextual differences.

## Culturally Responsive Instructional Approaches

Culturally responsive instructional practices offer the promise of providing opportunities to learn for culturally and linguistically diverse students and reducing disproportionate representation. What are the key ideas behind culturally responsive instruction? In order to delve into this concept, it is essential to acknowledge that culture plays a role in any kind of learning (Cole, 1998; Rogoff, 2003). Culture embodies complex and evolving characteristics (Gutierrez & Rogoff, 2003) and deeply influences how an individual relates to others and makes sense of the world around him or her. Therefore culturally responsive teaching requires that educators understand the sociocultural and historical contexts that influence their students' actions. We offer the following definition of cultural responsiveness (Klingner & Solano-Flores, 2007, p. 231):

> *Cultural responsiveness* is the extent to which research and practice in instruction and assessment take into consideration the cognitive, linguistic, and social assets of an individual (such as epistemologies, world views, and learning, teaching, and

communication styles) that are culturally-determined and shape the ways in which that individual learns and makes sense of his or her experiences. Cultural responsiveness refers to the fact that, in order to be fair and effective, education should be compatible with those assets and build on them, rather than disparage or ignore them.

Wiley (1996) provides a useful framework educators can use in implementing culturally responsive instructional practices:

- *Accommodation* refers to the need for educators, administrators, and school personnel to understand the cultural norms, communication styles, and literacy practices of their students in order to adapt their instruction accordingly.

- *Incorporation* takes accommodation one step further in that it requires that researchers and educators not only understand diverse cultures but also acknowledge that certain community practices have not been valued previously by schools and much can be learned from other ethnic groups (Wiley, 1996). It means letting go of the notion that mainstream Anglo-Saxon cultural norms completely drive standards of acceptability and success. The role of educators is not solely to teach families how "to do school" but rather to get to know the families and take time to build the social relationships needed to create meaningful links between a child's home life and what happens in the classroom (Moll, 1999). It is through the development of mutual understanding that schooling and curriculum can be adapted to serve the needs of families (Cairney, 1997).

- *Adaptation* relates to how children and adults go through a process of acculturating to the norms of those who control the schools, institutions, and workplace (Wiley, 1996). A key element of adaptation is that it be additive rather than subtractive. In other words, families and communities do not learn to manage in a new culture at the expense of losing their own cultural identity and practices. Supporters of adaptation claim that culturally and linguistically diverse parents and immigrant parents want to provide their children with the linguistic, social, and cultural capital needed to succeed in the marketplace of schools but may not know how to do so (Gallimore, Weisner, Kaufman, & Bernheimer, 1989; Super & Harkness, 1986). It is thus the responsibility of the school to give parents the information and support they need to help their children access new forms of cultural capital (Klingner & Edwards, 2006).

These three types of practice provide a framework for implementing culturally responsive teaching and working toward educational equity for culturally and linguistically diverse students in the United States. It is important to acknowledge that current educational practices are tailored to the dominant culture in society but are not responsive to communities with cultural practices different from mainstream culture (Ladson Billings, 1995; O'Connor & Fernandez, 2006). Research suggests that it is possible to design and implement culturally responsive interventions that enhance learning for diverse populations (Au, 1995; Cole & Engestrom, 1993; Engestrom, 1999; Ladson-Billings, 1995; Lee, 2001a, 2001b). The principle of cultural responsiveness also has important implications for RTI models.

## Response-to-Intervention Models

With its three-tiered structure, RTI models provide an alternative way of conceptualizing how we support student learning. Ideally implemented, RTI could help education move away from the deficit-based approach of labeling and sorting children and thus reduce disproportionality. The first tier of RTI is considered quality instruction with ongoing monitoring of students' progress within the general education classroom. At the second tier, intensive intervention support is provided to students who have not made sufficient progress or met expected benchmarks in the core program. This approach is very different from special education, in that this support is provided as part of general education to all students who are not progressing. When students do not adequately respond to the second tier of intervention, they move on to the third tier. In some versions of the RTI model, students then qualify for special education; in other versions, they are then evaluated for possible placement in special education (Fuchs, Mock, Morgan, & Young, 2003).

The RTI model is based on the idea that instructional practices or interventions at each level should be based on scientific evidence of what counts as effective practice. With the current emphasis on using evidence-based interventions, it is essential to ensure that decisions about instruction not be based on an assumption that one size fits all. The challenge educators and researchers face is to discover what works with which students in what contexts (Cunningham & Fitzgerald, 1996; Klingner & Edwards, 2006). Although issues of population and ecological validity should always be considered in any RTI model, they are all the more crucial with culturally and linguistically diverse students. In order for instruction to be deemed appropriate, of high quality, and evidence based, it should be validated with students like those with whom it was applied. Instructional methods should not be seen as decontextualized generic practices with no regard for the sociocultural contexts in which they are implemented (Artiles, 2002; Gee, 1999, 2001; Ruiz, 1998).

If children are not provided with appropriate, culturally responsive instruction, they are not receiving an adequate opportunity to learn. This concept of adequate opportunity to learn informs the RTI model and is a fundamental aspect of the definition of learning disabilities as part of its exclusionary clause: when children have not had sufficient opportunity to learn, the determination cannot be made that they have a learning disability. It follows that cultural responsiveness is an essential component of implementing an effective and fair RTI model (Klingner & Edwards, 2006).

## Considerations for Culturally Responsive RTI

What must be considered in order to create, implement, and research the most effective interventions for culturally and linguistically diverse students? How do we account for culture when designing and implementing interventions and conducting research? How can teachers reflect on and develop self-awareness of their own cultural background and beliefs about people different from themselves? What practices can we adopt in the design and reporting of research to make visible the cultural assumptions of researchers? Researchers must become aware of how their own assumptions about the role of culture in learning shape their research questions and the ways they collect data. Researchers' implicit assumptions influence the analytical and interpretive decisions they make about whether cultural factors and processes matter (Lee, 2002; Paredes, 1984; Walker, 1999, 2005). A cultural view of development and learning should be systematically incorporated into studies of best practices for diverse populations (Boesch, 1996; Goodnow, 2002; Rogoff & Angelillo, 2002).

At the same time, teachers, school leaders, and district administrators should become savvier consumers (and possibly creators) of research. When practitioners understand the importance of population and ecological validity, for example, they are better able to assess the appropriateness of a particular method or prepackaged program for their students and contexts. They also are in a better position to argue for adapting an approach to be more appropriate for their situations or for selecting one program over another. In sum, practitioners' and researchers' beliefs and practices and schools' curricula and structures must no longer turn a blind eye to the importance of culture in learning.

In conclusion, we are encouraged by the potential of RTI models to reduce inappropriate referrals to and placements in special education when they are implemented in culturally responsive ways. Yet for progress to take place, researchers and educators must alter the ways they think about language, culture, and learning. This will require a dramatic paradigm shift and changes at various levels of educational systems.

## A Multiple-Levels Perspective

The various planes of development are all critical in ensuring that learning and achievement are maximized. As others have argued (Artiles & Rueda, 2002; Klingner et al., 2005), specific approaches to addressing the needs of culturally and linguistically diverse students need to be embedded in culturally responsive systems rather than being considered as isolated entities. These "culturally responsive educational systems are designed to promote the creation of conditions, produce resources and tools, and support multiple stakeholders in the creation of educational systems that are responsive to cultural diversity" (Klingner et al., 2005, p. 8). Unfortunately special education has traditionally focused on the individual plane: the remediation of specific cognitive and learning problems of individual students. Some of this work has focused on instructional issues and the ways that instructional processes can improve student outcomes. In the context of reducing overrepresentation and addressing the needs of those groups most affected, what steps can be taken at each of the levels that might help alleviate issues of overrepresentation? We look briefly at each of the levels.

At the individual and interpersonal planes of development, recent focus has centered on thinking about instructional interventions and creating optimal instructional environments. Specific examples have been described in the earlier sections on early intervention and culturally responsive instruction. In the larger field of special education, for example, there is wide consensus on the use of primary and secondary tiers of intervention, RTI approaches, and specific types of interventions largely targeting cognitive skills and specific areas such as reading (see Swanson, Harris, & Graham, 2003). Much of this work stems from contemporary cognitive theory and targets specific cognitive strategy and metacognitive training. The area of reading interventions has been particularly visible in the literature (Vaughn, Gersten, & Chard, 2000: Vaughn & Linan-Thompson, 2003), partly due to the recognition of the effect of early reading to later school success. In general, the work on culturally responsive instruction supplements the work in the larger field of special education and seeks to consider cultural and linguistic factors specifically (Artiles & Ortiz, 2002).

Yet even as students and teachers find themselves engaging intellectually in culturally responsive classrooms, they may be doing so in spite of the systems in which they operate (Miramontes, Nadeau, & Commins, 1997; Townsend & Patton, 2000). An additional important consideration therefore is that just as teachers and students are embedded in particular schools, these schools are embedded in particular communities and are affected by policies and regulation at a multitude of levels (district, state, federal; see Klingner et al., 2005, for further discussion of these issues). Thus, school culture and leadership must be aligned to be consistent with the goals at the classroom level, and schools and districts must be aware of and responsive to the dynamics and concerns in the communities they serve.

It is in this last area that the least attention has been focused. Yet factors located within this plane of development can have important consequences on student learning. A previous study conducted by the first author focused on the issue of reading engagement among immigrant Latino students in central Los Angeles (Monzo & Rueda, 2001; Rueda, MacGillivray, Monzo, & Arzubiaga, 2001). Poverty, homelessness, and related social problems were commonplace among the families in the school where the work took place. Shortly after the study began, English-only legislation was put on the state ballot, and both advocates and opponents, including those within the school, took strong and vocal positions. Constant media attention kept this issue on the public's mind for an extended period of time. For a variety of reasons, this school became a focal point of the media, and the controversy was quite heated. At one point, a young student was overheard asking her teacher, "Why do people get upset because we speak a different language?"

During the same period when the study took place, periodic immigration sweeps were taking place in the central city. The area in which the school is located is surrounded by garment factories in which many of the parents work. These random checks, which could lead to deportation, were a strong source of fear and anxiety for many of the families, and as might be expected, these concerns filtered down to the students. In this context, it was clear that issues at the community and institutional plane seeped into the classroom and had a strong impact on students' learning and motivation. Fortunately, the teacher in this classroom was familiar with the families and the community and was able to deal with these issues in an instructionally responsive fashion. She organized debates around the salient issues so that students could both express their feelings and get a deeper sense of the issues from a variety of perspectives. She acknowledged the students' fears and anxieties and tried to be responsive to their questions. She maintained close contact with the parents of her students and in other ways tried to accommodate her instruction to focus on not only the intellectual aspects of their development but the concerns and issues from outside the classroom as well. This teacher could have chosen to ignore these factors as irrelevant to the increasingly standardized curriculum that the district was beginning to impose. However, she chose to integrate them in instructionally relevant ways to foster the engagement and intellectual development of her students. She thus was able to provide classroom experiences for these students in at-risk circumstances equivalent to those that are commonly found in classes of high-achieving and gifted students.

Teachers of diverse students must be familiar with and sensitive to the realities of students who find themselves in subordinated circumstances, including the many issues rooted in race, class, and gender that affect these students and bear on their ability or willingness to engage in academic tasks (Bartolome, 1994). Effective teachers of minority students think critically about the purposes of teaching and the values and beliefs embedded in the profession and make thoughtful and theoretically sound choices about when it is appropriate to apply them, modify them, or throw them out. Failing to consider all of the planes of development can lead to less-than-optimal educational experiences for students most in need of enriched environments. An imbalance in consideration given to the various planes of development is proposed as an important factor in overrepresentation.

## Context and Scale-Up

Currently there is a great deal of interest in the educational context to find what works and to promote evidence-based practice with an eye toward "scale-up," or widespread dissemination following the original implementation (U.S. Department of Education, 2003). For example, the federal What Works Clearinghouse is designed to provide "reviews of the effectiveness of replicable educational interventions (programs, products, practices, and policies) that intend to improve student outcomes" (Institute of Education Sciences, 2006). The gold standard in this effort is the randomized experiment using control groups to estimate the effects of specific interventions. In the light of this effort, most researchers would agree that accountability is a critical problem in education and that educators should be cognizant of their responsibility to be able to provide evidence for the validity of the interventions they develop and promote.

While the strength of evidence provided by randomized, controlled trial studies is not at issue, there is a danger in minimizing attention to features of local contexts that mediate treatment results. One implicit assumption in many approaches to scaling up an effective intervention is that context is largely irrelevant to how a particular approach fits in with students' developmental needs and what considerations might be relevant in considering all of the planes of development. The caution here is that what works in one setting will not always work elsewhere without conscious attention to features of the local context. As an example, a reading approach that teaches students how to decode but fails to consider that they come from environments that are not rich in conventional print materials or are not surrounded by adults who frequently engage in school-relevant literacy practices may be considered replicable and effective. But it is not likely to create engaged readers who are proficient in using literacy as a powerful tool to solve meaningful problems. Had the teacher in the example cited earlier focused solely on the prescribed curriculum and research-based approaches that she was required to use, she may have produced measurable change in her students, but the long-term goal of creating educated citizens may have suffered.

## Conclusion

We have provided an overview of the longstanding problem of the overrepresentation of culturally and linguistically diverse students in special education, including the historical events leading to the passage of P.L. 94–142 and the more recent IDEA legislation. This legislation provides important legal safeguards meant to ensure that all students are treated fairly and receive an appropriate education, and it represents an important achievement. Nevertheless, problems persist with respect to overrepresentation. Thus, we explored possible reasons for this persistent problem and some solutions proposed by researchers and educators who have grappled with this problem. We have focused on instructional approaches, especially those that occur early, are proactive rather than reactive in nature, consider the multiple planes of development, and are responsive to the cultural and linguistic characteristics of their students. While agreeing with the overall importance of evidence-based approaches that are replicable, we propose that equal attention needs to be paid to the features of local contexts that mediate the implementation of any instructional practices and characterize the ecological niches where students will need to transfer and generalize the skills and knowledge they acquire.

## Notes

1. In 1973, the American Association for Mental Retardation lowered the recommended IQ cutoff score for mental retardation from 85 to 70, or from one standard deviation below the mean to two standard deviations below the mean (Luckasson et al., 2002). This is the criterion subsequently adopted by P.L. 94–142 and then IDEA.

2. The risk index (RI) is calculated by dividing the number of students in a given racial or ethnic category served in a particular disability category by the total enrollment for that group in the school population. Thus, a risk index of 6 for African American students in a category means that 6 percent of all African Americans were given that label. The composition index is calculated by dividing the number of students of a racial or ethnic group enrolled in a particular disability category by the total number of students (summed across all groups) enrolled in that same disability category. The sum of composition indices for all the groups will total 100 percent. This index does not control for the baseline enrollment of a given group. Finally, the odds ratio divides the risk index of one group by the risk index of another (most often white) for comparative purposes. Odds ratios greater than 1.0 indicate greater risk of identification.

# FROM THE FIELD: REFLECTIONS ON DISPROPORTIONALITY

## Alnita Rettig Dunn

The overidentification of minorities within special education programs is a disturbing and complex problem. Robert Rueda,

Janette Klingner, Nicole Sager, and Alejandra Velasco provide a synthesis of this issue's historical roots. They briefly discuss alternative perspectives regarding its causes and review possible manners of addressing the problem.

As a practitioner within the field, it is this final point I wish to address here, and its application within my district. Specifically, Rueda, Klingner, Sager, and Velasco review several alternatives to reduce overrepresentation in the schools, including implementing culturally responsive instructional practices and introducing response-to-intervention approaches involving early intervention and assessment of students' academic performance. Given my current position as a special education administrator in a large urban school district, I can certainly attest to the harmful outcomes resulting from the over-identification of minorities within special education by educational professionals in our schools. But first I wish to discuss how I see schools consciously and unconsciously contributing to this problem and how parents address this dynamic. These comments are based on my twenty-six years of experience within the district, observations of my district's concerted and conscientious attempts to address this issue, and my thirty years of general experience within the field of education.

## Contributing to and Addressing Overrepresentation

Key stakeholders of special education programs include parents and school personnel representing different experiences, ethnicities, educational backgrounds, and income levels. In these stakeholder groups, the beliefs and practices of educators are influential in creating positive or negative decisions on behalf of students who are experiencing the most difficulty with learning. One group of educational personnel often perceives special education services as the only vehicle for students who are underachieving and possibly disabled. Be-cause special education services come with a funded service delivery structure of explicit procedures aimed at children who are having difficulty, some educators often view these services as the only mechanism for assisting children evidencing be-havioral or learning difficulties. At-risk or low-achieving stu-dents who are removed from general education programs and placed inappropriately in restrict special education settings miss out on opportunities to access the general education cur-riculum and interact with nondisabled peers. Moreover, when too many children are placed in special education programs, the effectiveness of these programs declines, and the provi-sion of intensive and individualized services to appropriately referred and eligible students decreases.

Another group of educational personnel believe that spe-cial education services and procedures are too cumbersome and deprive general programs of deserved funds and services for nondisabled students. These educators may avoid the pre-referral and referral process entirely, withholding struggling learners from much-needed assistance and possible services. There are other detrimental consequences of such practices as well, including resentment of special education teachers, students with disabilities, and their families and attempts by special interest groups to decrease funding for special educa-tion programs.

Both groups of educators have the potential to negatively influence school learning environments, service delivery, and student outcomes for struggling learners. Their behavior can also directly affect parents who seek the best educational options for their children.

Much like educational professionals, parents too have a powerful role in the education of children with disabilities. Particularly those parents who are knowledgeable about educa-tional systems and the laws governing general and special edu-cation may be dissatisfied with educational services and work toward making changes to those services. From this perspective, these particular parents understand the law and often obtain legal assistance to access appropriate services. They understand potential due process outcomes that may result when various compliance items have not been met. The knowledge and skills of this group of parents provide them with powerful voices for their children, allowing them to work within the system to facilitate what they perceive as the best educational situations for their children. Local school personnel view them as confident and able advocates. I have observed that these parents often come from what is considered mainstream society, are frequently well educated, and often come from middle or higher socioeconomic backgrounds.

Another group of parents may or may not be aware of the quality of educational services provided to children with disabilities and those experiencing difficulty at school. These parents are unable to make significant change given their lack of general knowledge of educational systems and the capacity to implement genuine change. When these parents realize that their children have not received adequate educational services, they may become quickly distrustful of the school system. They may feel that they are on unequal intellectual, cultural, or educational footing with school professionals and therefore unequipped to voice their questions or concerns. Moreover, they may lack the confidence to maneuver within a mainstream American educational system. More often, it has been my experience that many of these parents come from culturally and linguistically diverse, low-income backgrounds. In some instances, parents reveal having a history of previous negative educational experiences within the schools. In these cases, they relive their own experiences whenever they interact with school personnel on behalf of their children (sometimes in the same neighborhood school they attended). I find that educational programs within most urban student populations include more families from this group. What are the effects on educational policy when the most influential voices do not represent the majority of students and their families?

Schools benefit when parents are able to confidently advocate for their children and are knowledgeable of the educational system. Schools that have active and knowledgeable parents and families support higher levels of educational experiences for all students. In what ways might schools support families to become more knowledgeable about the educational system and promote effective change? How can educators assist parents to advocate for their children? I truly believe that as parents feel more confident in maneuvering through schools, understand their children's learning difficulties and strengths, and learn about the services that are available, they will become more involved and vocal within schools, and the educational system will benefit.

Our educational system has the capacity to reach out to parents, helping them to find their voice and identity within schools and classrooms. For example, districts may develop entire departments dedicated to parental involvement such as a parent community services branch. District offices and individual schools may initiate parent committees specifically aimed at providing information and support for culturally and linguistically diverse parents (such as a multicultural parent advisory committee) and those with children with disabilities. These groups can be powerful vehicles for parents to learn about district policies, procedures, and activities in accessible language. At a more local level, schools can reach out to parents by establishing parent centers on school campuses—designated spaces where parents can network, organize meetings, and participate in parent education classes. These centers can help parents feel validated as essential members of the educational community. Parents who participate on parent committees and use school parent centers feel more comfortable volunteering in classrooms, obtaining paid positions as support staff, and voicing their concerns about services and instruction.

## Culturally Responsive Instructional Approaches

Rueda, Klingner, Sager, and Velasco suggest that providing engaging, motivating, and culturally responsive educational experiences for all students will serve to improve the instruction provided to students of color. Students who feel alienated from the educational process are more likely to engage in behaviors resulting in suspension, exhibit low achievement, become truant, drop out, or be referred for special education. Recognizing and including the assets that these students and their families possess as part of the curriculum is a key aspect of cultural responsiveness that the authors highlight and probably the most difficult for many frontline educators to implement.

When children and their parents are respected and valued, the entire learning environment benefits by creating a supportive and improved school climate. Culturally responsive instructional approaches go far beyond the sharing of typical ethnic dishes and wearing of specific apparel on set days. Educators often miss opportunities to form strong connections with parents of color when they do not acknowledge that both parents and educators must work together as a team in order to attain what is best for children. For instance, when students and families are new to a school, school personnel should ask parents, "What can you tell me about your child that can help us teach her more effectively?" Or, "What does he like to learn from you?" Through these initial conversations, schools should acknowledge parents as their child's first and most important teacher. These conversations should emphasize not only what the child has previously learned but the context in which learning has historically taken place (both in school and within the home).

Culturally responsive pedagogy allows parents to feel more knowledgeable about the educational system because they are contributing to the instruction. Within this approach, parents become validated significantly as educational partners, sharing in the responsibility of their child's education. When recognition and appreciation of family practices are truly a basis for interacting with children and their families, educators help build an environment based on cooperation, mutual trust, and respect.

## Response to Intervention

Rueda, Klingner, Sager, and Velasco discuss another mechanism to perhaps address disproportionality: the implementation of response to intervention within a three-tier model of instruction. Depending on the district and its resources, a variety of factors within each tier may have a positive impact or hinder students' overall academic progress in the schools. For instance, curriculum companies may develop and standardize curricula and intervention programs on a population not reflecting the cultural or linguistic diversity of the students receiving instruction. Teachers may fail to implement these programs as intended by their publishers or neglect to implement them in a culturally responsive manner.

When considering how core curricula and intervention programs can best meet the needs of a given student population, districts and schools should ask targeted questions. How might teachers integrate culturally sensitive approaches and embed them into curriculum materials in order to maximize students' understanding? Do curricula contain stories or examples that students have experienced in their environment? Do purchased programs establish an appropriate pacing plan that will allow sufficient time for building strong foundations in basic skills, especially during the early grades? Are instructional approaches child focused in order to create independent learners? An effective core curriculum and intervention program that considers the characteristics of the school population combined with a culturally responsive approach to instruction may be the vehicle to create effective learning communities.

While using an RTI and three-tier framework, schools must be mindful of a myriad of other factors that have the potential to drastically influence student performance at school. This includes trauma or significant circumstances in the home (examples are homelessness and divorce) or community (such as violence and immigration raids). Children do not exist in isolation from their surroundings. Schools should become conscious of these and multiple other factors and their relationship to one another and the child. Mechanisms like student success teams and other types of early intervention should not erroneously conclude that students should be referred for special education services without an analysis of these systems and potential influence on students' functioning. Each of these factors requires a response from the educational system—either a referral to obtain additional resources or changes in the child's educational environment.

## Searching for Connections

When schools fail to provide culturally responsive instructional practices and create an environment where diversity and collaboration are absent, children cease to become excited about learning. Parents of color in larger numbers are searching for other educational opportunities for their children when they believe their neighborhood school's educational goals are not high enough, the school is not safe enough, or the school's doors are constantly closed to parental participation. Consequently I observe increasingly more parents of color placing their children in parochial, charter, and private schools and in some cases home-schooling their children. This flight from public schools may have direct implications on policy decisions for public education, because in some communities, the majority of children left in the public schools may represent families too poor to afford other educational settings for their children.

What students learn at school should become connected to their daily life and not be confined to the boundaries of the classroom. Educators should infuse examples that are familiar to students, thereby incorporating their knowledge and concerns around relevant current events and individual and familial experiences into daily teaching practices. The example that Rueda, Klingner, Sager, and Velasco provide highlights a teacher's efforts at discussing issues related to the English-only controversy within the students' community and finding ways to integrate this crisis into the instructional day. Teachers choosing to work in urban and diverse communities must provide instruction that connects students to their experiences and environment through authentic and meaningful practices.

## Final Thoughts

This country was diverse from its inception, encompassing groups escaping oppression, and was built on the ideals of freedom: freedom to live, work, and build, whereby each person contributes to the whole community. With changes in society, technology, and the global economy, the responsibility to educate future generations and prepare them for these changes has become even more important. The promise of a free quality education remains a hallmark of American society and has provided the foundation for our achievement as a country that continues to lead the world in the market of ideas and opportunity. Our educational system remains an indicator of our confidence and hope for the future.

Yet American public education is greatly limited by its continued failure to adequately serve children of color, many of whom continue to live in low-SES conditions. Our basic charge as educators must focus on providing equal quality educational access and not doing harm. There are negative outcomes when special education is used as the only mechanism for assisting students who are struggling academically, emotionally, or socially. Students who are given labels for expediency often experience unintended consequences. The significant overrepresentation of culturally and linguistically diverse groups in special education programs (Parrish, 1994) places them at greater risk for dropping out of school. Within three to five years of dropping out, students identified with emotional disturbance are often arrested (U.S. Department of Education, 2002). Students with disabilities are suspended at higher rates than their nondisabled peers, and they are enrolled in higher education at levels 50 percent lower than general education students (U.S. U.S. Department of Education, 2002). What kind of statement does a country make when disproportionately high numbers of its children of color experience poor life outcomes and inadequate public education?

Achieving this two-pronged goal of providing equal educational access and avoiding doing harm will ensure that our country is actively looking at today's America and seeing the potential of human resources that are being overlooked and untapped. Our children, the foundation of future generations, are our country's most valuable resource, and that resource is being neither nurtured nor protected. Perhaps the real definition of *mainstream America* is one that embodies and supports the belief that everyone can contribute to making our society better. Current educational and research trends offer hope that the promise of an effective education for all students can be realized. The work that we as educators need to accomplish is not beyond our competence levels or ability to implement. We can only trust that it is not beyond our will.

# 6

# EARLY INTERVENTION FOR STUDENTS IN GENERAL EDUCATION

## Promoting Academic Achievement for All

### Diane Haager

Prevention of academic failure is at the forefront of education. Although we have seen nationwide increases in students' reading and mathematics proficiency in recent years, many students continue to experience academic difficulties (National Center for Education Statistics, 2006). In urban areas, the rates of academic failure are particularly high. Schools with low achievement status and high numbers of students living in or near poverty are the focus of recent initiatives such as Reading First, a mandate that has provided an unprecedented amount of funding for improving reading instruction (Elementary and Secondary Education Act, 2002). This and other initiatives have led to widespread changes in elementary classrooms that focus more on catching struggling learners early, before their achievement lags so far behind that educators consider referrals to special education. Early intervention for students experiencing difficulty is the key to prevention. For example, in the area of reading, the National Reading Panel (2000) concluded that for all but a small fraction of students, it is possible to eliminate reading failure, given proper supports and conditions.

The identification of students with learning disabilities (nearly half of all students receiving special education services) has long been a topic of contention. Passage of the Education for All Handicapped Children Act (P.L. 94–142) in 1975 marked the first legislation that mandated special education services for students with disabilities. This law defined the condition of learning disabilities as a disorder in psychological processes that "may manifest itself in an imperfect ability to listen, think, read, write, spell or to do mathematical calculations." This definition was widely interpreted as the "discrepancy model," in which schools needed to demonstrate a significant discrepancy between a student's intellectual ability and academic functioning. Thus, students experiencing academic failure in one or more academic areas have historically been potential candidates for special education. How schools have determined that discrepancy has been the center of controversy. Critics have cited subjectivity in the referral process, flawed or inadequate tests, and ambiguous criteria as causes for concern about the definition and process of identifying learning disabilities (Vaughn & Klingner, 2007).

The reauthorization of the special education law, the Individuals with Disabilities Education Act (IDEA 2004, P.L. 108–446), brought special education into greater alignment with general education requirements included in the Elementary and Secondary Education Act of 2002, with such provisions as requiring highly qualified teachers and using scientifically based research to guide instruction. Relative to students with learning disabilities, however, the most significant change has to do with the process of identifying students with learning disabilities through an early intervention process called response to intervention (RTI). RTI places greater responsibility in the hands of general education teachers to identify struggling learners early and provide preventive intervention prior to considering a referral. This places greater emphasis on the nature and content of K-12 general education instruction and less on teacher referral. As students enter elementary school and experience academic failure, early intervention focuses on catching students who struggle academically early in the K-12 years and providing appropriate support, whereas in special education, we have often thought of early intervention occurring during early childhood, prior to kindergarten, for students with identified disabilities.

The focus of this chapter is the role of early academic intervention for school-age children in the RTI process. The first section explains important changes in the federal law with regard to RTI and how these changes came about. Then the chapter provides the historical context of prereferral intervention that led to the current focus on RTI, followed by an explanation of the basic components of the RTI model. Finally, it discusses a current research project that examined the use of RTI procedures to provide early reading intervention for English language learners (ELLs) with the aim of preventing academic difficulty.

## An Important Change in Federal Law

The changes in IDEA 2004 represent a conceptual shift for the field of special education as well as a response to abundant research documenting problems with past identification procedures for students with learning disabilities. The federal regulations indicate that states "must not require the use of a severe discrepancy between intellectual ability and achievement for determining whether a child has a specific learning disability" and that states "must permit the use of a process based on the child's response to scientific, research-based intervention" (34 C.F.R. sec. 300.307). Currently, state and local education agencies are developing procedures and criteria in response to the changes.

The use of discrepancy criteria has been standard practice since 1975, when services for students with learning disabilities were mandated in P.L. 94–142. Conceptually P.L. 94–142 and subsequent reauthorizations defined learning disabilities as significant underachievement based on what would be considered typical expectations for a student within the normal range of intellectual ability. In other words, for a student functioning in the normal range of intelligence, one would expect to see achievement within the same normal range. Achievement that dips significantly below the expected level may be due to an inherent disorder that prevents learning. Other provisions in the original definition of learning disability, called the *exclusion criteria*, further defined that this discrepancy in achievement may not be due to environmental or cultural factors or lack of instruction. In addition, some states required evidence that the student had a processing disorder, such as an auditory or visual processing disorder (Kavale & Forness, 2000b).

The discrepancy model poses several problems. The primary problem is that, using standardized tests, a discrepancy cannot typically be discerned until the student has been in school for several years, when the discrepancy finally becomes so severe that the student is hopelessly behind grade-level peers. This "wait-and-fail" approach, in which school personnel wait for the discrepancy to appear and allow the student to continue to fail for several years, delays the provision of special education services until third or fourth grade for most students, beyond the point where foundational academic skills are taught in general education classrooms, and creates a situation in which it is difficult to provide access to the general education environment and curriculum for students with learning disabilities (President's Commission on Excellence in Special Education, 2002; Vaughn & Klingner, 2007). Most students who are identified after two or more years of experiencing reading difficulty, for example, fail to fully benefit from special education help (Vaughn, Wanzek, Woodruff, & Linan-Thompson, 2007a), and will likely lag behind grade level for years following.

Further problems with the use of the discrepancy model for identifying students with learning disabilities have to do with the tests that are used to determine the discrepancy between intellectual capacity (IQ tests) and academic performance (standardized academic achievement tests). The use of IQ tests in a discrepancy model has been questioned repeatedly due to issues with the validity of IQ testing and its correlation with achievement (Fletcher et al., 1998; Speece & Case, 2001; Stanovich, 1991). The process to identify students with learning disabilities using the discrepancy model usually begins with a teacher referral. Some have criticized this process due to subjectivity and inconsistency in the criteria teachers use to make a referral decision (Egyed & Short, 2006; Klingner & Harry, 2006; Logan, Hansen, Nieminen, & Wright, 2001).

The definition of learning disabilities and the use of discrepancy criteria for identification have changed little since 1975, despite the fact that these problems have been apparent for some time (Kavale & Forness, 2000b). Many consider the IDEA 2004 recommendations for the use of RTI to determine eligibility for learning disabilities a welcome change because of the potential for more accuracy in identification and for earlier service delivery. Not only does this approach benefit students with legitimate learning disabilities by providing services earlier, but may also benefit students who struggle with learning for reasons other than learning disabilities. Early intervention may prevent the misidentification of some students while providing needed early learning support.

## Prereferral Intervention: The Roots of RTI

Early intervention is not a new idea in education. For many years, educators have documented attempts to remediate student difficulties in general education prior to making a referral to consider a special education placement (Graden, Casey, & Christenson, 1985; Rock & Zigmond, 2001; Safran & Safran, 1996). In fact, the law requires that educators document attempts to provide appropriate instruction in the general education program prior to special education placement, a process called *prereferral intervention*, though various other terms have been used, such as *intervention assistance*, to avoid an assumption that a referral for special education is expected (Graden, 1989; Whitten & Dieker, 1995).

Research has demonstrated that when effective prereferral intervention practices are in place, the number of spurious referrals decreases and the proportion of students who qualify for special education following assessment increases (McNamara & Hollinger, 2003; Safran & Safran, 1996; Whitten & Dieker, 1995). Many schools operate a prereferral process through a team approach. This collaborative process of prereferral intervention, also referred to as a student study team (SST), intervention assistance team, or other name, brings together teachers to discuss students' learning problems and work together to find solutions. Teachers have reported positive perceptions of the opportunity to work with peers to solve problems, as well as increased communication among staff members (Chalfant & Pysh, 1989). When additional support is provided by a specialist or colleague, teachers view the process in a more favorable light and are more likely to implement intervention (Lane, Mahdavi, & Borthwick-Duffy, 2003).

Despite the generally positive perceptions of the efficacy of prereferral intervention, there are several problems. Gersten and Dimino (2006) report that general education teachers tend to view the SST process as a special education function. It is important to note that most of the research conducted to study prereferral intervention practices has been published in special education journals even though the SST process is considered the purview of general education teachers (Haager & Mahdavi, 2007). Lack of consistency in implementation is the primary criticism of the prereferral process. Even when teachers are well prepared and knowledgeable about the process and the interventions that the team suggests are valid and appropriate, prereferral intervention is not always effective because of lack of consistency and fidelity of implementation of the interventions (Kovaleski, Gickling, Morrow, & Swank, 1999). Previous regulations governing special education services have been rather vague about what exactly is required in terms of prereferral intervention and have lacked teeth for mandating that effective systems should be in place.

## Overview of RTI Model

The idea of implementing a systematic approach for early identification and treatment of significant learning problems that would lead to positive learning outcomes for many children is intuitively appealing. Most agree that intervening early can prevent later, catastrophic academic problems for many children. Using an RTI model, teachers can identify students showing early signs of academic difficulty and then make instructional decisions based on students' responses to supplemental intervention. Some students may respond well to intervention and in a short time jump back in step with grade-level peers and discontinue intervention. Continued or more intensive intervention may be required for other students who have shown an inadequate response to intervention. Such students may be what Torgesen (2000) has referred to as "treatment resisters," who will require intensive, specialized instruction such as is offered in special education programs. Providing early intervention will not only help to prevent later academic failure, but may also prevent unnecessary identification of many students for special education.

As defined by Gresham (2002), "A *response to intervention* approach to eligibility determination [for special education] identifies students as having an LD [learning disability] if their academic performances in relevant areas [such as reading] do not change in response to a validated intervention implemented with integrity" (pp. 480–481). It is helpful to think of RTI as a layered, or tiered, model of intervention that provides schools with a means of catching struggling learners early, providing early support, and identifying students with significant learning disabilities somewhat earlier than is typical (Fuchs & Fuchs, 2007; Vaughn, Linan-Thompson, & Hickman, 2003; Vaughn,

Wanzek, Woodruff, & Linan-Thompson, 2007a; Vellutino et al., 1996).

Three-tiered RTI models have been conceptualized slightly differently across researchers, but the basic framework is similar. Figure 6.1 depicts a three-tiered RTI framework. In this explanation, I use reading as an example of how the model would be structured, but the model is likely to be similar with mathematics or other key skills. The first tier represents core reading instruction that is provided for all students. Instruction in tier 1 consists of a research-based core instructional program that is comprehensive in covering the essential early reading skills, is fully implemented, and is delivered by skilled teachers who have received adequate professional development. Tier 2 provides supplementary instruction beyond the core program for students whose performance is significantly below grade level as determined by reliable and valid assessments. Tier 3 consists of intensive and specialized instruction for students with significant reading difficulties that have not been remediated in a given amount of time in tier 2. Some consider tier 3 to be special education, while others conceptualize special education as a separate set of services to be used once the three tiers have been exhausted. Following is a description of a three-tiered reading intervention approach that has been used in urban schools serving large proportions of ELLs.

## PLUS Project: Promoting Literacy in Urban Schools

Through grants funded by the U.S. Department of Education, Office of Special Education Programs, my colleagues and I have implemented the PLUS Project in several urban schools serving a primarily Hispanic ELL population. Our goal was to create a sustainable model of prevention and early intervention for improving early literacy outcomes for ELL students who are likely to be identified in later years as having reading-related learning disabilities. Because schools and districts are constantly

### Figure 6.1    A Three-Tiered Model for Response to Intervention

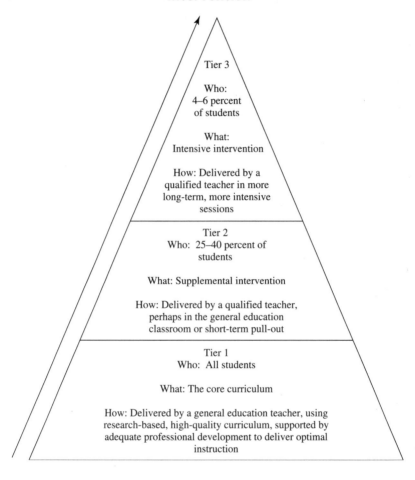

Tier 3

Who:
4–6 percent
of students

What:
Intensive intervention

How: Delivered by a
qualified teacher in more
long-term, more intensive
sessions

Tier 2
Who:  25–40 percent of
students

What: Supplemental intervention

How: Delivered by a qualified teacher,
perhaps in the general education
classroom or short-term pull-out

Tier 1
Who:  All students

What: The core curriculum

How: Delivered by a general education teacher, using
research-based, high-quality curriculum, supported by
adequate professional development to deliver optimal
instruction

juggling budget constraints, we felt it would be more sustainable if we could design a model that could be implemented at low cost, using existing personnel to provide intervention. Therefore, we provided extensive professional development to school administrators, general education teachers, and special education teachers. In the PLUS schools, tier 1 was implemented through the adoption of a standard reading curriculum throughout the district that had a strong research base and was supported by professional development for teachers. PLUS provided a second tier of reading intervention for these schools in which intervention was provided by classroom teachers within the context of their daily reading instruction. Tier 3 was provided by special education personnel following the usual referral and placement procedures.

The focus of the PLUS Project was to provide reading intervention and ongoing progress monitoring assessment for students supported by professional development in reading intervention for general and special education teachers. The project promoted collaboration between general and special education teachers and between researchers and school personnel. Table 6.1 depicts the roles of general and special education teachers in the PLUS model.

## Tier 1: Instruction for All

In 1999, California adopted rigorous academic standards for reading and language arts following Proposition 227, requiring that academic instruction be conducted in English for all students unless parents specifically request bilingual instruction (California Department of Education, 1999). This action was followed in the districts by widespread adoption of reading programs that exemplify principles of systematic, explicit, research-based reading instruction. Although there has been widespread concern that these initiatives would not benefit ELL students, most districts conducted extensive professional development for teachers to assist them in implementing these mandates.

In our PLUS schools, teachers received at least a full week of training in the newly adopted reading program, as well as additional training in English language development methods for ELL students. Teachers were required to fully implement the core program and district-required assessments in reading. Thus, we had reasonable confidence that tier 1 was well implemented in these schools. In addition, PLUS teachers assessed their students in basic early reading skills using the Dynamic Indicators of Basic

**Table 6.1   Teacher Roles in the PLUS Project**

|  | *Tier 1* | *Tier 2* | *Tier 3* |
|---|---|---|---|
| **General education teacher** | | | |
| Instruction | Provide core instructional program for all students | Provide 20–30 minutes of daily supplemental instruction to students who did not meet grade-level benchmarks | Provide mainstream instruction as specified on individualized education program (IEP) |
| Assessment | Conduct district assessments connected to core curriculum | Conduct progress monitoring assessment with intervention students every two weeks | Conduct classroom assessment only relative to mainstream instruction |
| Colla-boration | Work with literacy coach and site admi-nistrator to ensure quality implementation of instruction | Meet in grade-level teams with project consultant twice monthly to discuss and plan intervention activities and review assessment data | Meet in consultation with special education teacher to review student progress and plan mainstream instruction |
| **Special education teacher** | | | |
| Instruction | Maintain awareness of grade-level standards and curriculum | May provide supplemental instruction for selected students in general education classroom while simultaneously serving students with IEPs included in class, if general education students have instruc-tional goals similar to those of special education students | Provide specialized instruction as specified on IEP |

(*Continued*)

**Table 6.1   Continued**

|  | Tier 1 | Tier 2 | Tier 3 |
|---|---|---|---|
| Assessment | Maintain awareness of district assessments connected to core curriculum | May assist with conducting progress monitoring assessment with intervention for students every two weeks | Conduct ongoing progress monitoring assessment relative to IEP goals |
| Collaboration | May consult with classroom teachers, literacy coach, and site administrator to ensure awareness of core curriculum | Meet with grade-level teams and project consultant twice monthly to discuss and plan intervention activities and review assessment data | Meet in consultation with general education teacher to review special education student progress and plan mainstream instruction |

Early Literacy Skills assessment system (Good & Kaminski, 2002). At the beginning and middle of each academic year, teachers met in grade-level groups with research personnel to discuss the data results and identify students who might need tier 2 intervention.

## Tier 2: Intervention–Supplemental Instruction for Struggling ELL Readers

There is some evidence that the same intervention practices that are effective with native English speakers who are struggling with reading are also effective with English learners, especially at the word level of processing (August & Siegel, 2006; Carlo et al., 2004; Gersten & Baker, 2000; Gunn, Biglan, Smolkowski, & Ary, 2000; Haager & Windmueller, 2001; Linan-Thompson, Vaughn, Hickman-Davis, & Kouzekanani, 2003). However, intervention instruction may need some modification to incorporate support for vocabulary and language development

(Gersten & Baker, 2000; Gersten & Jiménez, 1994; Haager & Windmueller, 2001). The PLUS Project provided up-front and ongoing professional development for kindergarten through grade 2 teachers in participant schools regarding intervention practices and adjustments. Teachers learned how to analyze their assessment data to strategically group students according to areas of need (for example, phonological awareness, decoding, fluency). They learned a set of intervention strategies that could be implemented in small groups focusing on the core areas of beginning reading (phonological awareness, alphabetic principle, oral reading fluency, vocabulary, and comprehension). In addition, teachers were encouraged to reteach or preteach aspects of their core program during small group intervention sessions to reinforce the skills taught during reading instruction. Most important, teachers learned to integrate English language development instruction into their small group reading intervention instruction for ELL students. Although the teachers had time allocated in their day for English language development, they felt the small group reinforcement was particularly important for their struggling ELL students. Teachers met in grade-level groups to collaboratively plan how to schedule and implement intervention during their reading time block. Once or twice a month, teachers' planning sessions focused solely on intervention and their struggling readers.

## Tier 3: Pinpointing Specific Learning Disabilities

The PLUS model is essentially a prereferral intervention model designed to use the resources of general education to prevent unnecessary identification of ELL students for special education. Some of our participant schools implemented a collaborative model of special education in which the special education teacher went into general education classrooms to provide services. In these schools, the special education teacher quite naturally became involved in following the progress of the students who had been identified for tier 2 intervention. They often consulted with the classroom teachers regarding intervention techniques or about specific students. In some classrooms, the special education teacher included tier 2 students in instructional groups along with the special education students. In this way, tier 2 students often received intervention from the classroom teacher and the special education teacher. When it became clear that a student was not responding to intervention and the classroom teacher made a referral, the special education teachers were well aware of the students, and the assessment and eligibility process went quite smoothly. The teachers had quite a bit of documentation regarding the intervention process to take to an IEP meeting. In one school, the referral rate dropped by 40 percent during the first three years of implementation (Haager, Hunt, & Windmueller, 2003).

## Challenges Encountered in Implementing RTI

Implementing initiatives in schools, particularly in urban schools where large numbers of students and socioeconomic challenges abound, is difficult. Schools implementing RTI models will likely experience numerous challenges and will fare better if the challenges can be addressed as part of the planning process. Haager and Mahdavi (2007) describe the challenges encountered in implementing RTI in the PLUS Project, along with recommendations for addressing them:

• *Competing initiative and mandates.* Often schools take on too many special projects, initiatives, and mandated programs to successfully focus on RTI. For example, a single school might adopt a new textbook series, be involved in a special physical fitness program, or acquire new computers for a technology initiative, and lose its focus on early intervention. Too many initiatives occurring simultaneously dilute the energy and attention needed to achieve success with RTI. In planning the implementation of an RTI model, schools must work together to examine their programs and practices to determine which will support RTI and which will hinder implementation of the elements of the RTI model.

• *Negative attitudes or perceptions.* Resistance to change, insecurity about teaching "problem" students, feeling overburdened, and lack of knowledge about struggling learners or students with disabilities are all contributing factors to negativity about adopting an RTI model. Collaborative planning sessions that involve all teachers in some aspect of developing procedures and strategies is one way of heading off these problems before they escalate. In addition, creating a well-informed and knowledgeable teaching staff through professional development will help to offset potential problems.

• *Lack of time.* Many well-intended initiatives have failed due to educators' lack of time to devote to implementing them. Teachers may not have sufficient time in their daily schedule to work with struggling students in small groups. Also, they may not have regularly scheduled staff meetings for working through the planning and coordination required. A successful RTI model will be supported by careful scheduling that includes sufficient time for providing supplemental intervention. Intervention needs to be implemented systematically and be of sufficient duration to change students' responses to intervention. In many schools, finding additional time in a schedule is no small feat. It requires thoughtful planning and collaboration to determine where schedules can be shaved to make time for intervention.

• *Inadequate training.* Until recently, preservice teacher education has not included a focus on prevention and early intervention procedures. Therefore, general and special education teachers, as well as site administrators, may not have sufficient knowledge and skills regarding RTI and students with learning disabilities. General and special education teachers require professional development to better understand their roles in RTI implementation and to develop the skills and knowledge needed to work with struggling students. This will include rethinking traditional views of general and special educators' instructional roles. Preservice teacher education has not included training in RTI up to this point, and therefore teachers need in-service training and support to implement RTI successfully.

• *Lack of support.* Because schools are busy environments and administrators have increasing responsibility for accountability in all aspects of school operation, it is possible that administrators may not provide adequate administrative support for RTI implementation. This support may take the form of increasing professional development opportunities, managing the school schedule and structure, or providing time for teachers to collaborate. As schools take on RTI procedures, it is critical that site and district administrators provide support for implementation. Administrators play a key role in ensuring that teachers have the training, time, tools, and knowledge to conduct assessment and provide intervention.

## Recommendations for Implementing RTI in Reading

Several factors are important to consider for successful implementation of RTI in the area of reading:

• *Focus on the big ideas of reading.* Two panels, the National Research Council (Snow, Burns, & Griffith, 1998) and the National Reading Panel (2000), prepared syntheses of reading research that provide compelling evidence of the skills, experience, and knowledge children need to become successful readers in an alphabetic writing system such as English. Foorman and Torgesen (2001), summarizing the research over the past decade, describe the key elements of effective beginning reading instruction in the primary grades. A classroom exhibiting scientifically based reading research would likely have:

- Activities to develop students' phonological awareness
- Systematic explicit instruction in phonetic decoding strategies and spelling
- Activities that build fluency in both word reading and reading of connected text
- Explicit introduction of strategies for text comprehension
- A variety of vocabulary building activities

The Reading First guidelines recognize these areas as critical elements of reading instruction. These essential skills, or "big ideas" of beginning reading instruction, provide the foundation for literacy development.

- *Develop tiered reading intervention models.* Systematic and well-organized models of reading intervention need to be in place. An RTI approach to identifying students with learning disabilities focuses on providing early, preventive reading support to students showing early signs of reading difficulty and determining eligibility only when a student has not responded to a well-delivered intervention. Each tier must provide sound, research-based, systematic instruction in the core reading skills.
- *Use assessment data to guide intervention.* Having an assessment system in place is critical to successful tiered intervention models. To aid in accuracy of intervention and possible placement decisions, schools must use valid and reliable assessment tools. Screening assessment should include assessing all students to determine which students are demonstrating signs of risk and would benefit from supplemental intervention. In addition, for students receiving intervention, frequent progress monitoring assessments provide evidence of the student's response and the basis for decisions about continuing or exiting intervention or considering a referral.
- *Provide professional development and ongoing support to teaching staff.* Although many teachers are generally familiar with

assessment practices and small group intervention procedures, it is important for them to be consistent in their implementation and interpretation of data. Educators need sufficient professional development that addresses the skills and knowledge needed for RTI. In addition, opportunities for extended support, such as coaching or collaborative team meetings, are essential for ensuring a smooth transition from the traditional general and special education structures to an RTI model.

## Conclusion

RTI is conceptualized as an improved means of identifying students who truly have learning disabilities, compared to past methods, as well as supporting the goal of providing an appropriate education for all students. Key to a successful RTI approach is a well-designed core instructional program that is well delivered by highly qualified teachers. In addition, the supplemental intervention provided to struggling learners should reflect research-based practices and be responsive to individual student differences.

In order to provide students in special education with a free and appropriate public education as was established by P.L. 94–142, it is important that the referral process be well implemented with careful attention to accurately identifying learning disabilities that require specialized instruction rather than a more general academic difficulty that would best be addressed through a short-term intervention program. Educators must ensure that the referral of students for special services is done appropriately, following sufficient intervention and monitoring of students' responses to intervention. Early academic intervention in the general education environment is the first step in appropriately identifying students for special education.

Many students who are identified early as experiencing academic difficulty may not actually require special education, but instead may be successful following a period of focused academic intervention. Therefore, the process of monitoring students' responses to intervention, through systematic assessment with valid and reliable measures aligned to the curriculum, is a critical element of RTI. Only students who demonstrate a long-standing academic difficulty, despite the best intervention efforts and following progress monitoring assessment, should require the specialized instruction that is special education.

# FROM THE FIELD: ADDRESSING THE CHALLENGES OF EARLY INTERVENTION

## Jo Ann Isken
### with Terese C. Jiménez

During spring 2007 my elementary school staff and I (first author) convened a working group of approximately twenty teachers and staff to begin planning the implementation of RTI for our school of 950 students located in southern California. Although our percentage of English learners, 85 percent of our student population, may not reflect the current population of other schools, educational professionals, advocates and policymakers must acknowledge the rapid and pervasive increase in the number of English learners in school districts across the nation. In 2004, according to the U.S. Department of Education (2006), 9.9 million school-age children spoke a language other than English in the home. These numbers will continue to grow given the overall increase in immigrant populations in U.S. schools. The fastest-growing immigrant destinations in the United States between 1990 and 2005 were North Carolina, Tennessee, and Georgia (Frey, 2006). The states showing the fastest growth in their Hispanic population were Arkansas, South Dakota, and South Carolina, and the fastest-growing metropolitan areas in Hispanic population in 2004 were Fort Meyers, Florida; Charlotte and

Raleigh, North Carolina; Nashville, Tennessee; and Indianapolis, Indiana (Singer, 2003). Therefore, the issues we face as administrators and teachers in our school should not be unique to our context or our state alone. These will soon be, if not already, issues common to schools across the country.

Our working group was given several days to develop a response to intervention plan for English language learners (ELLs) not achieving grade-level benchmarks in English language development. Committed to the concept of early response and support for our students, we began to deal with the ground-level issues required in building an RTI pyramid for ELLs. The group consisted of myself (school principal), the assistant principal, the counselor, teachers representing grades K-5, the resource specialist, the special day class teacher, the speech/language specialist, the language arts staff development specialist, and the math staff development specialist. We began charting our students' English Language Acquisition profile results and drafting a preliminary school-wide early intervention plan. Fortunately, we had already comfortably dismissed three of the challenges to implementation that Diane Haager noted: negative attitudes and perceptions toward implementation, lack of time in the instructional day, and lack of support for planning and collaboration. Our group was committed, enthusiastic, and dedicated to designing and implementing a successful RTI program for our ELLs.

Feeling genuinely satisfied as a school staff that we did not face these challenges we moved on to discuss the issues at the heart of RTI implementation for our ELLs: curricula, assessment, intervention pedagogies, and the organizational structure that would support and define each tier of instruction. It was here that we began to redirect our discussion in search of answers to questions we felt less prepared to adequately address.

## Question 1: What Core Programs are Appropriate for English Language Learners?

Our first question focused on a lack of information related to effective core programs designed for ELLs. In the area of reading, the literature clearly identifies explicit instruction in phonemic awareness, phonics, oral reading fluency, reading comprehension, and vocabulary as essential components for monolingual learners (National Institute of Child Health and Human Development, 2000). A substantial amount of evidence and research supports this claim. Although instruction in a second language should focus on the same components as first-language literacy instruction, inherent differences in children's proficiency in the second language necessitates particular adjustments (August & Shanahan, 2006). However, research to date provides "a sketchy picture of what some of these adjustments might be" (August & Shanahan, 2006, p. 16). Undoubtedly we understand more about reading for monolingual speakers of English than we do about other areas for all learners, including mathematics, oral language development, and writing (Fuchs & Deshler, 2007).

In order to support our existing core programs, teachers have needed to heavily supplement these programs for their students. "The lack of detailed guidance and workshops on how to create a curriculum for English-language learners means that districts often are on their own in figuring out how to use the new standards in the classroom" (Zehr, 2007, p. 20). Core material does not reflect all the necessary standards or differentiated activities for diverse levels of English language development or learning needs. Often materials we receive do not report how they reflect scientifically based research practices. And if they do, these general instructional practices are conducted with students from other regions of the country, lacking the diversity and unique needs of our particular student population and community. Our teachers recognize that they must define the core program, develop accompanying materials, and determine how general progress in the core curricular areas may look different for students of varying levels of English language development.

## Question 2: What Types of Assessments are Appropriate for English Language Learners?

Response to intervention within a three-tier model depends on clearly defined, reliable and valid assessments (benchmark and ongoing progress monitoring) as indicated by Haager, that guide instruction and yield identification of students in need of intervention. Assessment measures and established benchmarks for these measures are currently in greater abundance in the area of reading. Other areas outside of reading in need of assessment and monitoring lack reliable and valid measures to assess our students. Moreover, current measures overall are admittedly not sensitive to the varying linguistic needs of ELLs. Shouldn't we expect students with certain levels of linguistic proficiency in English to differentially perform on measures of reading fluency or other skill area in comparison to same-age monolingual peers? When examining assessment results for diverse learners, including benchmark scores to determine risk status and intervention selection and implementation, our teachers recognize that they must also consider a student's rate of language acquisition, level of English and primary language proficiency, and general familial and school history.

The harm resulting from the unavailability of sensitive assessment measures for ELLs may contribute to the over-identification of students for intervention. If tier 1 core instruction should successfully meet the needs of 70 to 80 percent or more of students in a school, what happens when, according to benchmark measures, consistently fewer students are found successful with core instruction even after implementing class-wide interventions? Large-scale professional development is necessary in these instances; however, should teachers use existing measures and identify larger percentages of their students as at risk and in need of intervention? Some people may argue that these false positives may be a necessary technical glitch in the search for students who genuinely need this assistance.

However, as a result of using these measures, many schools send home countless letters during the first reporting period alerting parents of their children's "at-risk" status given their "lack of progress" on grade-level standards and the assessments used to measure such progress. Given this occurrence I urge schools to take all necessary steps to avoid such situations. Just as disability labels have the potential to cause harm to students' self-esteem and their overall perception of themselves as competent learners, so too being labeled at risk can carry similar consequences for these students and their families. We will not take this process of identification for intervention lightly or simply accept measures developed exclusively for monolingual learners as appropriate for children attempting to learn academic skills in a language they are only beginning to acquire. Our teachers realize they have an ethical obligation to be certain these decisions are made properly and from multiple pieces of information, especially in the case of linguistically and culturally diverse populations.

## Question 3: Which Interventions are Most Suitable for English Language Learners?

Most of the professional development workshops and trainings my staff and I have attended have provided good overviews of RTI yet little guidance regarding recommended, scientifically based interventions specifically designed for ELLs. With regard to areas of instruction outside of beginning reading, the same argument applies: schools currently have less access to ready-to-use programs and materials for classroom teachers in the areas of mathematics, language development, and written expression (Fuchs & Deshler, 2007) for monolingual and English learners. We also lack specific interventions and resources regarding what to do with older struggling learners in these areas. Schools need more specific information on what constitutes scientifically based interventions for diverse populations.

Our working group can appreciate this genuine lack of guidance given the extremely limited nature of research in this area. Few published studies give evidence supporting successful interventions for ELLs (August & Shanahan, 2006) or genuine models reflecting culturally responsive approaches (Klingner & Artiles, 2006; Klingner & Edwards, 2006; Klingner, McCray, Sorrells, & Barrerra, 2007). "The success of the RTI process for culturally and linguistically diverse students depends on teachers having access to appropriate evidenced-based instructional approaches that have been validated with diverse populations" (Klingner & Edwards, 2006, p. 113). Currently very limited access exists leaving many schools, pushed by urgent mandates to implement a model, to search for *any* program promising to deliver results.

To address the unique needs of our largely diverse student population, our teachers will supplement or modify existing research-based strategies and intervention programs. Given that such alterations will obviously affect the fidelity of an intervention's implementation, we must document whether such modifications produce positive changes in student outcomes. We encourage other schools to also become critical consumers of intervention programs and recognize their students' unique needs. Moreover, we invite local universities and research centers to assist schools with this process and learn from our students and our initial attempts at implementation. Now more than ever before, educators and researchers must work collaboratively to decipher what works with whom, by whom, and in what context (Cunningham & Fitzgerald, 1996; Klingner & Edwards, 2006).

## Question 4: How Can We Change Our Current School Organization and Structure to Facilitate RTI Implementation?

Nothing will truly change within a school system if there is a failure to study the organization (in this case, individual schools) and the capacity of schools for initiating real change prior to implementing a new initiative (Fullan, 2006). This issue became relevant as we began moving toward our school's implementation of an early intervention, RTI model. One's initial impulse with such mandates is to rearrange existing pieces while attaching the "vocabulary of the moment" to potential models, thereby avoiding the need to make genuine large-scale change (Fullan, 2006).This occurred during a workshop our staff attended in preparation for our RTI implementation. During this training, we were asked to sketch on a piece of paper how our school's current programs, resources, and services might fall within each tier of the RTI pyramid. I observed how diligently we inserted, erased, and reinserted various items on our papers. These models looked quite good on paper and seemed to address what we understood as elements of RTI. However, we immediately asked ourselves how our school would function differently within this new framework of instruction, intervention, and progress monitoring.

As a staff, we discussed wanting to avoid the mere labeling of existing practices—what we fear may be the general practice of other schools. We wanted to seriously change how we use these practices to facilitate better outcomes for struggling learners. We also wanted to consider what might be missing from our structure. Merely inserting new elements into our existing school structure without taking the time to make adjustments to the school's organization and function will not ensure that true change will occur. How, then, will our structure look and function differently within a new RTI three-tier model?

Our group proposes the following perspective. RTI is most often described as an intervention pyramid, yet only a flat, single face or triangle is delineated in workshops and training manuals — the face describing the tiers of instruction and use of assessment to identify students. This single-face, unidimensional representation does not reflect the true complexity of implementation of a pyramidal structure. Pyramids are constructed one layer at a time, with a strong core and equally strong foundation to support the topmost levels. One would never consider building a single face at a time because the single face would immediately collapse for lack of adequate support. In order to construct a true early intervention pyramid, our working group is committed to develop the tiers of intervention and assessment and simultaneously identify the staff development needs and changes in the organization. The model requires a strong sense of teacher and organizational efficacy—a recognition of the role of schools as capable assessors and instructional decision-makers.

## Final Thoughts

We will continue the implementation of our early intervention, Response to Intervention model enthusiastically, yet thoughtfully. Throughout this process we ask that educational professionals, researchers, and policymakers avoid the oversimplification of what it takes to implement mandates in general and RTI specifically. Moreover, school administrators need more opportunities for collaboration and hands-on support from the research community. We need assistance in establishing a process, as suggested by some, to help teachers and administrators distinguish good programs and interventions from bad ones (Fuchs & Deshler, 2007). Given that research examining the tiered system is in its infancy (Fuchs, Deschler, & Reschly, 2004; Mellard, Byrd et al., 2004) schools need permission to develop more long-term plans for implementation, recognizing the complexity of what these mandates require.

Finally, I challenge educational professionals, researchers, and policymakers to take frequent opportunities for research and reflection on RTI as an approach to early intervention, and to help answer the very difficult yet real questions we face in the field. For instance, what early intervention programs might more appropriately assist those students with limited prior schooling, English proficiency, or interrupted school histories? Should schools see decreases in intervention programs for students in the upper grades with the virtual elimination of intervention programs in middle and high schools? Should schools see consistent decreases in the number of students being referred for special education evaluation? Should we see a decrease in high school drop-out rates for diverse learners? We believe Response to Intervention as an early intervention approach is necessary but not sufficient to answer these very complex questions our schools face today.

We enthusiastically and thoughtfully move forward with our first steps toward implementing a better core program and early intervention system while fostering a strong collaboration with the research community in our endeavor. As schools begin to develop their own indicators of success, we encourage that they share their results with fellow educational professionals and schools around the country, so we may all learn from one another's challenges and successes.

Terese C. Jiménez assisted Jo Ann Isken in developing and writing the current chapter. The chapter's content, ideas and opinions entirely reflect Ms. Isken's experiences and perspectives regarding the topics discussed.

# 7

# DIFFERENTIATED INSTRUCTION

## Legislative Support and Classroom Practices

### Tanya Santangelo, Greg Knotts, Katharine W. Clemmer, Marianne Mitchell

> Listening to the voices of a multicultural
> community and providing effective learning
> experiences for all students will be the most
> difficult, but also the most interesting, challenge of
> your generation of teachers.
> —*Richard I. Arends (2000)*

Public Law 94–142 (The Education for All Handicapped Children Act) introduced the legal mandate that children with disabilities be educated in the least restrictive environment. Since the passage of that landmark legislation, schools and teachers have faced the omnipresent challenge (some would say, opportunity) of effectively providing special education services in general education settings. Most commonly, the response has been to create inclusive classrooms comprising students with and without disabilities (Mastropieri & Scruggs, 2007). This increase in academic diversity, juxtaposed with increased diversity in culture, language, and background experiences, means (as Arends, 2000, noted) that today's teachers face difficult, but most interesting, challenges. They must be able to design and implement instruction that maximizes learning experiences and outcomes for all students within their classrooms, including those with disabilities (Darling-Hammond, 2006; Pugach, 2005; Stodolsky & Grossman, 2000).

Differentiated instruction (DI) is a pedagogical approach through which teachers are able to achieve this goal of effective inclusive instruction (Haager & Klingner, 2005; Salend, in press; Tomlinson, 2005a, 2005b).

> In differentiated classrooms, teachers provide specific ways for each individual to learn as deeply as possible and as quickly as possible, without assuming one student's road map for learning is identical to anyone else's. These teachers believe that students should be held to high standards. They work diligently to ensure that struggling, advanced, and in-between students think and work harder than they meant to; achieve more than they thought they could; and come to believe that learning involves effort, risk, and personal triumph. These teachers also work to ensure that each student consistently experiences the reality that success is likely to follow hard work (Tomlinson, 2005a, p. 2).

In this chapter, we emphasize the practical, realistic use of DI as we seek to capture the essence of what it means to be a teacher in an inclusive classroom. First, we review legislation relevant to the need for and use of DI. Second, we provide an overview of the theoretical framework for DI and discuss strategies that are appropriate for a variety of content areas. Third, we present a case example that highlights how DI can be used to promote positive experiences and outcomes for students with and without disabilities in an inclusive classroom. Finally, we briefly discuss some of the challenges, remaining questions, and future directions for DI.

## A Legislative Backdrop for Differentiated Instruction

The need for, and use of, DI is supported by two primary pieces of legislation: Public Law 94–142: The Education for All Handicapped Children Act (EAHCA) and The No Child Left Behind

Act (NCLB) (Mastropieri & Scruggs, 2007). The EAHCA, passed in 1975, mandated that all children with disabilities were entitled to a free and appropriate education in the least restrictive environment. The importance of access to nondisabled peers was emphasized, and it was clear that schools were expected to provide a full continuum of alternative placements from least (for example, general education classroom) to most restrictive (for example, special schools), depending on students' needs. However, ambiguity in the language of the law meant that many students with disabilities had less access to the general education curriculum and settings than was intended.

When the EAHCA was reauthorized in 1990, it was renamed the Individuals with Disabilities Education Act (IDEA). This version of the legislation continued to reflect the desire for access to general education by stipulating:

> To the maximum extent appropriate, children with disabilities, including children in public or private institutions or other care facilities [be] educated with children who are not disabled, and that special classes, separate schooling, or other removal of children with disabilities from the regular education environment [occur] only when the nature or severity of the disability is such that education in regular classes with the use of supplementary aids and services cannot be achieved satisfactorily [20 U.S.C. 1412(5)(B)].

It did not, however, provide schools with explicit direction regarding least restrictive environment settings; decisions were based on individual education program (IEP) teams' determinations of students' needs.

When IDEA was reauthorized in 1997, it reflected still greater momentum for increased access to general education instruction, specifying "the education of students with disabilities can be made more effective by having high expectations for such children and ensuring their access in the general curriculum to the maximum extent possible" (20 U.S.C. sec. 1400 (c)(5)(a)). The most recent reauthorization of IDEA in 2004 codified the importance of least restrictive environment as "the regular classroom, to the maximum extent possible" (20 U.S.C. sec. 1400 (c)(5)). Whereas previous versions of the legislation advocated consistent inclusive practices, IDEA 2004 mandates their existence. It also stipulates that students with disabilities receive specialized instruction that includes ongoing adaptation of necessary content, methodology, or delivery of instruction in order:

(i) To address the unique needs of the child that result from the child's disability; and

(ii) To ensure access of the child to the general curriculum, so that the child can meet the educational standards within the jurisdiction of the public agency that apply to all children [(Part 300(A)300.39(b)(3)].

Schools must also "ensure that regular education teachers have the necessary skills and knowledge to provide instruction to students with disabilities" ((Title I)(D)(662)(a)(4)).

Along with outlining services for students who are officially classified as having a disability, IDEA 2004 includes provisions designed to address the needs of general education students who are experiencing learning difficulties (Mastropieri & Scruggs, 2007). Specifically, schools must implement and assess the effectiveness of research-based instructional strategies using a three-tier system, each level involving a sequentially more intensive and individualized form of DI. In tier I, the general education teacher implements a variety of best practice strategies, including DI. If that level of core instruction does not successfully address the student's difficulties, tier II interventions are employed. At this level, instruction continues in the general education setting, but interventions and differentiation are more intense, individualized, ~nd focused on identified needs. If sufficient progress is still realized, the student may move to tier III. In most cases, this involves a referral for special education evaluation and, where appropriate, the provision of special education services. At this level, the student receives the most differentiated and individualized instruction.

The No Child Left Behind Act (NCLB), passed in 2001, further supports the use of instructional practices such as DI that promote academic achievement and progress for all diverse learners within general education settings (Mastropieri & Scruggs, 2007). Although this landmark education act is not specifically special education legislation, it applies to all students and teachers in the United States. The intent of this legislation is to focus on children with the greatest needs, including children with disabilities. NCLB is based on four principles: increased accountability for states, school districts, and schools; greater choice for parents and students, particularly those attending low-performing schools; more flexibility for states and local educational agencies in the use of federal education dollars; and a stronger emphasis on reading, especially for young children. For the first time in educational history, states and school districts are mandated to hire qualified teachers to deliver standards-based instruction to all children in both general and special education settings. In addition, schools must demonstrate annual progress by systematically assessing all students, including students with disabilities whenever possible, using a predetermined standardized instrument. NCLB thus placed a new emphasis on accountability and progress for all students, including those with disabilities.

Collectively, IDEA 2004 and NCLB unequivocally mandate that schools and teachers provide effective and appropriate instruction for all students. Specifically, general educators are required to design materials and activities that can meet the needs of all students in an a priori fashion rather than making modifications only after realizing students have not been successful. This can be achieved, at least in part, through the use of DI (Haager & Klingner, 2005; Lawrence-Brown, 2004; Olenchak,

2001; Piggot, 2002; Salend, in press; Tomlinson et al., 2003). Thus, it is imperative that teachers understand the philosophy of DI and can effectively and efficiently implement corresponding strategies (Darling-Hammond, 2006; Pugach, 2005).

## An Overview of Differentiated Instruction

Differentiated instruction is a student-centered pedagogical approach that helps ensure all learners, including those with disabilities, have meaningful and enriched opportunities that result in measurable progress toward mastering grade-level academic content standards (Drapeau, 2004; Montgomery, 2001; Tomlinson & Eidson, 2003a, 2003b; Tomlinson & Strickland, 2005). This is achieved when teachers modify *content* (what is taught and how students access the material), *process* (activities that help students make sense of the content), and *product* (the ways students demonstrate what they learn) in response to students' unique characteristics. Specifically, decisions are made based on students' knowledge base, the content and activities that motivate students to learn, and students' preferred modalities of learning. The literature refers to these characteristics as students' *levels of readiness, interests,* and *learning profiles,* respectively (Hall, Strangman, & Meyer, 2003; Tomlinson et al., 2003).

Although a comprehensive review of the theoretical framework supporting DI is beyond the scope of this chapter, it is critical to briefly discuss several of the essential elements (or fundamental nonnegotiables) that allow teachers to evolve from making a few modifications from time to time, to creating classrooms that offer consistent, robust, and meaningful differentiation (Tomlinson, 2003b, 2005a, 2005b). These essential elements are using high-quality curriculum, focusing on the most important learning goals, using assessment to inform instruction, providing all students with respectful learning opportunities, collaborating with students, creating a positive learning environment, maintaining high expectations and goals, and demonstrating flexibility and creativity.

## Essential Elements

First, effective differentiation is predicated on the use of high-quality curriculum (Tomlinson, 2005a, 2005b; Tomlinson & McTighe, 2006). It must be relevant and meaningful for students, and it must promote both engagement and understanding.

Second, within the context of high-quality curriculum, teachers must identify and focus on the most important knowledge, understandings, and skills (Armbuster, Lehr, & Osborn, 2006; Tomlinson, 2003b). This clarity ensures struggling learners will be able to focus on prioritized topics, and advanced learners will be guided through more complex instruction rather than material they already know.

Third, effective and appropriate differentiation is possible only if teachers infuse assessment throughout the instructional process and, perhaps more important, use the data to inform their decisions about content, process, and product (Fuchs & Fuchs, 2006b; Tomlinson, 2005a, 2005b). Assessment takes a variety of forms (for example, whole class and small group discussions, journal entries, skill inventories, homework assignments, interest surveys); is necessitated before, during, and after a lesson or series of lessons; and is diagnostic in nature. It should focus on students' levels of readiness, their interests, their learning profiles, and their acquisition of the knowledge, understandings, and skills being taught. When benchmark assessments are used, they are constructed in ways that ensure all students will be able to demonstrate what they have learned.

Fourth, it is essential that all students consistently participate in respectful learning experiences (Tomlinson, 2005a, 2005b).

This guiding principle aims specifically to avoid the pervasive pattern where advanced learners are given motivating, creative, and important tasks, and struggling learners are required to complete tasks that are redundant, insignificant, and decontextualized.

Fifth, collaboration between the teacher and students is critical (Tomlinson, 2005a, 2005b). This does not imply the teacher relinquishes control; rather, he or she actively seeks input from students. Their ideas and insight are then used to promote a democratic classroom environment and collaboratively designed learning experiences.

Sixth, the learning environment, which consists of the concrete operations and physical attributes of the classroom as well as the overall tone, must be structured to support students' overarching needs for affirmation, contribution, power, purpose, and challenge (Tomlinson, 2003b, 2005a, 2005b). Teachers create a positive environment in many ways, including arranging the classroom to promote student interaction; ensuring all facets of the curriculum affirm the value of diverse cultures, languages, talents, and learning needs; providing students with individualized attention; demonstrating enthusiasm for, dedication to, and unconditional acceptance of each learner; and providing opportunities for choice whenever possible and appropriate. For example, students benefit from choices regarding what will be learned, how activities are completed, and how competency is demonstrated. Overall, the learning environment needs to be process based, supportive, and focused on individual growth.

Seventh, the potential benefits of differentiation are realized only when teachers maintain high expectations for all students and establish goals that focus on maximizing individual growth (Tomlinson, 2005a, 2005b). The essence of this is captured by Tomlinson's (2003a) edict:

> We would differentiate better if we always expect too much of kids, rather than expect too little. When in doubt, teach up.

I've never met a kid who couldn't do more than I thought he or she could. Under the right circumstances, every kid can do more than we believe; we compliment them by giving them something that's a little too hard and then by helping them get there.... A classroom in which differentiation is the best is one in which the teacher shoots high and expects all kids to rise to something that's a little more elegant than we might have assumed would be possible.

Finally, effective differentiation requires that teachers demonstrate flexibility and creativity (Ames, 1990; Gregory & Chapman, 2001; Tomlinson, 2005a, 2005b). This relates to the use of materials, instructional strategies, instructional formats, pacing, time, and space. Although technology is not a required tool for DI implementation, its use is an additional resource that reflects this flexibility. Of particular importance to DI is the effective use of flexible grouping (Haager & Klingner, 2005). Students should have opportunities to work in a variety of grouping formats (whole class, small group, pairs, and independently) and with a variety of their peers. Teachers accomplish this goal by purposely forming and restructuring groups across contexts during relatively short spans of class time.

There are times when it is appropriate and beneficial to organize students so they can work with peers who possess similar levels of readiness (Tomlinson, 2005a, 2005b). On other occasions, it is preferable to create groups that represent heterogeneous levels of readiness. Similarly, there are times when groups should contain students with similar interests or learning profile characteristics, whereas other tasks are best accomplished by groups of students who have diverse interests or learning profiles. Some circumstances necessitate that teachers create the groups; others provide options for student self-selection. Finally, it is essential that group activities are structured in ways that ensure each student can offer a significant and meaningful contribution beyond pedantic roles such as timekeeper.

Collectively, these essential elements guide decisions about how to differentiate content, process, and product based on students' levels of readiness, interests, and learning profiles (Tomlinson, 2003b, 2005a, 2005b).

## Readiness, Interest, and Learning Profile

The concept of student readiness encompasses students' knowledge, understanding, and skill in relation to the instruction a teacher is planning (Tomlinson 2005a, 2005b). Readiness is not synonymous with intellectual ability; it is a much broader and deeper construct that is shaped by prior learning and life experiences, attitudes about school, and cognitive and metacognitive proficiency. The goal of readiness differentiation is to ensure students are provided with tasks that are moderately challenging and then provide support to help them reach the new level of attainment. Differentiating based on readiness does not imply that students receive an alternative curriculum; rather, the teacher adapts instruction to provide access to and promote understanding of the standard curriculum.

Students' interests are the topics and processes that evoke curiosity and inspire passion (Tomlinson, 2005a, 2005b). Differentiating instruction according to students' existing interests promotes engagement, facilitates motivation, and helps them connect what is being taught with things they already value. Interest-based differentiation can also be structured to encourage students to discover new interests.

A learning profile describes the ways in which a student learns most effectively (Tomlinson, 2005a, 2005b). Salient factors include group orientation (for example, whole group instruction, small group activities; working with a partner or working independently), cognitive styles (for example, whole to part versus part to whole, linear versus nonlinear, reflective versus action oriented), intelligence preferences, learning environment preferences (for example, quiet versus noisy, still versus active, flexible versus fixed, warm versus cool), gender considerations (for example, competitive versus cooperative), and cultural considerations (for example, reserved versus emotionally expressive). Differentiation based on learning profile allows students to learn in ways that are natural and efficient.

Summarizing the importance of differentiating based on students' characteristics, Tomlinson (2005a) explains, "We know that students learn better if tasks are a close match for their skills and understanding of a topic (readiness), if tasks ignite curiosity or passion in a student (interest), and if the assignment encourages students to work in a preferred manner (learning profile)" (p. 2).

We next offer an overview of how teachers can use their knowledge of students' readiness, interests, and learning profiles to effectively and appropriately differentiate content, process, and product.

## Content

Content consists of both what is being taught and how students access that material (Tomlinson, 2005a, 2005b). In the vast majority of instances, it is preferable for what is taught to remain relatively constant across learners, with teachers varying how students gain access to essential elements of content based on learners' needs (Tomlinson & McTighe, 2006). In other words, if the goal of a lesson is to help students learn how to multiply two-digit numbers, that goal should apply to all students; some may need to work in ways that are more complex and with more independence and others with greater scaffolding (support) from the teacher and peers. Exceptions to this guideline occur in two instances: when a student has already mastered complex understandings and applications of that goal, or if a student has gaps in prerequisite elements (for example, fundamental understandings of number sense or basic operations) such that there is little or no likelihood of successfully reaching the goal, even with support (Tomlinson, 2005a, 2005b).

Effective content differentiation begins with the teacher identifying what exactly it is that students should know, understand, and be able to do at the end of an instructional sequence (Tomlinson, 2003b, 2005a, 2005b). Questions that help distill and prioritize content include, "What is this subject really about?" "What will be of enduring value to my students?" "What must I share with them to help them understand how this subject relates to their lives?" Then students' levels of readiness, interests, and learning profiles are used to determine whether differentiation is necessitated and, if so, how it will be successfully achieved.

A number of strategies promote content differentiation based on readiness (Adams, 1990; Cass, Cates, Smith, & Jackson, 2003; Cruickshank, Jenkins, & Metcalf, 2003; DuPaul & Stoner, 2003; Eggen & Kauchak, 2006; Strangman, Hall, & Meyer, 2003; Tomlinson, 2005a, 2005b; Vygotsky, 1987; Wisniewski & Smith, 2002):

- Providing text materials at varied reading levels and levels of complexity (and languages, if appropriate)
- Using small group instruction, also termed mini-lessons, to reteach or reinforce content
- Accessing computers to facilitate writing
- Providing text on audiotape
- Supplementing oral presentations with videotapes and visual demonstrations
- Using multimodal instruction
- Providing note-taking organizers
- Highlighting key portions of text
- Providing summaries of key topics
- Using manipulatives

- Providing vocabulary lists
- Using reading partners or adult mentors

Examples of strategies for content differentiation based on interest include allowing students to focus on an area they select, focusing the overall content on student-derived topics and questions, and offering examples that relate to students' experiences and areas of interest (Tomlinson, 2003, 2005a, 2005b). Examples of strategies for content differentiation in response to learning profiles include presenting material in visual, auditory, and kinesthetic ways; using examples and illustrations that represent varied ways of thinking; and presenting information in both whole-to-part and part-to-whole formats. Access to technology is beneficial for differentiating content based on readiness, interest, and learning profile.

## Process

Process can be thought of as sense-making activities that allow each student to increase his or her level of understanding about the topic being taught (Tomlinson, 2005a). Although there is inherent overlap between content and process, a simplistic way to decipher the two is to think of process as being the task (or series of tasks) that allows students to begin thinking about, working with, and personalizing information after they stop listening to the teacher or reading materials (the content). High-quality differentiated activities are those that are clearly focused on essential learning goals, facilitate students' ability to understand content, are interesting and engaging, require students to use higher-level thinking, and involve use or application of content rather than rote recall. Flexible grouping is integrally tied to process activities.

As with content differentiation, process can be differentiated by readiness, interest, and learning profile (Tomlinson, 2005a, 2005b). This is achieved by selecting from a plethora of strategies that vary in level of sophistication and preparation—for example:

- Providing directions at varied levels of specificity
- Varying the pace of work
- Providing graphic organizers and structured activity guides
- Using small group instruction for reteaching and extension
- Providing choices of topics
- Offering multiple options of expression, such as writing, typing, drawing, or creating a video

Learning contracts, cubing, and tiering are examples of more comprehensive strategies to differentiate process.

*Learning Contracts.* A learning contract is an agreement between a student and the teacher outlining a series of activities that will be completed within a specified time frame (Tomlinson, 2003b, 2005a, 2005b). Contracts lend themselves to differentiation based on readiness, interest, and learning profile and can be used effectively in any subject area or grade level. They are usually structured to allow students to choose activities, and they can involve individual or group work, or both. The self-directed nature of contracts provides teachers with opportunities to focus on small groups or individual students, and it fosters students' assuming responsibility for their learning.

Students' needs dictate whether it is appropriate to create a common contract for everyone in the class or whether multiple versions are necessary (Tomlinson, 2003b, 2005a, 2005b). For instance, a teacher who decided to use contracts for interest-based differentiation reflecting the most popular interests of the class (for example, sports, music, animals, and movies) would create a different version of the contract, each focusing on a particular category.

A standard contract has these components:

- A list of the essential knowledge, understandings, and skills being targeted
- Descriptions and directions for each activity
- The anticipated timeline and schedule
- The evaluation criteria
- The working conditions—for example, required meetings with the teacher, designations about what will be done in class and at home, procedures for organizing and storing work, and whether activities will be done independently or with peers
- The expectations and consequences associated with the contract (working quietly results in continued freedom and choice; inappropriate behavior leads to more teacher-directed activities)
- Signatures from the teacher, student, and sometimes parents or guardians

A contract can also be written as a learning menu (Cummings, 2002; Tomlinson, 2003b). Menus typically contain three sections: a "main course" that all students must complete, a designated number of "side dishes" (that are either selected or assigned), and "desserts" that are optional extension activities. At the secondary level, the terminology for this format of contract is adjusted to make it age appropriate. They are called *learning agendas* and contain "imperatives," "negotiables," and "options."

A third contract format, the think-tac-toe (Tomlinson, 2003b), is created by placing a different activity description into each of nine cells on a three-by-three grid (in other words, a tic-tac-toe board). Typically each row is thematic. For example, after completion of a book, students might work on a think-tac-toe that contains three character-related tasks in the top row, three setting-related tasks in the middle row, and three theme-related tasks in the bottom row. Students complete the contract by selecting and finishing one activity from each row. The case example later in this chapter highlights the use of a think-tac-toe in an elementary classroom.

*Cubing.* Cubing is a strategy that allows students to review, demonstrate, and extend their thinking about content that was presented (Tomlinson, 2003b, 2005a, 2005b). As the name implies, students use a cube that can be constructed out of sturdy paper consisting of four flat squares in a column and three flat squares in a row, or purchased assembled. Each of the six sides contains a statement, task, or question that is either predetermined by the teacher or created by students. Cubing activities can be completed independently or with a group and can be required in their entirety or a portion thereof.

For example, after reading a book, students might be told they can either work independently or with a partner to complete at least four of the following six prompts on their cube:

- Draw the main character (side 1).
- Use a Venn diagram to compare this book with another one we have read (side 2).
- Create a storyboard that shows the most important features of the plot (side 3).
- Predict what happened to the main characters during the year after the final chapter (side 4).
- Make a poster that highlights the author's theme (side 5).
- Write a letter to a friend explaining why he or she should, or should not, read this book (side 6).

In math, students can use cubing to review solving essentially any kind of problem (for example, addition, multiplication, or algebraic equations). Prompt ideas include:

- Describe how you would solve…
- Explain how each step of the problem leads to a solution.
- Compare this problem to…
- Explain how this kind of problem could be used in real life.
- Change one or more [parenthesis, numbers, signs] and explain what happens.
- Create an interesting and challenging word problem using the example, and show us how to solve it.
- Diagram or illustrate the solution to the problem.

Cubing can be used to differentiate based on readiness by having prompts at varying levels of difficulty (Tomlinson, 2003b, 2005a, 2005b). For example, if four students have demonstrated mastery of a topic but the remainder of the class has not, it might be appropriate to create two cubes at different levels of complexity and have students work through the activities in groups of similar readiness. Alternately, one cube with prompts at varying levels of complexity could be created and used by groups of dissimilar readiness. Cubing can also be used to differentiate based on interest (for example, one cube that presented the content using references to animals, one to sports, and one to automobiles) and learning profile (for example, one cube that contained written tasks, one musical, and one kinesthetic). ThinkDots is a strategy similar to cubing, except that rather than having the six prompts on the sides of a cube, they are placed on six index cards held together by a loop of string or metal clasp (Tomlinson, 2003b).

**Tiering.** Tiering is a strategy that allows all students to engage in tasks that focus on the same concept, but approach it in different ways that have appropriate complexity, abstractness, and open-endedness (Pierce & Adams, 2005; Salend, in press, Tomlinson, 2003b, 2005a, 2005b). Tiering can be used effectively at any grade-level or subject area and applied to any instructional format (for example, writing prompts, science labs, learning centers, homework activities, and tests). As with all other differentiated process activities, the first step in developing a tiered assignment is to clearly identify the essential knowledge, understandings, and skills to be targeted. Next, one high-quality activity is created. Preferably this initial activity is the most advanced, because that helps establish high expectations for the other versions. Then, based on knowledge of students' readiness levels, the teacher decides how many other versions (tiers) are needed to ensure that each student will be appropriately challenged. In some circumstances, two versions are sufficient; in other cases, it may be three or more. Adjusting the difficulty for each tier is accomplished by changing one or more dimensions, such as the materials required, the form of expression, the degree of complexity, the level of abstraction, the level of structure, the number of dimensions, the degree of familiarity, and the pacing.

Although tiering typically focuses on providing tasks that match students' readiness levels, the activities should also be created in response to knowledge about interests and learning profiles (Tomlinson, 2005a, 2005b). Prior to implementing a set of tiered activities, it is critical to review each version and verify that they are equally enticing, meaningful, and important. While students are working through tiered activities, they should be provided with support and scaffolding as appropriate. After they have finished, closure is established by having them share what they learned with others.

## Product

Products are student demonstrations of how much they understand and how well they can apply their knowledge and skills after a significant segment of instruction—for example, a two-week unit on animal habitats or a semester-long study of mechanical drawing (Tomlinson, 2005a, 2005b). Tomlinson (2003b, p. 5) explains, "While an activity will often ask students to produce a tangible outcome, here product does not describe what a student produces at the end of a day or two of learning. Rather, product describes a major assessment." Products can take many forms—such as a research project, a written composition, a visual display, a demonstration, or a portfolio—and should be appropriately differentiated in response to students' readiness, interests, and learning profiles. For example, a musically inclined student could demonstrate the knowledge she acquired during her first semester of French by writing a song that incorporated key vocabulary, usage, and grammar.

Contrasting the performance orientation of differentiated products with more traditional, formal assessment procedures, Tomlinson (2005a) explains, "Teachers may replace some tests with rich product assignments, or combine tests with product options so the broadest range of students has maximum opportunities to think about, apply, and demonstrate what they have learned" (p. 85). Hallmarks of effectively differentiated product assignments include providing clear and appropriate criteria for success, focusing on real-world relevance and application, promoting creative and critical thinking, requiring the analysis and synthesis of multiple sources of information, and allowing varied modes of expression. Throughout product development, it is also important for teachers to provide students with adequate scaffolding and support, as well as opportunities for peer and self-evaluation.

## Summing Up Differentiated Instruction

DI involves adapting content, process, and products in ways that respond to students' readiness levels, interests, and learning profiles. Effective implementation is achieved when the strategies are embedded within essential elements. Specifically, instruction must be grounded in high-quality curriculum and focused on essential knowledge, understandings, and skills. Assessment must be infused throughout instruction, and all activities must be equally engaging and meaningful. The learning environment must be supportive, inviting, and motivating. Teachers need to actively involve students and maintain high expectations for each one. Finally, teachers need to be flexible with materials, instructional strategies, instructional formats, pacing, time, space, and grouping. Effective implementation is supported by establishing collaborative relationships with other educational professionals (for example, special and general educators, other service providers, and administrators). The following case example illustrates how all of these components and strategies work in concert with one another within the context of an inclusive classroom.

## Case Example

This case example demonstrates how DI is used to support the achievement of Jake Cota, the fourth of five children in a low-income Latino family in a small neighborhood community. Jake's parents and extended family place a high value on education and consistently make efforts to support him in school. First, we present some background information regarding Jake's early elementary experiences. We then describe Jake's experiences in a third-grade cotaught classroom and later in a ninth-grade language arts class, taught by a single teacher. In both classroom examples, the essential elements that guide differentiation are evident, and the teachers demonstrate the use of a wide repertoire of strategies. Finally, we discuss some of the common themes that emerged from the two diverse settings.

### Elementary School

Jake's kindergarten experience is positive; he enjoys interacting with his peers, engaging in hands-on activities, and learning about new topics. His basic skills do not progress as quickly as most of his peers, but the class is structured in such a way that he is able to participate and feel successful. His difficulties with early literacy and numeracy skills become more evident during first grade, and he is unable to keep up with the rest of the class. His frustration and declining sense of self-efficacy lead to a pattern of scribbling on his work and defying adults. A student study team is convened to discuss the concerns of Jake's teacher and his parents. Several interventions are implemented and monitored during the next few months, but Jake shows little progress.

At the end of second grade, Jake's reading fluency, reading comprehension, and writing skills are at the beginning first-grade level; he is nearly two years behind grade-level expectations. He also struggles with critical mathematical skills such as counting strategies and algorithms. Given the severity of his difficulties and lack of response to interventions, the team refers Jake for a special education evaluation over the summer. When the team reconvenes to review the evaluation, the school psychologist explains that Jake has a learning disability, making it difficult for him to process information and attend to tasks independently. She then emphasizes his many strengths, including expressive language, motor skills, auditory processing, creativity, artistic ability, social skills, and motivation to complete tasks that are appropriate and engaging.

The team develops an individualized education program (IEP) to be implemented when Jake enters third grade in September. This plan includes support from a resource specialist for ninety minutes a day to help develop Jake's reading, writing, and math skills, using multisensory instructional techniques whenever possible. Jake's special education services will be provided within his general education classroom. The team also identifies several classroom accommodations for Jake, including extended time on assignments and tests, audio books or reading buddies for text above his instructional level, graphic organizers, and technology to support writing.

As Jake begins third grade, Ms. James, the general education teacher, and Mr. Wassell, the resource specialist, introduce their first thematic unit of the year. The theme is family history, and the unit will focus on three big ideas: we all face challenges, we all have triumphs, and we all have culture. They introduce the first series of interdisciplinary lessons centered on immigrant experiences using a K-W-L (what I know, what I wonder, what I learned) chart to help activate students' background knowledge and create enthusiasm. Knowing that many students in the class, including Jake, express their ideas better orally than in writing, Ms. James gives the students six minutes to discuss what they know and what they wonder with their desk buddies (groups of four students who are seated together). She explains that each group member will assume the role of "awesome thinker," but the group must also select a recorder and a reporter. Jake's group selects him to be reporter because he enjoys talking in front of the class. Both teachers circulate throughout the room during the discussion. Mr. Wassell then asks each reporter to share the group's ideas so he can add them to a large chart that will remain posted in the front of the classroom.

Next, Ms. James explains they will read several stories about immigrants during this portion of the unit so they can better understand the experiences of immigrants from different cultures. She gives each student a copy of the first book and instructs them to look through the pages and predict its content. After making sure all students have enough time to preview the text, she asks them to share their ideas with the class and then gives them the option of reading silently, with a buddy, or in a small group guided by herself or Mr. Wassell. Many students, including Jake, recognize they understand a story better when they read it aloud, so they are eager to join a small group. The ten students who want to read in a group are randomly divided into two groups and guided through the text.

After reading the first book, Ms. James and Mr. Wassell noticed everyone in the class could benefit from strategies to improve reading comprehension; they bring the class back together and collaboratively model how to complete a story map. They emphasize that this form of graphic organizer helps everyone better understand important story elements such as plot sequence and character relationships.

While they were planning this unit, Ms. James and Mr. Wassell had decided to structure the activities focusing on immigrant experiences using a think-tac-toe learning contract. Recognizing that reading proficiency varied greatly among their students, they created two versions, each written in the same format and containing activities reflecting students' interests and learning profiles. What differs is the level of complexity of each task, the level of structure and specificity associated with the directions, and the criteria for evaluation (see Figure 7.1). Using a whole group format, the teachers introduce students to the think-tac-toe by discussing the format, goals, and procedures. They also explain that students will receive either a red or blue version, based on the teachers' assessment of which tasks would be more interesting and challenging for them. The class decides that after completing their think-tac-toe activities, they want to have a showcase celebration: each student can invite an important person in his or her life to share the project about which he or she is proudest.

Students divide into the two color groups to learn about their activities in more detail. Ms. James begins working with Jake's group but soon realizes that many of the fourteen students are having difficulty focusing. It seems they are somewhat overwhelmed by the amount of text on the page and are also very excited about what they keep calling "cool stuff." She has each student select two pieces of construction paper and demonstrates how to cover everything above and below the section they are discussing. She lets them pick a highlighter and helps them mark key words for each activity (for example, create a pair of collages, write a poem or song, draw a story board). After making sure each student understands the nine activities, she has them select one from each row. Jake picks these:

## Figure 7.1

**Think-Tac-Toe (Red Version)**

**Directions:** Select and complete one activity from each horizontal row to help you and others think about how learning about immigrants helps us understand, "We all face challenges, we all have triumphs, and we all have culture."

**All your work should be thoughtful, detailed, original, and accurate. Use the rubrics that go with the activities you selected to help you do your best work.**

| | | | |
|---|---|---|---|
| **Culture** | Develop a trunk that contains special items you would want to bring to a new country. The items can be pictures, replicas, or actual artifacts. Be able to explain why each one is meaningful to you. Calculate the value of all the items in your trunk. **Jake's 1st Activity** | Create a skit that shows how culture and traditions may have influenced an immigrant family the day before they left for a new country and the day they arrived. Video tape your final production. | Interview an immigrant child who just started school in a new country. Focus on how he or she is impacted by culture. Present your interview in written, audio, or visual form. |
| **Triumphs** | Write a series of letters from a child who immigrated to this country to someone who stayed back in their home country. Describe his or her experiences, making sure to highlight some important triumphs. Your letters can be typed or handwritten. | Create at least two journal entries that would have been kept by a child who just immigrated to this country. Describe his or her experiences, making sure to highlight some important triumphs. Your journal entries may be typed or handwritten. **Jake's 2nd Activity** | Draw a story board showing the journey of an immigrant child. Include pictures that describe his or her experiences, making sure to highlight some important triumphs. |
| **Challenges** | Create a pair of collages. One should show the challenges faced by a child who immigrated to this country and the other should show some of the challenges you face. Include captions or speaking bubbles to explain your thinking. | Write a poem or a song about the challenges immigrant children and families faced and how they overcame them. Make an audio or video recording of yourself reading or singing your piece. | Interview a family member or other important person in your life to learn about the challenges associated with immigration and some of the ways they are overcome. Use a question and answer format to present what you learned. **Jake's 3rd Activity** |

- *We all have culture.* Develop a trunk that contains special items you would want to bring to a new country. Be able to explain why each one is meaningful to you. Calculate the value of all the items in your trunk.

- *We all have triumphs.* Create at least two journal entries that would have been kept by a child who just immigrated to this country. Describe his or her experiences, making sure to highlight some of the child's triumphs. Your journal entries may be typed or handwritten.

- *We all have challenges.* Interview a family member or other important person in your life to learn about the challenges associated with immigration and some of the ways that they are overcome. Use a question-and-answer format to present what you learned.

Ms. James then walks the students through the criteria on the rubrics they will use. She also helps all students establish one individual goal that will apply to all three of their think-tac-toe activities. Jake decides his goal will be, "Use correct punctuation in my writing." Finally, she helps each student fill out the schedule sheet that outlines the steps they will take to complete their think-tac-toe during the next few days.

As students begin working on their first activity, Mr. Wassell meets with Jake and the six others who are developing a trunk. He briefly reviews the task and shows them a crate filled with relevant books (each with a colored sticker on the inside cover corresponding to readability ranges) and other resources that list, picture, or describe possible items for their trunk. He asks if anyone has an idea about how he or she might begin this task. Jake offers, "Maybe we could look through the crate, get some ideas, and make a big list together. Then we can each pick what we really want in our trunks." His peers agree, and they ultimately create a list that includes twenty-six items.

Jake selects five items and estimates the cost of each. He reviews his best guesses with two peers and then shows them to Mr. Wassell for a final check. Mr. Wassell tells him his numbers are very reasonable and then generates a TouchMath worksheet with the costs he listed. Jake sums his numbers by quietly counting the touch points on each digit. Mr. Wassell uses TouchMath with Jake because it allows him to capitalize on his strong auditory processing skills, motor skills, and kinesthetic orientation. Jake completes this activity by drawing colorful and elaborate pictures to represent each of the items. Rather than constructing a trunk, he plans to bring in a real one from home.

Jake's second activity is to create two journal entries. Both teachers were surprised and thrilled when Jake initially selected this task, hoping it would provide an opportunity to develop his writing skills and confidence as a writer. Ms. James meets with the four students who chose this task and gives them the option of beginning independently or with their peers. Three students remain with her and review exemplary journal entries. Together they generate a list of necessary components they should include in their entries. Each student then copies the final list on an index card for later reference. Ms. James shows them three graphic organizers (varying in complexity) for organizing the ideas they want to include in each journal entry and helps each student make an appropriate choice.

The students begin organizing their ideas independently. Ms. James quickly notices Jake and another student are having difficulty. She lets everyone know she will give a mini-lesson to review brainstorming, and anyone who wants a little help getting started is welcome to participate. Jake and two other students join her and generate a list of prompts:

- Pick his or her biggest accomplishments.
- Describe how they came to be and how they changed him or her.
- Tell about the people who helped him or her succeed.
- Help your reader understand how he or she felt and why.

The students eventually compose their entries using an AlphaSmart portable word processor with word prediction software. This technology is especially beneficial for Jake because it helps minimize the visual-motor difficulties with handwriting, supports his vocabulary and spelling (with a dictionary and spell-checker), and allows him to revise his work easily.

After observing Jake during his first two think-tac-toe activities, his teachers are genuinely impressed by his increased engagement, improved work quality and completion rate, and willingness to try more challenging tasks.

Jake informs Mr. Wassell he is going to interview his grandparents for his third activity and that he feels comfortable working independently. To ensure Jake's success, Mr. Wassell has him explain the steps he plans to follow. Jake begins this task at his desk by listing ideas for questions on a graphic organizer. However, Jake decides he will be more comfortable and will work better sitting on a beanbag at the back of the classroom. Using an AlphaSmart, Jake drafts twelve questions and prints them out so he can share his work with a friend during a peer conference. He incorporates the friend's suggestions, revises his work, and signs up for a conference with a teacher.

During the conference with Ms. James, Jake mentions he is worried he will not be able to write as fast as his grandparents talk, so he might not be able to remember all the important things they say. Ms. James asks, "What do you think we should do about that?" After thinking a moment, Jake suggests that a tape recorder might help, but he would need to borrow one. Ms. James congratulates his innovative idea and lets him use one from the classroom. During the final showcase celebration, Jake invites his grandparents and proudly describes his interview project.

## High School

When Jake enters high school, he is excited about the prospect of playing on the football team, joining the art club, and participating in other social activities with his friends. The special education services and DI he experienced during elementary and middle school helped him make significant progress with reading fluency and decoding; he is performing at grade level in both areas. He does, however, still experience difficulty with reading comprehension (especially with lengthy or complex text), using appropriate sentence structure when writing, and applying math reasoning skills. His IEP for ninth grade includes goals in each of these areas and stipulates he will receive consultative rather than direct support from the resource specialist. His classroom accommodations include extended time on assignments and tests, reading comprehension supports (graphic organizers, text summaries, highlighted text, and guiding questions), note-taking supports, and technology to support writing.

During the second month of school, Jake's English teacher, Mr. Silverstone, tells the class they are going to begin a unit on different kinds of poetry and the grammatical conventions commonly used in poems. At the beginning of every class, students select a journal prompt and write or type a response for ten minutes. Today's prompts will help Mr. Silverstone gain a better understanding of their readiness levels and interest regarding their new unit. On the board he has written:

Option 1: When I think of poetry . . .

Option 2: The Book Authors of America have recently proclaimed that poetry is not "real writing." Defend or refute this statement.

Jake selects the first topic and composes his entry using an AlphaSmart. Knowing his work will be reviewed by both Mr. Silverstone and a peer motivates him to write well. Specifically, they will consider whether Jake has met the three criteria the class developed during the first week of school (writing must be well organized, concise, and interesting to read), as well as his individualized goal (use complex sentences). Jake will use their feedback to revise his work.

After students complete their journal entries, Mr. Silverstone initiates a class brainstorming session about poetry, listing "short" and "rhyme" on the board as examples. As students generate ideas, he records them and includes a brief definition for any he thinks might be less familiar. Jake offers "literation," but jokingly adds, "Just please don't ask me what it means!" Mr. Silverstone proclaims, "Now there's a million-dollar term," while writing *alliteration* on the board. Knowing that using humor and popular phrases can help reduce the stigma associated with soliciting help from other students, he asks if Jake would like to "phone a friend." Jake responds, "Oh yeah!" and a classmate respectfully explains, "It means using words with the same first letter or sound." Mr. Silverstone writes the definition on the board and then tells students to take a scrap piece of paper and generate as many examples of alliteration as they can. He casually walks around the room and, after glancing to verify Jake generated an accurate answer, asks him to share one of his examples with the rest of the class.

After students exhaust their ideas, Mr. Silverstone brings closure to the brainstorming activity by adding a few more words he believes are important. He tells the class, "Now you are going to take all these great ideas and create a poster-size concept map using 'Poetry is...' as the central theme." Noticing that some students, including Jake, appear puzzled, Mr. Silverstone has another student "remind" him what a concept map is and quickly sketch an example on the board. Following that clarification, Jake and two friends decide to work together; ultimately Jake explains the group's concept map to the class. All of the posters are displayed in the classroom for the duration of the unit.

At the end of the period, Mr. Silverstone explains that tomorrow's lesson will focus on self-portraits and similes. He reminds them to take a handout from the "Sneak Peak" folder if they would like to preview the content he'll be presenting and review the important vocabulary terms at home. Most students, including Jake, grab a summary on their way out the door.

The following day, after completing their journal entries, Mr. Silverstone distributes an outline corresponding to the lecture he will give on self-portrait poems and similes. It contains several blank spaces and is designed to facilitate their ability to take notes. He always offers an outline to everyone in the class and allows them to decide individually whether it is beneficial. Jake consistently takes advantage of this strategy. Throughout the lecture, Mr. Silverstone makes a concerted effort to include examples that reflect his students' interests. He also stops approximately every five minutes to give the class an opportunity to process what they heard using the think-pair-share technique: he poses a question based on the material that was just presented and then has students respond individually in their notebooks (think), talk about their ideas with a partner (pair), and summarize what they discussed with the class (share).

At the conclusion of his lecture, Mr. Silverstone tells the class they will now have several opportunities to practice writing self-portrait poems and using similes. First, they will write collaboratively (with Mr. Silverstone as the subject of focus), and then they will write independently using what he calls "secret categories." On the board he writes:

His hair is as _____ as a _____.

His eyes are like _____.

His clothes are as _____ as a _____.

He travels like _____.

Together the class generates, "Mr. Silverstone's hair is as black as night. Mr. Silverstone's eyes are like cameras. Mr. Silverstone's clothes are as colorful as a rainbow. Mr. Silverstone travels like a snail."

In preparation for the independent practice activity, students form groups based on the category they find most interesting: presidents, movie stars, sports heroes, cartoon characters, or famous authors. Jake and three other students select cartoon characters, and Mr. Silverstone gives them an envelope containing pictures of Mickey Mouse, Bart Simpson, Charlie Brown, Calvin, and Garfield. He also gives them a short stack of worksheets, each printed with the same four prompts on the board. Their task is to create at least two self-portrait poems based on the pictures in their envelope. While the class is working on their poems,

Mr. Silverstone circulates throughout the room, making sure everyone is participating and able to apply the content he presented in his lecture. After each group has successfully completed the activity, students read the poems aloud.

At this point, Mr. Silverstone passes out a worksheet that explains the final activity and tells students they will be starting this task in class and, most likely, finishing at home. He asks Jake to read the directions aloud so everyone understands what they are required to do. They state:

1. Your task is to write a self-portrait poem that is actually based on *you.*

2. It must have at least five stanzas (lines) and at least three similes. Aim to exceed these criteria!

3. You may create your poem by selecting from the twelve prompts listed below, or use your own ideas.

4. If you're having trouble, use your resources. You can: look at your notes; review the poems you wrote in class; check out the Web sites listed at the bottom of this page (they have text and audio-recorded examples); or call your homework buddy for help!

5. If you would like to enhance your poem, feel free to draw (or attach) a picture of yourself.

6. Work hard! Be proud! I have confidence in you!

Mr. Silverstone asks another student to summarize what Jake read, inquires whether there are any questions, reminds them to use this worksheet as a reference while working, and then allows them to begin their assignment.

Three students go to the computers located in the back of the room to see and listen to the online examples; the rest of the class starts drafting their poems. Mr. Silverstone circulates throughout the room offering positive feedback, answering questions, and monitoring progress. He pays especially close attention to the performance of students who typically find writing challenging (such as Jake), as well as others he observed having difficulty during practice activities. However, he does it inconspicuously so as not to draw negative attention to anyone in the class. Today he is pleasantly surprised to see everyone completing the assignment successfully. Jake finishes his poem at home that evening. It contains six stanzas, five similes, and an expertly sketched self-portrait. He is very excited to share his work in class tomorrow.

## Discussion

This case example described Jake's experiences within elementary and secondary settings. The first scenario featured an interdisciplinary unit in an inclusive third-grade classroom cotaught by a general education teacher and a special education teacher. The second scenario featured a poetry unit in a ninth-grade English class taught by one general education teacher. Both classrooms demonstrated a blend of essential elements and a variety of differentiation strategies resulting in an effectively implemented IEP and a positive and inclusive classroom experience for Jake. DI looked very different in the two settings, but two overarching themes help us answer the question, "Why was Jake successful?" First, the classroom environment at each grade level provided all students with appropriate levels of support. Second, Jake's teachers selected and integrated a variety of differentiation strategies to scaffold and optimize his learning.

*Classroom Environment.* Both classrooms were structured so all students, including Jake, received the support they needed in natural and affirming ways. As a result, Jake was not stigmatized for having a learning disability, and other members of the class were able to benefit from the strategies that may have initially been intended primarily for Jake. In Jake's third-grade classroom, both Ms. James and Mr. Wassell assumed responsibility for supporting all students; thus, when Jake received help with a task, often with other peers, it was viewed as a natural part of the classroom routine and culture. Another example was Mr. Silverstone's "Sneak Peak" handout that allowed Jake to preview the major concepts and relevant vocabulary prior to a lecture, allowing him to access the content when it was presented in class because he had a foundation to further his understanding. This handout was made available to the entire class, allowing each student to choose whether to use it.

**Differentiation Strategies.**  All three of Jake's teachers carefully selected and integrated a variety of strategies to scaffold and optimize his learning. The techniques they used represent the full spectrum of complexity, preparation, and duration. Their efficacy with implementation was integrally tied with their skillful use of assessment throughout instruction; they knew his readiness levels, his interests, his learning profile, and his acquisition of what was being taught. Specifically, Jake benefited from:

- Content differentiation
- Process differentiation
- Proactive and reactive differentiation
- Differentiation capitalizing on his strengths
- Opportunities for choice
- Flexible grouping
- Access to technology

Although these subcategories are integrally tied and frequently overlapping in actual practice, we discuss them individually to highlight the unique benefits of implementation. (Product differentiation will not be discussed given that Jake was not featured creating a culminating project or given another form of assessment after completing the units on family history and poetry.)

The variety of strategies used to differentiate content enabled Jake to learn the same information as his classmates. Ms. James and Mr. Wassell scaffolded his comprehension of the immigrant stories in several ways. Prior to reading, Jake was asked to preview the text and predict the story content. Then Ms. James included him in a small group for guided support, and he completed a story map to help him understand and remember important elements of the text. Mr. Silverstone's guided outline facilitated Jake's note taking during the lecture on poetry and similes. He also enhanced Jake's ability to maintain attention and see relevance in the poetry unit by using examples that incorporated Jake's interests and featuring Mr. Silverstone in the guided practice poem. Finally, the use of explicit instruction, concrete modeling, and the think-pair-share meant the content was readily comprehensible and presented in manageable quantities.

The variety of strategies used to differentiate process enabled Jake to understand and personalize the topics of study. Ms. James and Mr. Wassell used the think-tac-toe learning contract as an overall format to differentiate process. Jake successfully completed his three activities because his teachers appropriately and effectively scaffolded his learning. They walked him through each of the activity descriptions and rubrics and helped him develop a schedule in order to understand the steps and timelines. During the writing tasks, Jake benefited from strategies such as using graphic organizers (of appropriate complexity), reviewing sample journal entries, having an index card listing important elements, and collaborative brainstorming.

Mr. Silverstone increased Jake's engagement and willingness to practice writing self-portrait poems by using cartoon characters. During that activity, Jake worked with his peers, used a model poem, and had guiding prompts. These critical scaffolds allowed him to participate actively and successfully complete the task. Because Mr. Silverstone circulated throughout the classroom while the groups were working, his assistance was readily available.

Jake benefited from the use of differentiation that was proactive as well as responsively used. As part of the instructional planning process, Ms. James and Mr. Wassell wrote the think-tac-toe contract, and Mr. Silverstone designed the poetry practice activity around several categories. In addition, differentiation resulted from Jake's teachers' vigilant assessment of his performances during various tasks. Ms. James noticed that Jake and many of his peers were having trouble focusing on the think-tac-toe contract. She gave them construction paper to cover up everything above and below the section they were discussing and use a highlighter to mark key words. In another example, Mr. Silverstone recognized that Jake did not understand alliteration, so had a peer give a definition and asked everyone to generate a quick list of examples on scrap paper. After verifying Jake had a correct response, Mr. Silverstone invited him to share it with the class. During the third-grade journal activity, Ms. James noticed that Jake and another student were having difficulty organizing their ideas, so she held a mini-lesson to brainstorm some prompts that would help them begin writing.

Jake's teachers made a concerted effort to differentiate instruction in ways that allowed him to capitalize on his strengths. At both instructional levels, the teachers frequently structured activities that allowed him to discuss ideas with his peers rather than write them, drawing on his strengths in auditory processing and expressive language. Jake's teachers also integrated art into activities knowing that was an area of strength and interest. Capitalizing on Jake's strengths helped him compensate for his difficulties and allowed him to demonstrate his talents.

Jake benefited from having many opportunities to exercise choice. Using the think-tac-toe contract and being able to choose from multiple journal prompts enabled Jake to select appropriately challenging, interesting, and meaningful tasks. At both instructional levels, he was allowed to establish individualized goals, which helped him focus on his unique needs. He had opportunities to participate in the grouping format of his choice with the level of teacher support he felt was appropriate. As the class moved to each think-tac-toe activity, Jake was given the option of beginning independently or working in a small group with teacher guidance. He chose to work collaboratively for the first two tasks and independently for the third. Collectively, the opportunity to exercise choice strengthened Jake's sense of ownership and responsibility for his learning.

Jake benefited from his teachers' effective and integral use of flexible grouping. He had opportunities to work in a variety of formats (independently, with a partner, in small groups, and with the whole class). He successfully participated in groups with classmates with similar readiness levels and similar interests, as well as in groups with classmates whose attributes differed from his own. Each of Jake's teachers thoughtfully considered what grouping format and composition would be most appropriate for a particular task. Ms. James and Mr. Wassell recognized that Jake and some of his peers might have difficulty reading their first immigrant story independently, so they offered students the option of participating in a small group guided reading. On other occasions, such as when the think-tac-toe contract was introduced, they used a large group format to promote a sense of community and common experience.

Finally, Jake benefited from access to technology at both instructional levels. The AlphaSmart enhanced his ability to write in several ways: it minimized his visual-motor difficulties that challenge his handwriting, supported his vocabulary and spelling (with a dictionary and spell-checker), and allowed him to revise his work easily. The word prediction software helped to increase Jake's typing speed, and its portability allowed him to work within the classroom or to take his assignment home to complete.

In summary, this case example demonstrated how a blend of the essential elements and a variety of differentiation strategies resulted in a positive experience and outcomes for Jake and his classmates. Jake benefited from a positive classroom environment and his teachers' skillful ability to select and integrate a variety of differentiation strategies to scaffold his learning.

## Conclusion

We began this chapter by explaining P.L. 94–142's original mandate, that children with disabilities are entitled to a free and appropriate public education in the least restrictive environment, and its evolution over three decades. Today IDEA 2004 and NCLB collectively require schools and teachers to design instruction to meet the needs of all students, including students with disabilities, in an a priori fashion. We then provided an overview of how Tomlinson's model of DI (2003b, 2005a, 2005b) facilitates teachers' ability to achieve this goal of effective and appropriate inclusive instruction. The essential elements as well as the framework for considering how content, process, and product can be differentiated in response to students' levels of readiness, interests, and learning profiles was highlighted. Finally, we offered a case example that described how DI was used at the elementary and secondary levels to promote success for one student with a learning disability as well as his classmates.

Within the context of that legal mandate and recommendations for implementation, the proverbial challenge in education is to translate research into practice, and DI is no exception. Research suggests that teachers currently make few changes in response to individual student needs (Tomlinson et al., 2003). This is not surprising because, as Mehlinger (1995, p. 154) explains, to "customize schooling for individual learners, rather than mass produce students who have essentially been taught the same thing in the same way in the same amount of time . . . is not a superficial change; it is a deep cultural change." This drew Tomlinson et al. (2003, p. 134) to elaborate, "We can dismiss neither the need to make classrooms a good fit for the range of learners in them nor the immensity of the challenge in doing so."

To meet this challenge requires a robust multidimensional effort at all levels of the educational system. At a fundamental level, preservice and in-service teachers, administrators, other school professionals, and teacher educators need to gain a deep understanding of DI. Among the most important areas of focus is to understand the effect of culture, language, background experiences, and disabilities on individual students. Educators need to have knowledge of effective instructional strategies and assessment techniques and be able to implement them with proficiency. They need to understand how to create a positive and flexible classroom environment. Finally, a critical component to successful DI implementation is the belief that a teacher's role is to address the individual learning needs of all students. When realized, this results in a classroom teacher's philosophical belief that "all children belong here."

Two factors will facilitate classroom teachers' ability to make instructional decisions based on the needs of their students. First, teachers' efforts need to be meaningfully supported by collaboration with other school professionals. This may occur with direct involvement in the classroom (coteaching, for example) or may involve consultation outside the classroom and focus on the sharing of ideas and resources. Second, school structures are needed to support implementation by flexible time, access to resources including technology, and support for collaboration among professionals. With that support, more students with disabilities will experience a positive and inclusive classroom experience. Finally, to expand and refine our knowledge of DI, future research should be a collaborative effort between institutions of higher education and schools. We need to investigate the relative impact of differentiating instruction based on readiness, interest, and learning profile; we need to carefully examine the effects of learning environments on achievement; and we need to continue evaluating the efficacy of specific differentiation strategies.

# FROM THE FIELD: BENEFITS AND CHALLENGES OF DIFFERENTIATED INSTRUCTION

## Savina Woodyard

Tanya Santangelo, Greg Knotts, Katharine Clemmer, and Marianne Mitchell provide a wonderful overview of differentiated instruction (DI), its components, and its application with learners of varying needs. The implementation of DI methods has become an essential aspect of my instruction as an English teacher in an inner-city high school in order to ensure my students' access to the often challenging general school curriculum. Currently I provide instruction in modern literature, Advanced Placement English Language, and expository writing at David Starr Jordan High School, centralized in the Watts area of Los Angeles. To the west of the school are the Jordan Downs Housing Projects, a community lodging mostly low-income African American and Latino families. A majority of the Jordan High School students come from that housing community. Eighty percent of the students at the school are Latino, and 20 percent are African American.

Considering that my students come from different ethnic, cultural, and linguistic backgrounds, I largely shape my instruction to fit their personal experiences and varying learning needs. Given existing diversity within the classroom, both veteran and first-year teachers alike often fall into the trap of designing one lesson for one class, failing to recognize the varying abilities of individual students and the need to modify instruction. Differentiated instruction is a method that is important for all educators.

## Benefits of Differentiated Instruction

Differentiated instruction plays a critical role in allowing students to recognize their own skills and strengths. Too often, struggling students become comfortable in accomplishing the bare minimum given years of frustration and failure with schoolwork and their inability to demonstrate their knowledge. With DI, teachers encourage students to develop their skills by communicating that students can and will achieve when they are provided appropriate assistance. Teachers who implement DI strategies regularly in their instruction will see benefits of more positive student attitudes toward learning, growth in students' academic skills, and greater access to the general curriculum for all learners.

Differentiated instruction can change students' negative attitudes toward learning given its focus on student choice throughout the learning process. By providing choices to students, teachers give students control over their learning environment and encourage student buy-in during lessons. In the case example presented in the chapter, Jake's teachers infused student choice in learning center activities, problem types, and writing topics. In this way, they gave students the opportunity to play an active role in the learning process.

Within my own classroom, I try to take students' general interests and incorporate them into my lesson planning. For example, when introducing students to the concept of rhetorical devices (imagery, symbolism) I use their favorite songs from the hip-hop genre in order to familiarize them with the concepts I'm teaching. In my experience, incorporating student choice within my lessons helps my students feel more comfortable with the material, eventually resulting in a better attitude toward learning.

By helping students become more motivated about their learning, teachers will observe their students improve in a variety of academic areas. The more students are engaged in their learning, the more they acquire the skills necessary to master content standards. The AlphaSmart, for example, was a motivating tool that provided Jake the necessary support to more efficiently draft and review his writing. When I recently asked my students to write an introductory paragraph on a particular topic, several students hesitated at this request given their previous difficulties with the writing process, in spite of the previous guided instruction I provided. I scaffolded the assignment by using additional graphic organizers and step-by-step instruction packets for how to write an introductory paragraph. As a result, my students became more familiar with the process and developed the skills necessary to write an effective paragraph on their own.

Finally, by improving students' attitude toward their learning and enhancing their general academic skills, DI allows more students greater access to the general education curriculum. Struggling learners can become complacent as a result of their academic deficits and consequently disengage themselves from their learning environment. However, with DI, teachers provide students with greater and more frequent opportunities to learn and engage in the academic curriculum. Jake was able to better understand the curriculum when his general and special education teachers took the time to present information in accessible ways and require assignments that would truly demonstrate Jake's knowledge. Similarly, within my classroom, I use surveys and questionnaires to gauge where students continue to have challenges and questions regarding lesson material and differentiate accordingly. As a result, an increased number of my students are better able to access grade-level material throughout the year.

Although there are several benefits and outcomes of DI, it is important for teachers to understand the potential challenges teachers may face when implementing it in real classrooms.

## Challenges of Differentiated Instruction

Santangelo, Knotts, Clemmer, and Mitchell define and provide several examples of how to apply DI but stop short of presenting the genuine challenges to implementing it successfully. One need not think too long to imagine what these challenges may include. Once schools genuinely recognize and reflect on these obstacles, they may be better prepared to address them successfully. Common challenges educators may face when implementing DI practices are limited time for lesson planning and preparation, limited opportunities for collaboration, and lack of adequate training.

A primary challenge lies in the planning and preparation time needed to implement DI successfully. It can become increasingly difficult for teachers to plan for several classes, especially at the secondary level, where they may see at least one hundred students in the course of a day. Differentiating instruction may also become difficult when teachers must prepare for a variety of content areas, typically the case in elementary settings. Teachers may need to outline an assignment for science, develop graphic organizers for history, or consult with the resource teacher to help students complete complex math functions. Furthermore, the planning that DI requires becomes increasingly difficult when teachers are responsible for assisting in a variety of school activities, such as coaching a team or chairing a department or committee, while maintaining outside obligations such as continued course work and family obligations. In my experience, differentiating my instruction for upcoming lessons becomes challenging when I also need to complete assignments for graduate classes or attend to various credentialing requirements. Juggling these responsibilities places heavy limitations on how much time I can spend adjusting lessons, projects, or lectures to adequately meet my students' individual needs. When teachers are overwhelmed by these obligations, they tend to gravitate toward the one-lesson-fits-all ideology.

These same time constraints also limit teachers' ability to meet, consult, or collaborate with other teachers. Although Jake's teachers find a mutually convenient time to meet, my experience is often that collaborative meetings of this sort are more often few and far between. Realistically, a teacher may have several students in need of extensive support based on previous difficulties or disability status. There is no guarantee that the general and special education teachers will be able to meet to discuss a lesson or instructional unit and how to address the needs of specific students requiring more specialized instruction.

I have collaborated on many occasions with colleagues and special educators in order to design more appropriate lessons for my classes. Through this interaction, I have learned several strategies to scaffold my instruction, including using double-entry journals for struggling readers and prereading strategies to engage students in reading activities. If general education teachers like me learn and accumulate appropriate methods over time to improve our instruction through initial collaborative efforts with colleagues and specialists, then perhaps these meetings may only occasionally be required.

A final challenge to successful implementation of DI involves obtaining the appropriate training it requires. Teachers need critical professional development, including training in collaborating with specialists, working more with students of diverse backgrounds, and effectively differentiating instruction. They need guidance as well in how to differentiate instruction within their content areas and support students with varying needs. For example, they may need assistance in how to scaffold a lesson for an English language learner or for a student with a specific processing deficit. I previously experienced difficulty supporting a student diagnosed with aphasia, an inability to easily use or understand language, spoken or written. This student struggled with reading, learning vocabulary, and memorizing definitions given the nature of his disability. I needed specific training for issues related to assisting students with disabilities and was able to support this student only by consulting with my resource teacher and a previous university professor.

Although my efforts to obtain training through my district and local university have generally been successful, veteran teachers, after numerous years in the profession, can lack updated training on such methods. In fact, some teachers oppose additional training entirely, declaring they are sufficiently prepared to meet the needs of their students. Other experienced teachers emphatically profess that students must be responsible to adapt to their teachers' instruction. These teachers neglect to acknowledge the changing social, economic, and cultural climate of their school and community or recognize how these factors affect students' learning in the classroom.

Considering the context of my teaching environment, some students arrive at Jordan after recently relocating from another country to Los Angeles, perhaps with or without having previous school experiences. These students are often thrust into English-only classes with teachers who fail to differentiate their instruction in order to meet their students' specific needs. As a result, many of these students become increasingly dissatisfied with school given their repeated failure and their inability to demonstrate their ideas and true knowledge. With this common discrepancy between students' and teachers' skills and needs, further professional development is becoming critically necessary. When teachers are better prepared to meet the diverse needs of the students they teach, student buy-in and performance will increase.

## Solutions and Final Thoughts

Given the enormity of these issues, how can teachers effectively practice DI within urban and highly diverse classrooms? Although several practices may address the challenges previously discussed, two essential methods rise to the forefront: collaboration and administrative support.

Collaboration with other teachers can help alleviate the pressure surrounding lesson planning and preparation. For example, several teachers within the same grade level can arrange a time to meet twice a week and assist one another, with the help of a specialist, to develop lesson plans and materials. Furthermore, they can share their knowledge regarding their efforts at differentiation within the classroom. Teachers need to prioritize time in their schedule to attend these meetings and participate in the collaboration process. Thus, time management plays an important role in a teacher's ability to differentiate instruction, glean useful ideas from colleagues, and implement those within the classroom.

Teachers should also begin to collaborate with individual students and their families in order to address individual needs. These lines of communication must be readily available, safe, and open. Should students not feel comfortable speaking with adults, teachers can review student files and consult with previous teachers and the student's parents or significant family members. By having ongoing communication with students, teachers can create lessons with objectives and activities their students can successfully accomplish with support.

Administrators also need to play an active role in assisting teachers to implement DI. Administrators often arrange for professional workshops and trainings without consulting with teachers regarding the areas they feel necessitate additional support. These trainings may lack sufficient material, instructional strategies, or classroom examples that can readily be used with students. Often administrators have the authority to hire additional staff to support classroom teachers, including instructional assistants, coaches, specialists, or resource teachers. They can schedule additional time for teachers to meet for planning and develop materials for lessons with other colleagues. Administrators can provide teachers with opportunities to observe colleagues implement certain strategies, supports, or methods in their classrooms. Teachers who observe a differentiated lesson or activity can better replicate those methods in their own classroom. Thus, the role of administrators is to ensure that teachers receive adequate training and sufficient time to collaborate with other teachers and observe genuine classroom practices that support their instruction.

Through ongoing collaboration with colleagues and proper administrative support, teachers can access the skills and time necessary to implement differentiated instructional practices. Differentiated instruction provides an opportunity for teachers to reach all students, meet high expectations, and assist learners—including students with disabilities—to engage in the learning process. By implementing this approach within the classroom, teachers demonstrate a devotion to the teaching profession as well as a belief in the success of all their students.

# 8

# TRANSITION SERVICES AND EDUCATION FOR ALL

## Ernest Rose

The Education for All Handicapped Children Act of 1975 (EAHCA, P.L. 94–142) focused on such critical issues as identification, educational planning, service delivery, placement, and due process. These issues were of primary concern because of numerous court challenges that had taken place since the late 1960s (Hardman, Drew, & Egan, 2004). Thus, it is no wonder that at the time, little attention was paid to defining the continuing needs of individuals with disabilities once they left the K-12 school system. However, from the passage of the EAHCA forward, the ideas and definitions of transition have become a critical element in educational planning for individuals with disabilities (Neubert, 2000; Steere, Rose, & Cavaiuolo, 2007; Wehman, 2001). In addition, a series of highly cited studies emphasized the plight of individuals with disabilities when compared with their nondisabled peers in terms of employment, postsecondary education, independent living, and general failure to thrive after high school (Hasazi, Gordon, & Roe, 1985; Mithaug, Horiuchi, & Fanning, 1985; Wagner, 1989; Wagner, Newman, & Cameto, Garza, & Levine, 2005). Because of the significant, continuing needs of individuals with disabilities as they progress from the teenage years into adulthood, this chapter focuses on the importance of transition language in the public law, as well as definitions of transition and how they direct planning and service delivery; specific differences between legislative acts of entitlement and acts of eligibility; and some continuing challenges for individuals with disabilities under the revised act, IDEA 2004.

## Legislating Transition Planning and Services

Public Law 94–142 stated that children and adolescents with disabilities had the same access to programs as students without disabilities, including all available vocational education programs. However, the law contained no concrete language related to transition services or guidance on moving from the world of special education to the world of adult services. Without a future orientation to programming and services, students with disabilities and their families were left to fend for themselves. The Education of the Handicapped Act Amendments of 1983 and 1986 included discretionary funding for school-to-work model programs, but did not require transition services for children and adolescents with disabilities. The amendments did not address the use of the individualized education program (IEP) for developing a full range of transition planning and programming to prepare individuals for life beyond high school (Steere et al., 2007). In addition to preparation for the critical world of work, other equally important aspects of adult life, including postsecondary education options, were not covered. By the time the act was due for full reauthorization, families were aware of the lack of transition planning and service options and had formidable studies to back them up (Hasazi et al., 1985; Mithaug et al., 1985; Wagner, 1989).

In 1990, the reauthorized act, named the Individuals with Disabilities Education Act (P.L. 101–476), included provisions requiring identification of necessary transition services in the IEP by age sixteen or younger if deemed necessary. The definition stated:

> a) As used in this part, transition services means a coordinated set of activities for a student with a disability that—

(1) Is designed within an *outcome-oriented process* that promotes movement from school to post-school activities,
   including postsecondary education, vocational training,
   integrated employment (including supported employment), continuing and adult education, adult services,
   independent living, or community participation [italics
   added; Section 300.29].

The definition emphasized student participation in the planning process.

(2) Is based on the individual student's needs, *taking into
   account the student's preferences and interests* [italics
   added]; and

(3) Includes-
   (i) Instruction;
   (ii) Related services;
   (iii) Community experiences;
   (iv) The development of employment and other post-
       school adult living objectives; and
   (v) If appropriate, acquisition of daily living skills and
       functional vocational evaluation [Section 300.29].

From the original EAHCA to IDEA, the legislation moved
from a concept that access to traditional vocational education
programs would be appropriate to an understanding that specific activities and specific individuals must be identified to
ensure appropriate transition planning and services for students
regardless of the range or severity of disability. This concept
was expanded in the Individuals with Disabilities Education Act
Amendments of 1997 (P.L. 105–17), which changed the required
age from sixteen to fourteen to allow additional planning and
education for full community integration. However, the latest
reauthorization of the act, the Individuals with Disabilities Education Improvement Act of 2004 (P.L. 108–446), has changed

the service age language to "beginning not later than the first IEP to be in effect when the child is 16, and updated annually thereafter" (sec. 614, VIII). This language gives planning teams an upper age range starting date while providing some latitude on beginning transition planning and services at a younger age if needed. Nevertheless, the adoption of this revised language on age goes against the thinking of most researchers and professionals and, as noted later in this chapter, can be problematic (Etscheidt, 2006; Madaus & Shaw, 2006; Szymanski, 1994).

As the official definition of transition services in IDEA 2004 now stands in continuation of earlier legislation, some terms are important to consider. The first is *coordinated set of activities*. This identifies a number of people with responsibilities for planning and implementing transition services, including teachers, specialized service providers from the school district, in many cases adult service providers from outside the school district, the student, and the student's parents. Depending on the academic potential of the individual, high school counselors who advise students and parents on postsecondary education options can play an important role as well. These individuals charged with determining the transition services that are part of the student's IEP are required to update the services annually as needed. The 1997 amendments had extended the definition of coordinated services by including such related services as speech and language pathology, physical and occupational therapy, social work services, and rehabilitation counseling services. Like the IDEA of 1990, such services could come from outside the school district and be included as part of interagency planning in a student's IEP.

The term *outcome-oriented process* was introduced in the 1990 reauthorization, but in 2004 Congress adopted the term *results-oriented process* to stress the issue of improving academic and functional achievement in children with disabilities. This new term refers to the movement toward greater accountability expected of schools that receive federal and state funds, and conceptually links it with the No Child Left Behind Act of 2001. Transition services provided by a school should make a positive difference in the life of a student, but they have been less effective than anticipated (Johnson, Stodden, Emanuel, Luecking, & Mack, 2002). The individual's prospects for successful employment or postsecondary education or both, participation in community activities, and living an independent life outside the family home (with or without supports) should be accomplished by the transition planning and service process (Etscheidt, 2006; Shaw, 2006). During the school service years, IEP teams must develop measurable postsecondary goals that come from age-appropriate transition assessments based on training, education, employment, and independent living skills as appropriate. The team must also specify transition services, including classes that will support students in reaching the goals set forth in the IEP (IDEA 2004). To this end, schools must provide a summary of performance (SOP) when special education services end due to graduation or age limitation (IDEA 2004). The SOP is a summative evaluation on whether a student has met the goals set forth in the IEP and the student's continuing need or lack of need for disability support services.

Finally, *taking into account the student's preferences and interests* is a phrase that affirms an individual's right to have significant input over her or his life choices. This means that any outside public or private agency participating in the transition planning and service delivery of a student must invite the student and representatives of other agencies who will interact with the host agency in providing or paying for the transition services under consideration.

This language of "taking into account the student's preferences and interests" has spawned an important area of training and research called *self-determination*. The Beach Center on Disability at the University of Kansas (2004) defines self-determination as "the concept that a person with a disability should have the opportunity to choose what happens to the person, to receive education that enables the person to make a choice, to have support to make a choice and to carry out the choice, and, consistent with law governing the age of majority and competence/incompetence, to be assured that those people already in the person's life will heed the choice."

According to this definition, the concept of self-determination follows the IDEA Amendments of 1997 in that transition planning must include the student's preferences and interests. However, as Field, Sarver, and Shaw (2003) note, many high schools pay little attention to this requirement and tend to rely primarily on the preferences of parents and teachers. This is poor preparation for students who choose to enter into independent employment or attend postsecondary education programs because their rights are protected by the Rehabilitation Act of 1973 and the Americans with Disabilities Act (ADA), which assume the individual, not parents or others, is the initiator of services and accommodations (Sitlington, 2003). Thus, it is critical that high school teachers, paraeducators, counselors, and certainly parents understand the essential components of and differences among the Rehabilitation Act, the ADA, and the IDEA. In addition, parents must understand that under the regulations of the Family Educational Rights and Privacy Act (FERPA), they cannot have access to specific information about their adult sons and daughters (those age eighteen and over) without their permission. Occasionally some parents become exceedingly frustrated over this regulation in the FERPA after spending years advocating for their child's special needs. The Rehabilitation Act of 1973, especially section 504, the ADA, and FERPA, are covered in greater depth later in this chapter.

It is clear that transition from high school to adult life is but one of many important life transitions. Thus, an increased perspective on transition is discussed in the following section.

## Broadening the Perspective on Transition

The topic of transition from school to adult life has typically focused on students from ages fourteen through twenty-one. However, this is only one of many points of transition in a person's life. For example, children make a transition from home to preschool or day care settings. Later, they make a transition to kindergarten or first grade for their initial school experience. These transitions lead to transitions from grade to grade and from one teacher to the next. Maturation brings additional transitions in terms of physical changes, skill development, and changes in self-image.

Szymanski (1994) emphasized this point in discussing a "life-span and life-space" orientation to transition and highlighted the importance of experiences in early childhood on later transition success. For example, the responsibility for chores within the home provides a foundation for adult work. These early experiences regarding career awareness, adult roles and responsibilities, and the development of a work ethic are cumulative and are a foundation for longitudinal planning and service efforts. Szymanski also posited that career development is a developmental process and is usually not complete by age twenty-one. Her essential point was that parents and educators cannot wait until a child is fourteen years old to begin to think about transition to adult life, because of the many foundational skills, habits, and attitudes that need to be developed. Nor can parents and educators stop transition planning and service efforts when the young person turns age twenty-one, assuming this is a magic age when all life's lessons have been learned. These recommendations have important implications for collaborations with other professionals, the role of the family in transition planning and services, and the importance of educators at the elementary and intermediate levels. Given this position, it is understandable that those who study the process and effects of transition planning and programming are discouraged by the designation of age sixteen for the onset of transition services in IDEA 2004.

## An Alternative Position and Definition

The official definition of transition brought forward in IDEA 1990 and the amendments of 1997 made transition planning and delivery part of the IEP, but the language and scope were too narrow for many in the transition field. Halpern (1994) wrote a position paper for the Division on Career Development and Transition (DCDT) of the Council for Exceptional Children that he called "a framework for guiding future work in this area" (p. 117). He proposed that

> transition refers to a change in status from behaving primarily as a student to assuming emergent adult roles in the community. These roles include employment, participating in post-secondary education, maintaining a home, becoming appropriately involved in the community, and experiencing satisfactory personal and social relationships. The process of enhancing transition involves the participation and coordination of school programs, adult agency services, and natural supports within the community. The foundations for transition should be laid during the elementary and middle school years, guided by the broad concept of career development. Transition planning should begin no later than age 14, and students should be encouraged, to the full extent of their capabilities, to assume a maximum amount of responsibility for such planning [p. 117].

Halpern (1994) explained the definition in two parts: one related to transition planning and the other to the delivery of transition services. For the planning stage, he stressed that students should develop an emerging sense of empowerment, which will foster self-determination in the transition planning process. Here, DCDT was emphasizing student interests and preferences and their primary importance in developing the transition plan. Second, student self-evaluation was emphasized. Special education has a history of standardized assessments for eligibility and program services. DCDT advocated that student self-exploration be a pivotal part of the evaluation process, and students, whenever possible, should direct the goals of their transition plans.

Third, student postschool transition goals must be consistent with the results of the student's self-evaluations. For example, if the student's goal is employment, professionals should work with that student to ensure he or she finds competitive employment, with support if necessary, and with benefits to promote financial security as much as possible. In addition, students should be encouraged to select appropriate educational experiences in school and in the community that fit their transition goals. It is important to promote classroom and school inclusion and to use the community as a fully integrated educational experience that will better prepare students for success after leaving high school (Rose, Rainforth, & Steere, 2002; Steere, Rose, & Fishbaugh, 1999).

Halpern (1994) also described the delivery of transition services as following the four criteria of planning. He stressed that DCDT does not advocate a specific approach to delivery, but it does recommend that selected approaches conform to the planning criteria. Halpern identified five issues that should help guide the delivery of transition services. The first issue urged that services and programs be based on a student's interests, preferences, and skills with an orientation toward the future. Although this to some extent mirrors the language of IDEA 1990, Halpern and others believed that greater emphasis was needed given that the traditional practice of special education has been based on the choices of parents and professionals. The second issue reemphasized inclusion in general school programs. The third stressed the importance of community-based programs as learning environments, including transportation systems, whenever appropriate. The fourth promoted the linkage of adult service agencies as needed, especially as postschool providers. And the fifth emphasized the need to involve community organizations, such as service clubs and independent living centers, in addition to service agencies, such as the Department of Rehabilitation Services and Department of Mental Health Services. Thus, the definition of transition that Halpern (1994) proposed on behalf of the DCDT invites innovation and creativity while emphasizing that the individual is the most important initiator of the transition plan and delivery of services.

## Comments on the Alternative Definition

For students with disabilities to gain the most benefit from their education, support systems, and learning experiences, a method of planning including family, friends, and advocates must be enacted during the school years. An important element of such planning is the individual's preparation to assume as much self-involvement as possible (Martin et al., 2003; Wehmeyer, 1996; Wehmeyer & Schwartz, 1997). The amendments to the Rehabilitation Act in 1992 and 1998 specified activities related to self-determination (West, Kregel, & Revell, 1993–1994). The amendments required individualized plans for employment (IPE) cowritten by the client and the vocational rehabilitation counselor with consideration of the individual's employment goals and job choices (West et al., 1994). Hence, the importance of individuals' learning to contribute to their own advocacy from the school years through the adult years is now a well-recognized practice (Steere et al., 1999; Wehmeyer & Schwartz, 1997).

Within the context of IDEA 2004, the student's interests, preferences, and skills continue to be emphasized, but studies have suggested that student involvement is often lacking in IEP meetings and, thus, transition planning is lacking as well (Etscheidt, 2006). That is, students are too often not invited to IEP meetings, and when they are, they tend to be passive participants because they have received little preparation to understand the program and service options available to them (Martin, Huber-Marshall, & Sale, 2004; Williams & O'Leary, 2001). Recall that the language on student involvement in transition planning first appeared in IDEA 1990, but a number of investigations indicate disappointing progress. However, studies of students who attended IEP meetings and were prepared to participate in transition planning demonstrated improved high school graduation rates and employment results (Etscheidt, 2006).

If the educational needs of children and youth with disabilities are addressed in school classrooms only, those needs will not be sufficiently met (Rose et al., 2002; Steere et al., 1999). The school, home, and community are essential domains in integrated curricula and have been proven to be productive environments for teaching and learning (Rose et al., 2002; Steere, et al., 1999; Steere et al., 2007). The responsibilities of teachers are more expansive in an extended classroom model in that teachers in this model work as service coordinators organizing the activities of parents and other family members, friends, related-services personnel, public agency providers, and employers. By extending the classroom into the community, students with mild, moderate, and severe disabilities are, for example, able to develop and sustain a larger and more stable network of friends and advocates than with school peers alone (Rose et al., 2002; Steere et al., 1999).

## Beyond IDEA: Laws and Regulations for Adults with Disabilities

One of the benefits of IDEA is that as a single law, it comprehensively addresses the legal rights of students with disabilities in K-12 education and lays out a process for eligibility and reasonable support services in all areas of school activity, from the classroom to after-school events. However, the provisions of IDEA end when a student leaves the K-12 system, and other laws take its place in protecting the rights of adults with disabilities. To make sure students and their families understand their rights and the laws that protect those rights, special education teachers, administrators, and counselors must make sure they can facilitate the transition from IDEA to the laws that govern adult disability services and postsecondary education, specifically section 504 of the Rehabilitation Act of 1973, the ADA, and the Family Educational Rights and Privacy Act (FERPA).

## The Shift from Entitlement to Eligibility

As students with disabilities prepare to graduate or leave school, one factor that challenges them is the shift from an entitlement program to an eligibility-required adult service system. Unlike the special education system, in which identified students are entitled to a full range of services, adult service programs require applicants to meet eligibility criteria for gaining access to their services. Furthermore, meeting the eligibility criteria does not guarantee immediate services, and waiting lists are common. This factor is one that families of students with disabilities are the least prepared for in the transition from high school to adult life (Steere et al., 2007). It also seems to be one of the least understood factors by special education teachers and school administrators. There is an assumption among high school educators and counselors that once a student leaves the special education system, he or she will have little trouble becoming eligible for the adult service system. When students leave a special education program, schools do not typically track their outcomes and placement. The concept of creating a seamless transition between high schools and adult service systems has been voiced as a significantly needed change to the service delivery system (Sax, Noyes, & Fisher, 2001). At this point, it is too early to determine if the SOP documentation required in IDEA 2004 will result in a better communication of service results that can be effectively shared among high schools, adult service agencies, and postsecondary education programs.

After years of learning and negotiating the special educa- tion system in school districts, students and their families are faced with learning a completely different set of systems for adults with disabilities that can vary from state to state. In an eligibility-driven system, there are no guarantees of funding for needed services or programs. It is a system in which individuals have to continuously prove their eligibility, despite what may be an obvious disability or need for services. Families find this process time-consuming and frustrating, and it sometimes leads to giving up their search for services. In such cases, the individual with the disability may become homebound and regress in the skills he or she has learned at school (Steere et al., 2007). The fol- lowing sections provide an overview of legislative acts that cover the rights and responsibilities of individuals with disabilities once they leave high school.

## Rehabilitation Act of 1973, Section 504

In 1977, after a delay of four years and sparked by protests of people with disabilities, including a takeover of a government building in San Francisco (Shapiro, 1994), the former U.S. Department of Health, Education, and Welfare established regulations for implementing section 504 of the Rehabilitation Act of 1973 (P.L. 93–112). The regulations stated that individuals with disabilities must be provided equal opportunity to achieve the same results, earn the same benefits, or attain the same levels of achievement in the most integrated settings that fit the individual's needs. Section 504 was the first congressional action to mandate that individuals with disabilities could not be discriminated against or denied benefits by any program (or activity) receiving federal funding solely based on being disabled.

Subpart E of the regulations addressed postsecondary edu- cation and established that institutions of higher education must adapt academic requirements and methods of evaluating academic progress to meet the assessed needs of individuals with disabilities. However, postsecondary education institutions do not have to modify requirements that are vital to the integrity of a program or course of study directly related to licensing or accreditation requirements, or that change the concentration or processes necessary for assessing the performance of individuals (*Southeastern Community College* v. *Davis*, 1979). Importantly, postsecondary education schools cannot establish practices that restrict the participation of students with disabilities. Thus, where appropriate to the individual's disability, reasonable accommodations must be provided, such as extended time on examinations, the use of note takers and tape recorders in classes, course materials provided in large print or recorded formats, and sign language interpreters (*Guckenberger* v. *Boston University*, 1997). Section 504 ensures that college students with disabilities do not have to fight groundbreaking battles for admission, accessibility, and accommodations.

## Americans with Disabilities Act

The Americans with Disabilities Act (P.L. 101–336), signed into law in 1990, extended the reach of section 504 to cover employment settings and all educational programs and services, whether they receive federal funding or not (Sitlington, 2003). It clarified that methods or other criteria for work settings and programs of study may be subject to reasonable accommodations without altering the integrity of the scope of work or the rigor of educational programs. In the case of postsecondary education programs, institutions of higher education do not have to modify the structures and requirements of degree programs, but they do have to allow students with disabilities the opportunity to use reasonable accommodations to meet the criteria for passing courses and earning degrees. Likewise, employers are not required to alter the quality and timeliness of their work or products, but they must allow for accommodations so individuals with disabilities can fully participate as employees in all areas of the organization.

In the example of higher education, students and designated officials of the college or university determine specific and reasonable accommodations for each case. Students initiate the process by identifying and documenting their disability and requesting specific reasonable accommodations within a workable timeline. The designated officials, usually staff personnel in an office of services for students with disabilities, determine the eligibility of the student and the reasonableness of the requested accommodation. Reasonable accommodations may include assistive technologies and variations in the uses of technology.

## Family Educational Rights and Privacy Act

For individuals who continue their education beyond high school, the Family Educational Rights and Privacy Act (FERPA), also known as the Buckley Amendment, is a federal law that protects the privacy of student education records. Schools receiving funds from federal programs must comply with FERPA regulations. The law gives parents certain rights to their children's educational records prior to adulthood. These rights transfer to the children when they reach the legal age of majority (age eighteen) or when they attend an educational institution beyond high school. When the rights transfer to an individual at the age of eighteen, she or he becomes referred to as an "eligible student." At this point, parents no longer have the right to request the educational records of their child without the child's permission.

Parents have the right to inspect and review the education records kept by the school only with the permission of their child or eligible student. Schools are not required to provide copies of records unless it is impossible for parents or the eligible student to review the records at the school because of great distance or hardship. Schools may charge a reasonable fee for copies of records.

Qualified parents or eligible students have the right to request that a school correct records they believe to be inaccurate or misleading. If the school decides not to amend the record, parents or eligible students then have the right to a formal hearing. After the hearing, if the school continues its position of not amending the record, parents or eligible students have the right to place a statement in the records declaring their position on the contested information.

In general, schools must have written permission from parents or the eligible student to release any information from the student's education record. Nevertheless, FERPA allows schools to disclose those records, without consent, to various parties under the following conditions (34 C.F.R. sec. 99.31):

- Another school to which a student is transferring
- School officials with legitimate educational interests
- Specified officials for audit or evaluation purposes
- Appropriate officials in connection with financial aid to a student
- Parties conducting certain studies for or on behalf of the school
- Accrediting associations
- To comply with a judicial order or lawfully issued subpoena
- Appropriate officials in cases of health and safety emergencies
- State and local authorities, within a juvenile justice system, pursuant to a specific law

In addition, schools may disclose, without consent, directory information such as a student's name, address, telephone number, date and place of birth, honors and awards, and dates of attendance. However, schools must tell parents and eligible students about the directory information and allow them a reasonable amount of time to request that the school not disclose such information. Schools must annually notify parents and eligible students of their rights under FERPA. Eligible students seeking assistance from vocational rehabilitation agencies or other adult service systems while attending a college or university should check to see if FERPA regulations apply to the disclosure of their educational records and if they must provide written permission.

## Continuing Challenges and IDEA 2004

Previously I noted the challenge of moving from the entitlement program of special education to the eligibility system of adult services. The 2004 reauthorization of IDEA extends this challenge through the language of its assessment and evaluation procedures (Etscheidt, 2006; Madaus & Shaw, 2006; Shaw, 2006). Beginning with the IDEA Amendments of 1997, school districts were no longer required to conduct full reevaluations of disability identification and educational achievement. This continues in IDEA 2004 and creates problems for families and students with disabilities that need current evaluations for a less cumbersome transition to adult services or postsecondary education. Because IEP teams can choose the type and frequency of assessments they use to reevaluate students with disabilities, it is possible that many students leave the school system with dated evidence as to their disability and its effect on their education, work, or life skills performances. This may well translate into additional costs for individuals or families because they are responsible for providing current eligibility information to adult service providers and postsecondary education providers (Shaw, 2006). Thus, it is critical for parents and school personnel to understand that the law does not prompt them to provide regularly scheduled comprehensive reevaluations. A comprehensive evaluation provides information on the status of an individual's disability, his or her continued need for special education services, the level of academic achievement and developmental needs, and the determination of additional or modified special education and related services required. Results of the evaluation are checked against the measurable annual goals identified in the IEP, as well as the opportunity for appropriate participation in the general education curriculum. All of this information is valuable for adult service providers and postsecondary educators, but unless the information is current, the individual's eligibility and service needs will be in question until such information is updated.

The good news is that the parents or school members of a student's IEP team can request an evaluation based on any of the points presented above. However, they must know their rights and responsibilities in this matter. Thus, more than ever before, parents and school personnel must be educated in the nuances of the IDEA and understand how to use the regulations of the law for the equal opportunities it provides.

In IDEA 2004, annual transition planning for students with disabilities begins with the IEP enacted just prior to age sixteen. Most transition advocates believe this is far too late for maximum benefit and are perplexed as to why it was moved from age fourteen as identified in the 1997 amendments. For students who will move on to postsecondary education campuses, planning for an academic course of study that will prepare them to be accepted and successful in college must begin at least by middle school. From that point forward, college preparatory programs increase in rigor throughout the high school years and often require additional tutoring in English and mathematics. Parallel to the proper academic preparation are plans and training to become an independent, self-determining individual who can cope with the rigors of college life outside the classroom (Steere et al., 2007).

Students with severe and multiple disabilities need even more time for planning and implementing transitions from home to school, school level to school level, school to community, and school to employment (Steere et al., 1999). To assume that transition planning for all the complexities an individual with severe disabilities must encounter can begin at about age sixteen is truly uninformed and suggests a naiveté about the needs of these individuals. Clearly, students, parents, and school personnel must be far more aggressive in their transition planning than stipulated by IDEA 2004. To do so, they will need to understand the obvious and most subtle features of the law, and that may be the biggest challenge. My hope is that future reauthorizations will take a fuller account of the importance of transition from school to adult life and the continuing service needs of individuals with disabilities, their families, and their friends.

Clearly there has been progress in the past thirty-three years from an act that had no provisions on preparing individuals with disabilities for life after the school years to amendments and reauthorizations that tie transition planning to the IEP. Nevertheless, there is a continuing need to improve the legislation in ways that recognize the many life transitions of individuals with disabilities and require greater participation from them in designing their futures. To do so will help individuals with disabilities live more active and productive lives and ensure opportunities for greater inclusion in their homes, places of employment, and communities.

# FROM THE FIELD: SUPPORTING THE TRANSITION OF INDIVIDUALS WITH DISABILITIES

### Gina Semenza

As a young adult with a disability, I know how confusing and intimidating the transition process can be into postsecondary education and employment. I am honored to share my transition experiences and thoughts at this point in my life. I am in my mid-twenties and have successfully made the transition to adulthood. I have a college degree and have completed a post-graduate fellowship program in public affairs. I drive an adapted vehicle and am the proud owner of a wheelchair-accessible home. Today I am employed as a field representative for a U.S. senator.

Despite examples of transition success stories like mine and the amazing progress in legal rights, such as the Individuals with Disabilities Education Act (IDEA), youth with disabilities are still at great risk and continue to have significantly lower school graduation and employment rates than their nondisabled peers. This reality is appalling and unacceptable, but I know the youth with disabilities of today can and will improve these odds in their favor. Although much advancement has been made, much more must happen to meet the intent of the laws passed to protect these youth and future generations.

As Ernest Rose explained, youth with disabilities had no guarantee of equal access to education before 1975. The potential opportunities youth with disabilities have today are unlimited compared to a little over thirty years ago. A clear illustration of this generational contrast exists in my family. My great uncle Angelo grew up in the early twentieth century with the same disability that I have, spinal muscular atrophy, a form of muscular dystrophy that often requires the use of a wheelchair. Uncle Angelo did not have access to the same schools his brothers and sisters attended; rather, he attended a segregated institution for children with disabilities until he turned eighteen years old. Because he did not have the option to go to college, he sold newspapers part time. He never had a career or lived independently in an accessible home. I often think of my great uncle's life and realize how privileged I am in today's world, even when I continue to fight for my basic civil rights.

The implementation of laws like IDEA does not always accomplish the original intent of such laws. I have been fortunate to mentor some amazing youth with disabilities and have learned a few things along the way: (1) individualized education programs (IEP) are not always fully carried out or implemented as indicated by law, (2) youth are not often empowered or encouraged to be self-determined, (3) youth and their families are not consistently made aware of their rights, and (4) the transition planning process can be an afterthought at too late of an age. With such broad guidelines for IEPs in an age where administrators and educators are inundated with heavier demands and less funding, the ineffectiveness can vary due to a myriad of factors, such as a family's awareness and level of advocacy, the financial well-being of a school district, the cumulative desire to empower youth, and the genuine belief in the abilities of youth with disabilities.

I believe the IEP process can dramatically affect a youth's life and his or her ability to make a successful transition to adult-hood if certain components are strongly present. One person can have the top educators and administrators and the most informed and active family involved in an IEP, critical factors in youth succeeding, but too often, the most significant stake-holders, the youth themselves, do not actively participate. If we say we want to empower youth and give them a voice and oppor-tunities to grow and contribute, we must include them in an act-ive way on every level. True youth participation benefits both the youth and the system as a whole.

Many people in the field of education often discuss the vital role self-determination plays in the IEP and transition process. I know for a fact that youth with disabilities must be proud of who they are in order to fully develop their self-esteem and ability to be self-determined. Rose mentions the importance of self-image, and I believe that it is not uncommon for youth with disabilities to feel ashamed of their disabilities because our society over-whelmingly casts both obvious and hidden disabilities in a neg-ative light. Our culture often enforces the notion that one must ignore disability and not embrace it as a diverse and important aspect of life. The consequences of such attitudes are detrimental to the development of positive self-image and one's ability to be self-determined.

One of the best ways to strengthen the process of self-determination and support successful transition outcomes is to provide disability awareness to all students. No act of legislation can force society to regard disability as a diverse aspect of life. However, I strongly believe that administrators, educators, and families can help reverse these stigmas by teaching youth with disabilities about the history of the disability rights movement and the culture of full inclusion. When they learn about disability within this context, they develop a comprehensive sense of who they are and how they fit into the world. It is priceless when youth learn that adults with all different types of disabilities accomplish amazing things and lead fulfilling lives. There is no substitute for knowing that your life matters and that disability does not prohibit you from realizing your personal potential.

Families, educators, and administrators ought to teach all children about the role of disability. Children grow to become well-rounded individuals when they are encouraged to understand and embrace diversity that includes disability. The Disability History Week Act is an example of how to address this vital issue with legislation. It was passed by the State of West Virginia in 2006 establishing a Disability History Week and requiring instruction in public schools on the disability rights movement, history, leaders, and general disability awareness. The passage of such legislation is a step in the right direction and will undoubtedly make a huge impact on all students. However, educators should not wait for legislation to pass in order to incorporate such instruction into the curriculum.

In addition, families and communities should not solely rely on schools to teach children about disability history and culture; rather, they too should take proactive measures such as (1) emphasizing awareness of and respect toward people with disabilities, (2) encouraging the use of respectful disability terminology and proper disability etiquette when talking to or about people with disabilities, (3) creating situations in which youth are exposed to role models with disabilities in the community, and (4) routinely seeking relevant books, movies, and Web sites that teach something about disability.

In addition to encouraging pride, awareness, and self-determination in youth, the IEP process itself must address transition issues throughout their education to prepare youth for the shift from an entitlement program to an eligibility-required adult service system. Although moving to adulthood can be challenging for any adolescent, youth with disabilities often have additional circumstances to navigate—such as personal assistance, health care, and social security benefits—making it is critical for youth with disabilities to begin the transition process early. IDEA 2004 mandates age sixteen as an age in which transition planning must begin. Unequivocally, I agree with Rose that age sixteen is far too late in a youth's development to set as the minimum age requirement. Transition planning ought to begin as early as possible and should encourage and enable the youth to adopt growing levels of responsibility, self-awareness, and communication.

Unfortunately IEPs do not address transition in a comprehensive and fully realistic manner. For instance, benefits planning for social security, health care, and personal assistance can be extremely confusing and intimidating to even the most informed adults, youth, and families. I believe that including benefits planning in the IEP process will drastically reduce the huge number of adults with disabilities living in poverty. Regrettably, when these issues are not addressed with transition-aged youth, many grow to be adults who struggle to gain financial independence or live an independent life outside the family.

An effective way to tackle the need for benefits planning can be through the active participation of community-based resources and adult service agencies in assisting youth in developing an IEP. Individuals with disabilities and their families have no central place from which to access information regarding all appropriate agencies or community resources. This is why it is critical for youth to learn how to use and work with community resources at an early age. Individuals such as local benefit planners and independent living specialists should be included in an IEP to address the transition process. Only then will youth have a higher likelihood of becoming effective, independent, and employable adults who are truly equal in our society.

I personally contribute much of my success to having had mentors with disabilities who I could look up to. Educators stress the vital role a mentor can play in the lives of youth at risk, and this especially holds true for youth with disabilities. Mentors can influence a youth's career awareness and self-realization by reaching out beyond the basic mandates of the IEP. Community resources and support personnel could potentially provide opportunities for youth to work with and look up to role models with disabilities.

The IEP process must also be youth friendly. It can be quite intimidating for a young person to sit in a room with adults focused entirely on him or her while listening to ongoing prescriptive suggestions about his or her life. Some youth find themselves uncomfortable in this overwhelmingly adult-oriented experience. Yet there are a few basic steps that may help incorporate the youth as a central and active participant in the process: (1) believing that youth can and will be successful when they are properly and thoroughly empowered; (2) using youth-friendly language in both communications and written materials; (3) focusing on the youth's abilities and interests; (4) fostering independence by providing opportunities for their input, leadership, responsibility, and personal voice; and, most important, (5) listening to youth.

Families play an integral role in supporting youth and must empower and encourage them to become active members in the community in which they may live independently, with or without supports. Children with "special needs" eventually grow up to be adults with disabilities who, regardless of the severity of the disability, desire to realize their full potential. We must be keenly aware of IEPs that become more about the wishes of a parent or an educator than those of the youth.

Moreover, success is possible when youth and their families understand their legal rights, proper courses of action, and available due process. Knowing one's rights is more than a tool to help people navigate the programs that are designed to assist them; for me, understanding my rights and knowing how to advocate for them was necessary. From social outings at restaurants and bars, to hotel accommodations, physical access in college classrooms, and reasonable accommodations in the workplace, self-advocacy is central to my full participation in life.

Although laws like the Americans with Disabilities Act guarantee the right to equal access and treatment, the fact remains that disability discrimination exists. More often than not, society's unconscious discrimination overwhelmingly affects people who have visible or hidden disabilities. Keep in mind that youth with disabilities grow up to become adults who will require reasonable accommodations at one or many points in their lives, which is why they must learn about their rights, what reasonable accommodations exist, and how to advocate for themselves and others. This awareness will empower youth to live life to their fullest potential and reverse existing disability discrimination.

I am proud to be a young adult with a disability who has made a successful transition from postsecondary education to meaningful employment. Despite what I have personally accomplished and the great strides disability laws have made, I am continuously frustrated knowing that youth with disabilities remain at risk. This is a reality I refuse to accept given the tremendous possibilities that exist to genuinely empower youth with disabilities.

It would be insincere of me to say that living with a disability is effortless or that transitioning and benefits planning were not complex. However, embracing my disability and learning about disability history have made me a better person. I love my life and deeply respect my friends and mentors with disabilities who have taught me how and why to fight for equality. Frequently used educational terms like *self-determination, career awareness, student participation,* and *self-evaluation* really mean something in the practice of a successful transition from youth to adulthood. Successful and comprehensive IEPs will have a significantly positive impact on youth with disabilities by fully empowering them to graduate with the necessary tools to be independent, rise above poverty, and achieve their personal potential.

# 9

# PERSONAL EXPERIENCES WITH DISABILITY AND SPECIAL EDUCATION

## Sue Rubin, Olegario D. Cantos VII, Janeen Steel

Growing up with a disability is a personal journey, filled with countless moments of discovery, frustration, pain, hope, and joy. Growing up as a student with a disability soon after the passage of the Education for All Handicapped Children Act (Public Law 94–142) in 1975 challenged students, families, and educational professionals as they learned to understand the basic tenets of the law. No one at the time believed that enforcing its implementation within the public schools would be a simple endeavor. However, those early years today provide a foundation from which to learn how schools and families working together can better support learners with exceptional needs.

This final chapter provides the journeys of three individuals who navigated the systems of general and special education during the law's infancy, all successfully but not without individual hardship and struggle. These contributors include an author born with a severe developmental disorder, another with a disability resulting from complications after birth, and another waiting almost two decades until fully understanding her disability and receiving necessary supports and accommodations. Although their different paths have led them to fulfilling lives today, it is their progression within the school system we wish to explore. How did their formal education contribute to or was critical of disabling barriers often experienced by individuals with disabilities? How did these individuals navigate school systems barely prepared to support their needs and build on their strengths to later make their mark in the world? What helped and hindered them along the way? What made the greatest impression on them that contributed to their now illustrious careers and bright futures? The chapter concludes with the reflections of an English teacher and codirector of a small learning community. As an educational professional, she summarizes overlapping themes and draws on what can be learned from the experiences and insights of these incredible individuals.

By presenting these three personal statements, we by no means feel their stories fully describe their experiences within the schools or that they represent the experiences of all individuals with disabilities. We hope their accounts and recommendations will facilitate a better understanding of the issues they faced as we move forward.

## DISCOVERING THE REAL ME

### Sue Rubin

I am essentially a nonverbal person with autism. As I tell you my story, I want you to realize that I am not unique. What is unique is the educational opportunities I have had and the support I have received from my family. When people find out I am a student at Whittier College and an elected board member of the international human rights organization TASH (formerly The Association for Persons with Severe Handicaps) and have autism, they assume I have Asperger's syndrome or high-functioning autism. That assumption is quite wrong. I have classic autism as described in 1943 by Leo Kanner, the first person to name the disability. I am quite typical, with almost all of the symptoms listed in the diagnostic criteria for autistic disorder: lack of eye contact, lack of facial expression, body postures, repetitive speech (echolalia), very poor spoken language, lack of social imitative play when I was younger, routines and rituals, and attachment to objects (plastic spoons for me). I am a typical low-functioning person. I cannot dress myself or wash my hair. I have major movement problems and a strange gait. And although I've gotten much better, I must admit I am still an occasional head banger and engage in an occasional tantrum. People with Asperger's syndrome have normal speech, although they want to talk only about their favorite subjects, have normal self-help skills, and have major problems with social skills.

After reading this description of me, surely you can recognize students who are like me; however, I am a college student with an A– grade point average and a member of Phi Alpha Theta, the honor society for historians. Because I type slowly with one finger, I take only one class each semester. When I started Whittier College, I was taking two classes per semester, but when I reached my junior year, I found the classes required much more typing for papers. The college has been wonderful, treating me like a full-time student, even allowing me to keep a John Greenleaf Whittier merit scholarship for $38,000, which really should go to a full-time student; however, they decided that I would be a part-time student because of my disability and not by choice.

For people who are confused about a typical low-functioning person with autism who is succeeding in college, I will describe what enabled me to accomplish this goal. I was fortunate to be born in Whittier, California, where severely disabled children were being educated in the public schools even before the Education for All Handicapped Children Act of 1975 (P.L. 94–142) was passed. In 1956 eight small school districts combined to form the Whittier Area Cooperative Special Education Program (WACSEP) to serve severely disabled pupils in their districts by grouping together similar disabilities at one site. This model was later used by the state when it formed SELPAs (special education local plan areas). From its inception WACSEP staff were very progressive and often presented at conferences, including CalTASH and TASH, talking about the latest developments in special education. I started special education when I was twenty months old and was in an infant stimulation class. When I was three, the doctors thought I had hypotonic cerebral palsy, so I was placed in an orthopedically handicapped class. My mom thought I was autistic, but the doctors told her she was wrong. When I was four, a new pediatrician told my mom he thought I had autism, and the psychologist at UCLA agreed.

WACSEP reset the program to allow me to be in either a segregated autism county program or a noncategorical severely handicapped program in a local school where I would have opportunities to be with nondisabled peers. The choice was a no-brainer for my parents: they chose the less restrictive environment. I do not remember anything from that class, but my teacher made a book of photographs of me and others to bring to Maryland when we moved there for a year when I was six.

The school in Maryland was, sadly, a segregated site, and I was not around nondisabled students at all that year. When I came back to California, we were happy to be home and return to a WACSEP program; however, the class was very crowded, with thirteen students, one teacher, and two aides. WACSEP agreed this was not a good setting for me and encouraged my parents to file for a fair hearing. At the mediation, the WACSEP psychologist agreed with my parents, and the mediator said I should go to a nonpublic school. I went to the Speech and Language Development Center but was again on a segregated campus. When the year was over, I went back to a special day class with integration opportunities. I have no memories of this time either.

When I went into upper elementary special day classes, I had more integration opportunities, but I was not expected to understand or participate in the regular education classes. I still have no memories of this time in my life. I only know about this history and my nasty behavior from old IEPs [individualized education programs]. In 1982 when I was four, the psychologist described me as moderately retarded and recommended, "If Susan's behavioral excesses of biting and tantruming increase in frequency, a behavioral assessment is encouraged." In 1988 when I was ten and my cognitive development was at the two-year eleven-month level, the psychologist noted problem behaviors: scratching arms and forehead, yelling or screaming up to ten times a day, pinching and scratching others up to six times per week, biting adults, tantrums, leaving the house, removing my clothes, and dangerous car behavior (unbuckling my seat belt, climbing over the seat, grabbing the driver, touching the controls). At an evaluation two years later when I was twelve and scored a mental age of two years six months on the Leiter (nonverbal intelligence test) and one year four months on the Developmental Test of Visual Motor Integration, my behaviors were the same, except for the addition of operant vomiting.

When I entered middle school in 1990, I was a typical low-functioning person with autism functioning at the level of a two year old. I had no means of communication even though my speech therapist developed a book of pictures for me to reference. I didn't initiate communication and couldn't point to what I was trying to point to. The nasty behaviors and lack of communication prevented me from learning.

The next year when I was thirteen and in the eighth grade, my life changed. The educational psychologist, Jackie Leigh, had been asked to watch a graduate student of Ann Donnellan from the University of Wisconsin work with Shawn Lapin, an autistic young man who was being introduced to facilitated communication (FC). Jackie tried to convince the parents to stick with picture communication, which she thought was the better choice for Shawn, but agreed to attend the session. She asked Shawn some questions that the graduate student would not have known, and he typed the correct answers. She was amazed because she knew that

Shawn was mentally retarded and didn't know how to read, so how could he have answered her questions?

Jackie decided to try FC with me and my parents because she felt they would be honest if this was all a hoax. She and Darlene Hanson, my speech therapist at school, came to my house and tried it with me. I was not as successful as Shawn because they had no training as facilitators, but I was able to easily find some of the letters in single words. We were surprised; really, the most surprised person was me. I remember that day well. It was October 8, 1991—the beginning of my life as a thinking person. Before that, I was trained like an animal with rewards and punishments, like lost privileges. I became so dependent on outside forces to manage my behavior that after I was able to type, I actually asked for privileges to be taken away to help me inhibit nasty self-abusive behaviors. As early as four months after I was introduced to facilitated communication, I became an active participant in managing my behavior. On the psychological evaluation completed in late February 1992, the psychologist wrote,

> Extreme frustration may lead to yelling, grabbing others, head banging, or other self directed behaviors but these outbursts are infrequent and easily controlled. The most effective strategies for dealing with behaviors at this point involve determining how much control Susie has over the behavior, providing feedback to her as to how she looks or sounds, and asking her, when she is able to respond, "What's wrong?". . . A communicative approach to problem behaviors is the most effective strategy.

When WACSEP saw that I was somewhat successful and could type with facilitation, the speech therapist tried it with the other eight students in my class. They could type too. With my ability to type words spelled correctly, Rita, my mom, cancelled the IEP meeting she had called to add goals and services related to direct instruction in beginning reading.

Words became phrases and sentences, and by spring I was typing paragraphs. With math, I was given a standardized test, and I could do simple addition, subtraction, multiplication, and division. We assume I had learned this when my brother, who is two years older than me, was learning math facts from flash cards. We then spent about an hour when I learned fractions, decimals, and percentages.

The speech therapist had taught my classroom teacher how to facilitate, so I was typing throughout the school day and at home. Rita was very persistent and made me type each day for longer and longer periods of time. I believe that this was what made me a thinking person. My autism was pushed away when I was concentrating on my typing. At school I was put into a regular science class and, toward the end of the year, an algebra class. I was able to do this because Rita had been working with me using a computer program called "School Mom" and, after that, "Algebra Blasters."

The principal of the middle school did not believe I was smart and didn't want me in regular classes. Fortunately I had repeated a grade in elementary school when I had surgery, so I was old enough to go to high school after only two years of middle school. We all decided at the IEP meeting that I should go to Whittier High School because it already had severely handicapped students in regular classes, although they were not in college prep classes and were not expected to do homework.

When I started Whittier High in 1992, I was in only three regular classes because my behavior was so bad. Every day I yelled and banged my head. Eventually my behavior got better, and I added more classes, so I was taking five regular classes each semester until I graduated. I did not have a modified curriculum but did have some accommodations. In math I didn't have to do as many problems as the rest of the class. In ceramics I wrote papers about techniques instead of producing pieces. When I took essay tests, I was given extra time and could take them in a separate room. However, I wrote the same length papers as regular students and took the required classes for college prep. I always had a regular education counselor at my IEP meetings during this time because special education staff did not know about college requirements. I participated in my IEPs so we could plan a college prep program and allow me to choose which courses I wanted to take to fulfill the requirements necessary to attend a college in the University of California (UC) system in case I decided to go to a UC.

The support I had in classes varied tremendously. Sometimes I had a special education teacher, and that was great. Some of the time I had aides who were not trained facilitators. That was difficult at school, but my mom was my major facilitator, and my dad facilitated for math homework so I could keep up with class work. The support I received from both parents made it possible for me to get a regular diploma. My mom often spoke to the special education teachers to problem-solve and called other students in my classes or the aides to be sure we were doing the right homework. The special education teachers often were facilitators so I could take tests. Sometimes students were facilitators and did homework with me. I really liked that, and they became my friends. I recently was a bridesmaid in the wedding of one of my high school friends who later worked for me as a support person in college and at home.

High school was an awesome time for me. Regular education students could get school service credit for spending time with the severely handicapped students, and some of them became friends. I became more relaxed at school and had fewer and fewer inappropriate behaviors. I also got better at typing, so school work and socializing became easier. Taking five years to graduate was awful because I didn't graduate with my friends. We did that so I could have one period a day for speech therapy or counseling. We also wanted me to experience transition services to prepare me for moving into my own home. During my fifth year of high school, I took academic classes in the morning and transition classes in the afternoon. Transition was a bit different for me since I knew I would be going to college and not into the workforce right after high school. Transition for me was learning how to take care of a house. I knew that I had a whole lifetime to master those skills, so I didn't mind leaving the public school system at nineteen with only minimal transition services. Academics were more important to my future, and I really wanted to graduate. I had taken a number of honors courses, and upon graduation I had earned a final grade point average of 3.98. Typing also allowed me to take the SATs; I received a 1370 and was accepted by my first choice of colleges: Whittier College.

I have talked about facilitated communication changing my life, so perhaps I should describe it to people unfamiliar with the method. I believe there are really two kinds of people who use facilitated communication. Some people are already thinking and are aware of the world around them. These people have been waiting for someone to devise a way they can communicate and do very well learning how to type with support. The second group is like me, who are so autistic that they are not processing information from the world around them. We need communication to organize our minds.

Facilitated communication begins with physical, emotional, and communicative support. The facilitator provides physical support, such as pulling back at the wrist or forearm, forcing the FC user to focus on where to direct his or her finger. The facilitator never guides the typer. In case the person can't isolate his or her finger, the facilitator may have to start at the hand or use a dowel. The goal of facilitated communication is for the user to type without physical support, so fading support should start immediately. It took me five years of typing with support before I was able to type independently.

The emotional support is more difficult to fade. I usually can't type when a total stranger sits next to me to act as my facilitator. It takes a new staff person anywhere from two weeks to two months of supported typing with me before I am comfortable enough with that person to type independently. When the new staff person already types with other people, it takes two weeks, but when they are new to facilitated communication, it takes two months. I need to develop a relationship with the person. Communicative support also is not easy to fade. The facilitator has to get me to focus on the world by repeating quietly what I should be doing if I am becoming lost in autism. Awash in autism, without the facilitator, I would wander around quite aimlessly spouting echolalia. The facilitator has to help me sit and focus. She then quietly arranges the environment so I can work. If I am using books, written notes, or anything else I will need to refer to, they must be to the right of the keyboard. She must also hold my keyboard where I want it if I am not using a computer and constantly keep me focused.

Clearly in my case and that of other nonverbal and limited-verbal people, what was most important in our lives was accessing a communication system. The scientific evidence already exists for the acceptance of FC as a legitimate method of adaptive and augmentative communication (AAC) (Bundschuh & Basler-Eggen, 2000; Calculator & Singer, 1992; Cardinal, Hanson, & Wakeham, 1996; Intellectual Disability Review Panel, 1989; Ogletree, Hamtil, Solberg, & Scoby-Schmelzle, 1993; Olney, 1995, 2001; Sheehan & Matuozzi, 1996; Simon, Toll, & Whitehair, 1994; Vazquez, 1994; Weiss, Wagner, & Bauman, 1996). I know of twelve peer-reviewed studies that prove people using facilitated communication can type their own thoughts. Critics of the method say that research shows it is the facilitator communicating. This is only partially true, because research also shows that typers are communicating their own thoughts. There is a very simple explanation for this. There are two different hypotheses being tested. One hypothesis is that influence can occur when someone is using physical touch. That has been proven to be true. The other hypothesis is that people using FC can and do communicate their own thoughts. That too has been proven to be true. Also, many of us are now typing without physical support. That is definite proof we are typing our own thoughts. Critics say they believe us when we type independently but not when we use physical support. How can we become independent if we do not go through a training period using physical support?

The fact that nonverbal and limited-verbal people with movement problems like I have can type means that we are not mentally retarded. Entire curricula for severely handicapped students are based on that myth. Often when students are not successful, teachers assume they are retarded, that they can't do the work. Movement problems may prevent some students from showing their ability, and other students may be so bored with preschool work that they refuse to do it.

When I am talking about nonverbal and limited-verbal people, I am not talking only about people with autism. Many other people are judged by their ability to take tests that require speech or movement ability. Teachers must recognize that these tests are meaningless and that their students may have processing, attention, or movement problems but not necessarily what we call mental retardation. Dependence on tests that were developed for people who don't have movement and attention differences is wrong. For example, I was a participant in a nationwide study conducted by the University of California, Irvine, among other places. As part of the study, I had to take a test requiring me to match pictures; however, I couldn't make my hands and fingers pick up the pictures and move them. Because I had been answering questions on a keyboard, the psychologist said I could name some pictures by letters and some by numbers and match corresponding pictures using the keyboard. Using this method, I got all of the items correct. If I hadn't been an FC user, I would have failed the test, like many other people with movement problems often do.

As for my attention problems, I often focus on the wrong thing. If I am supposed to be concentrating on a paper with questions I might be focusing on the tester's clothing instead. Also, we people with autism often have problems using two senses at the same time, so I might not be able to see what I should be looking at if I am listening to the voice of the examiner. We also focus on the smells and textures of the examination materials. All of these things interfere or prevent us from answering traditional test questions.

These examples illustrate how and why teachers and psychologists often think we are retarded. I was fortunate that once I began to type, my parents, teachers, and the school psychologist all realized that I was an intelligent person and attempted to seek answers to why I was originally tested as having mental retardation. Most school districts and families have not yet reached that point of understanding.

In Whittier, I received the best educational services possible for someone with my degree of autism. I was able to spend time in classes with nondisabled students from the time I was three years old. Even before I was able to communicate, I was spending time in academic classes. Once I was introduced to facilitated communication and I was seen as an intelligent person, the school district saw its duty as giving me the same rigorous academic program that all other students in Whittier were getting, even though I needed tremendous support to take advantage of that opportunity. I realize that I was very fortunate to be in a community that believed in me and other students like me and was willing to meet the challenges we presented.

# A LIFELONG JOURNEY

## Olegario D. Cantos VII

Special education students are general education students first. Fundamental to this assertion is the philosophy of physical, programmatic, and attitudinal integration of all children in every aspect of educational life. As such, both the formation and implementation of public policy must appropriately reflect a commitment to the individual child, with a strong and consistent emphasis on students' meeting high expectations and resisting the temptation to rationalize away lower performance on supposed realism. Indeed, my own perceptions of what was possible truly did pale in comparison to what has thus far ultimately come to pass.

I was born two months premature. The year was 1970. A series of preventable medical mistakes resulted in my overexposure to oxygen in the incubator; I became totally blind in my left eye and have minimal vision in my right. Such an outcome was the last thing to be expected to happen to the child of two healthy parents, Orlando and Linda Cantos, immigrants from the Philippines. It was difficult for my parents to accept the reality of disability because of their perceptions of what having a disability would entail. On the basis of how they recalled people with disabilities being treated back home, they imagined limited opportunity, exclusion from society, and social isolation. Clouded by this perspective, my well-meaning parents had a vested interest in hiding my disability and told only those who could potentially be of assistance or support. They always downplayed my blindness, equating it with the absence of a so-called normal life and a real ability to succeed. Against this backdrop, they made decisions about my upbringing that have forever shaped the course of my life.

My intent in the sections that follow is to foster a dialogue about the appropriate intersections of parental choice, wishes of the child, the intentions of general and special education professionals, and the views of those in postsecondary education, employers, and the public at large.

## School Experiences

My first exposure to education outside the home came very early. I was sent to the Blind Children's Center (BCC) in Los Angeles, where I began to be taught basic skills at the age of two. A woman named Darlene was my first caregiver there, though I have more vivid memories of childhood from three years old and on.

I learned early in life how I could familiarize myself with my surroundings. Every morning, five days a week, my mother and I took two buses to get me to school. When we arrived at 7:00 A.M. sharp, a grandmotherly woman named Beth, who prepared breakfast for the children, greeted us. Following breakfast, I went outside to play. At that time, I did not realize that the social interaction that I enjoyed was intended to help instill confidence in me as a young child figuring out his place in his ever-expanding world. It was at the age of three that I met my first mobility instructor, Mr. Fazzi. He took time to show me how to problem-solve and find my way to desired destinations. But no one ever taught me how to use a cane; indeed, one was never placed in my hand. Between the ages of three and five, I received instruction from other caring members of the staff. Consistent with principles of promoting age-appropriate development, I learned shapes tactilely, discovered the joy of counting, went on field trips to see wondrous new places, and continued to enjoy the carefree world of childhood.

When I left the nurturing environment of BCC, I entered public school in the first grade at Dalton Elementary in the

Azusa Unified School District, located roughly ten miles from home. It was 1976, the year after the Education for All Handicapped Children Act (since renamed the Individuals with Disabilities Education Act, or IDEA) was signed into law by President Gerald Ford. For the first time in my life, I was placed in an environment where the vast majority of children were not blind or visually impaired. Their acceptance of me was mixed at best. Although Mrs. Scott, my general education teacher, was as supportive as she could be, I had no self-confidence; I was an extremely sensitive child and did not feel that I fit in. I found the greatest acceptance among peers who had the same disability as I did. I was regularly subjected to mean-spirited taunts by other kids, disparaging and hurtful remarks about my disability, and exclusion from team activities such as kickball and tag.

I never seriously considered using a cane at that time, because I associated the cane with pity and felt that canes were only for children who were totally blind and not for me. I thought that not using a cane would make me more immune to negative treatment. I didn't realize at that stage in my life that the other children knew that I could not see well because of the large print I used and the Visual Tek (now called the closed-circuit television or CCTV) that was made available for my use to enlarge images that were otherwise too small for me to see. But the thought that never occurred at the time was that proper use of a cane would enhance independence and promote self-confidence. Instead, while dismissing occasions on which I would bump into physical obstacles, trip, or even slip down a step or two, I just did the best I could with what I had, and my itinerant teachers in the resource room would spend time with me during hours when I was pulled out of general education instruction to focus on basic reading, writing, and mathematics skills.

In second grade I was transferred to Victor Hodge Elementary School. My general education teacher, Mrs. Ortega, came to have a strong impact on my life. Room 13 was a special place because her nurturing disposition and belief in each child were unmistakable, as were her warmth and her commitment to each of us individually. I especially became fascinated by science. This was one of the twenty stations, or centers, set up between rooms 13, 14, and 15. My teacher asked, "What is the name of the system that revolves around the sun where the Earth is the third planet?" Other kids guessed, but I knew the answer: the solar system. I confidently raised my hand and enthusiastically yelled out the answer when called. The answer was correct, and for the first time in memory since I began public school, I felt that I could do well. That feeling was bolstered by the surprise I felt during a school assembly during which I was named Student of the Month. When my name was announced, the pride that I felt swelled up inside me, and that was the first instance in which I experienced what it felt like to achieve something big and to earn a coveted honor as the result of hard work. Although I didn't realize it at the time, my amazing teacher had awakened in me the vision of potential that laid dormant inside.

As a result of the constant love and support of my parents and the encouragement of my itinerant teachers that year, I began to internalize that I had the ability to do well. This was reinforced by my having listened to a classroom talk by a man named David. He was the first blind adult I met during my grade school years. I recall paying careful attention to how he was able to get around so well and how his guide dog, Princess, was always at his side. I am quite certain that since I was one of two dozen kids who met him that day, he would not remember me. That, however, does not detract from how his inspiring talk began to plant the seeds in my mind that there were positive role models with disabilities whom I could emulate. In retrospect, it underscores how, during the course of any person's efforts to make a difference, he or she may never fully realize the amazing good that is done simply by living life as a good role model and example to others.

More challenges came in fourth grade. By this point, I was in Mrs. Jeffrey's classroom. New subjects were California history, health, and cursive writing. I found achieving success in these areas to be extremely difficult, and I was struggling to stay on track as reading assignments became much longer. In addition, the print in the textbooks was much smaller as pictures gave way to more extensive content of the written word. I was provided with large-print textbooks and spent several hours per day in itinerant instruction to receive the backup assistance I needed.

Yet fourth grade was difficult at best. I spent all afternoons and evenings doing homework and battling the headaches that I endured on a regular basis. My one outlet was karate, but I had to stop that because my eye doctor was concerned that any accidental trauma to the head would cause permanent and irreversible loss of the little vision I had left. I was also extremely anxious. I worried a great deal about how I would be able to tackle mounting challenges with no prospect of relief in sight as work piled on and academic demands increased. But in spite of the challenges, I was able to succeed. Even at a social level, I was beginning to gain acceptance by peers. In fact, during elections for class president, I was nominated for a position of leadership for the first time in my life by a classmate named Leah Ludwig. She raised her hand and nominated me to serve the class as president. But I had little confidence and sheepishly declined. I could not imagine taking on a daunting responsibility of that nature, especially since I could not see.

In sixth grade, I was admitted to what was then called mentally gifted minors (otherwise known as MGM), more commonly referred to today as the gifted and talented program. For the first time in my life, I was pulled out of class for reasons that had more to do with my mental ability rather than the need to receive additional specialized instruction based on disability. Also, as part of my individualized education program (IEP), I was taught basic typing skills. This turned out to be one of the best moves the educators could have made. Sixth grade was also the year when I got to know Mr. Sandoval, whom I had met back at Dalton. One thing that he said to me has never left my mind: "Practice doesn't make perfect. Perfect practice makes perfect." I did not understand the nuances of his assertion right away, but over time, I came to see that he was teaching us that perfect is perfect and not merely the effort to attain perfection. He was essentially asserting that perfection must always be the goal, because the commitment to high standards is what will lead to success.

Seventh grade marked my transfer from the Azusa Unified School District to my home district in West Covina. Moving to Hollencrest Junior High was part of the growing trend of supporting students at the schools near their home rather than sending them to magnet districts farther away (in my case, an hour away because of the yellow bus picking up other students while en route). It was at this point that I met Mrs. Louise Newman, an itinerant teacher with a warm smile in her voice and an abiding belief in me that reflected itself well from that year through the day when I finished high school six years later. In addition to assisting me with class work and other assignments, she taught me the basics of learning how to use a new device that was just beginning to come to the fore: the computer. It was the Apple IIe, and I was one of the first to get to try it out. The year was 1982. I learned the basics of its operating system and witnessed a steady increase in my typing speed as I submitted work in typewritten format. Meanwhile, I was introduced to an organization now known as Recording for the Blind and Dyslexic (RFB&D), which provided textbooks in recorded format and enabled me to go through my textbooks more independently than I had previously done.

A significant milestone for me that year was an agreement by both the general and special education professionals, and supported by an academic counselor, Shirley Hargrave, that I be allowed to walk to and from school, forgoing the door-to-door bus transportation that I had known all my life. The one small pleasure that other kids had taken for granted was now a privilege that I had earned by proving I could walk to and from school quite safely. The victory was small but not insignificant. As I grew older and sought to attain greater independence, support for my efforts to walk to and from school served as yet another demonstration of others' confidence in my abilities. This led to a greater sense of self-confidence that would manifest itself in ways that I could scarcely have imagined at the time.

In eighth grade, for the first time ever, I earned straight A's and achieved the highest possible marks in citizenship in every class. By the end of the first semester, at the urging of my parents and teachers, I ran for and was elected student body vice president in a school of more than five hundred students. That proved to be a watershed year. At junior high school graduation that year, I was completely surprised by being called to the stage: the faculty, vice principal, and principal had selected me as the most improved and most inspirational student. Considering all that I had to endure to get to that point, I could not help but feel a deep sense of triumph and abiding gratitude to God, who had remained by my side as I prayed daily and often for strength to continue even when I did not think I could do well.

Ninth grade was a time of significant change, not only because I was by that point a full-fledged teenager but because I was in a new school. This move was counter to the advice of the West Covina Unified School District, which urged my parents to keep me in public school. Officials said that if I were to go to private school, I would not have the same level of access, such as bus transportation, daily itinerant instruction, access to current technology, future career counseling, and other academic support. Indeed, my admittance to Bishop Amat Memorial High School, a Catholic institution, was initially met with resistance from school officials themselves, who initially indicated to my mother that they could not serve me. They let me take the entrance examination only after my mother vigorously protested. I earned passing scores as the result of being given the examination in large print, and I proceeded through school with Mrs. Newman continuing to provide itinerant instruction to assist me with each of my classes. I was not provided with transportation support, so my parents were left with no alternative but to change their work schedules and make arrangements with other parents. While at Bishop Amat and with strong parental support, I gradually got involved in extracurricular activities. Among other things, I was active in speech and debate competitions, participated extensively in community service projects, wrote for the school newspaper, and was elected junior class president in my class of five hundred. My final year in high school was capped off when I was elected student body president in a school of two thousand. I graduated with high honors.

Yet despite the goals I attained, I never received braille instruction. And although I learned braille when I was in my early twenties, I remain functionally illiterate: I have significant difficulty reading on my own at the same speed as those who read print. I was mistakenly taught that braille was only for those who were totally blind; in reality, braille should be taught to every child with a visual impairment if the use of technology does not enable him or her to read at the same level of efficiency and for the same length of time as those with full vision. Although I have become a braille reader, I am nowhere near as efficient as those who learned braille as children and who read several hundred words per minute.

This state of affairs was an unnecessary tragedy for me that could have been prevented.

## Recommendations for Educators

Based on my personal experience, I believe that the best way for students to make the transition into adulthood is for general and special education professionals to work actively and consistently to facilitate an environment in which children learn life skills at every stage of educational development. As soon as possible, students with disabilities must learn the basics of how to interact appropriately with others in social situations. They also need opportunities in an integrated setting to be exposed to other children, including those who may not necessarily have a good understanding about the nature of disability and may initially make fun of disabled students as a result. As difficult as those times were, such situations actually brought out both the best and worst in others. Fellow students who failed to understand me as a person with a disability were chastised by peers for saying what they did. Those not subscribing to bad treatment by others came to me individually to say they did not agree with such assertions. In effect, I was exposed to the raw attitudes of fellow students, both good and bad. The very act of having to confront those attitudes was a learning experience in and of itself. Although adults with disabilities may no longer have to deal with blatant negative attitudes, negative ways of thinking based on outdated stereotypes may nevertheless be present. Their subtlety must never be mistaken for their absence.

In addition to social integration, acquisition of academic skills is paramount. In my grade school years, I distinctly recall instances in which I neither believed I could do a certain task nor wanted to do so. But my parents held fast and insisted, and at times even demanded, that I do well. They did this out of love, and they made it clear that they applied this pressure because of their fundamental belief in what I could do. They emphasized to me repeatedly that their allowing me to accept less than my best would be the worst thing they could do to me or to the prospects for my future. They said that my acceptance of any level of mediocrity would be the biggest insult of all.

Social integration and adherence to high academic standards are but two elements of the overall formula for success in transition. Of equal importance is the need for students to become and stay involved in activities beyond schoolwork and homework: community service, active membership and leadership in clubs and organizations, and the meaningful pursuit of other hobbies such as sports or music, or both. I played the organ for five years and enjoyed bowling, horseback riding, and interactive sports with my family. All of these helped make me a well-rounded person. They also helped me to have things in common with peers at school as well as with friends outside school. In time, the disability itself becomes more and more incidental, as should be the case, since disability is only a part of who we are and must not itself define the whole of who we are.

When I was about twenty years old, I came to what was then the most groundbreaking realization of my life: the biggest obstacle to my disability of blindness was not the disability itself but what people thought about it. The earlier that children understand that their disabilities do not in any way diminish them as a person but are merely part of their personal characteristics, the more quickly they may fully embrace their whole person. These individuals must realize that they need never directly or indirectly apologize or otherwise sugarcoat their disabilities as motivated by any level of shame associated with possessing such traits. As such, efforts to substitute *handicapable, differently abled,* or *physically or mentally challenged* for *disability* are unnecessary. People of all ages with disabilities need to have true pride in who they are and for their families to be just as proud (if not more so).

This philosophy carries over to those in the field of education, both general and special. Outside the home and especially during the early years of a child's development, teachers are the greatest influence, and the attitudes of educators and administrators about the abilities of students with disabilities will necessarily manifest themselves in the policy decisions they make, the financial resources they dedicate, the programs they put into place, and the integration efforts they implement. Educators, parents and other family members, and students with disabilities alike must continually challenge their own beliefs in the abilities of people with disabilities, and they must ask themselves how something may be done rather than assume that a particular goal is impossible.

## Final Thoughts

The most important and critical element to a child's success is support in the home. Although educators have a vital role to play, the home is where basic principles are taught and enforced and where attitudes are formed, strengthened, and solidified. For better or worse, what takes place within the life of the family and outside the school setting is what will play the defining role in shaping the early development of children. Such is the case for children both with and without disabilities.

As educators and school administrators, psychologists, social service providers, paraprofessionals, and others seek to play a critical role in forging lasting impact on the lives of children with all types of disabilities and of every age, quality early intervention is key to maximizing awareness by parents and guardians about options available to assist children with disabilities in maximizing their potential. Such intervention, to be most effective, must entail empowering children to grow up to have the ability to make meaningful choices about their lives. In order for them to know what is truly possible, they must be exposed to role models, both with the same disability and other disabilities, so that they have an opportunity to emulate the admirable qualities they see in these individuals. They must also be exposed to role models without disabilities who embody positive traits they admire.

As these children progress to adulthood, they must have opportunities to interact with individuals pursuing different careers and not merely careers felt "most appropriate" for people with a certain type of disability. For instance, for those with developmental disabilities such as mental retardation, janitorial work at fast food restaurants may be felt to be best aligned with their skill sets. However, efforts by Children's Hospital in Cincinnati, Ohio, shatter that way of thinking: the hospital employs people with disabilities to sterilize and prepare medical instruments for reuse. As another illustration, though it is traditionally believed that those who are blind are best suited for careers in massage, piano tuning, or music, current success stories clearly illustrate how those who are blind pursue careers as teachers, medical doctors, lawyers, artists, automobile mechanics, scientists, engineers, computer programmers, and organization executives.

In order to pave the way for a more inclusive environment, schools must seek successful individuals with different types of disabilities in their local communities and invite them to speak to individual classrooms and large assemblies about how people with disabilities can and do succeed. During such programs, students must be taught that disability itself need not be the characteristic that drives them apart but may, to the contrary, serve as yet another example of how all students are equal, even though the presence of visible disability may in some ways set them apart as different. By the same token, attention must be devoted to educating students of all ages that not all disabilities are visible; learning disabilities, psychiatric disabilities, and other medical conditions may not be outwardly evident. Particular attention must be given to eliminating the stigma surrounding certain types of disabilities whose prevailing myths and misconceptions still rear their ugly head.

"Full inclusion" must be the watchword of every leader charged with meeting the needs of students with disabilities. Any absence of success in integration must be examined within the context of whether or to what extent appropriate resources or supports were put into place to facilitate a smooth process leading to an effective outcome. In examining the costs associated with special education, accountability is critical. So is the need to continue to put into place efficient service delivery systems that promote excellence in educational instruction, the appropriate measurement of quantifiable outcomes, and the commitment in letter and in spirit to promoting a climate in which students with disabilities are supported in their goals and are themselves meaningfully included in the IEP process as the Individuals with Disabilities Education Act requires and with good reason. For students who are blind or visually impaired, keeping in mind that the law has an inherent presumption favoring braille instruction, quality instruction must be provided to ensure that such students read at or above grade level. In providing transition services, advancement of the principle of self-determination is also important while making sure to provide a variety of options so as to facilitate true choice. Such choices should include attending and completing college, pursuing vocational or technical instruction, and moving from high school to the world of work. If or when work is considered, students must be provided with up-to-date information about work incentives that serve to minimize dependence on government income assistance and maximize economic self-sufficiency by taking full advantage of the programs put into place to enable them to become taxpaying citizens.

Decision makers in every quarter must keep in mind the role that cultural background plays in perceptions about disability. This necessarily means that such decision makers must understand how some cultures to this day still believe that disability is a source of shame and should be hidden to the greatest extent possible. Here is where role modeling may play a particularly pivotal part in highlighting what success truly is possible. If individuals from diverse ethnic backgrounds are introduced to individuals with similar backgrounds who have attained success, beliefs about disability may change, resulting in a higher level of activism by parents and family members in promoting quality instruction for their children with disabilities.

Above all, parents, students, educators, and administrators must set expectations high, recognizing that achievement itself must be limited only by the imagination. Indeed, the rich and priceless rewards of life come not just to those who are initially perceived to have the most ability, but also to those who harness the power found in perseverance, determination, drive, passion, and energy to strive and then attain high goals.

In my case, after completing high school, I made an effective transition into adulthood, successfully attaining academic excellence in college while being involved in extracurricular activities and enjoying rollerblading, horseback riding, ice skating, and jogging to keep my life fun, balanced, and well rounded. I then went to and completed law school, worked as an attorney in Los Angeles for three years, and then was recruited to work in Washington, D.C., as general counsel and director of programs for an organization with sixty-five thousand members. Two years later, I became special assistant to the assistant attorney general for civil rights in the U.S. Department of Justice. Less than two years after that, by the age of thirty-five, I was privileged to begin two consecutive appointment terms of service as associate director of the White House Domestic Policy Council, working for the president of the United States. Back at the Justice Department as of April 2007, I am now special counsel to the assistant attorney general for civil rights, and my story continues.

# FROM INSTINCT TO INTELLECT

### Janeen Steel

When I was asked to write a section for this book, I was extremely honored. What I was not prepared for was the personal journey I would make during the process of writing about my experiences growing up with a learning disability. As the executive director of the Learning Rights Law Center and a graduate of UCLA Law School, I should be confident in my ability to write and describe my experiences. Yet my feelings associated with years of failure in this area quickly resurfaced. As I reflected on this history, I realized once again how lucky I am to have accomplished so much. I am successful today due to the laws protecting individuals with disabilities and because of my family, teachers, and professionals who believed in me when I did not believe in myself.

## Grammar School: Reading, Writing, and Arithmetic

At an early age, I can remember avoiding reading books whenever possible. I would not pick up children's stories or attempt to read them for enjoyment. In school I excelled at reading single words and could read sentences easily. The class used a phonics approach to teaching reading, which helped me quickly learn how to sound out words and put them together. No one really noticed I wasn't picking up books to read or really understanding what I was reading. Reading for me as a young child was lifeless, bland, and boring. I would much rather watch *Gilligan's Island, I Dream of Jeannie,* and *Scooby-Doo.*

As a young child, I would have amazing thoughts and complex ideas, but I struggled to convey these in my writing. In order to compensate for my frustration, I began distracting teachers by talking during class and subsequently getting into trouble. Thinking I was just a social child, my teachers did not realize I was avoiding my work. Even during these early years, I felt like a fraud in school. Receiving good grades required luck, not skill. To add insult to injury, my sister was brilliant, and my mother had been a straight A student through high school. All I knew was that I was very different from them.

In 1973 our family moved to Bedford, Texas, a small town outside Fort Worth. My ability to escape school work by socializing with friends followed me to Texas. Because I was slightly ahead of the class academically, school became very boring, prompting me to spend my time writing letters to friends, talking in class, and gossiping, much more fulfilling pastimes than anything happening at school or at home. As the class clown, I received a lot of recognition from peers and could deflect my classroom boredom.

In fifth grade, my life changed dramatically as my family moved to Ohio and then again to California after my parents divorced. My mother and I moved to an apartment in Hollywood, where she started working full time as a file clerk. I attended Cheremoya Avenue Elementary School for the fifth and sixth grades, now the fourth school I had attended. My experience with school continued to include feelings of boredom and frustration. I was adjusting to meeting new friends and taking care of a household when my mother was not doing well. For several years after the divorce, she suffered from severe depression and bouts of alcoholism.

School was never a complete escape for me. When you are bright but learning disabled, day-to-day classroom activities become painfully simple and predictable. I became quickly bored when teachers repeated information I felt I already knew. But when I was given an assignment and had the information in my head yet could not describe it in writing, I became frustrated and would quickly abandon my work. I adopted the attitude that teachers did not understand me while my friends did. I could make people laugh and make friends easily. My creativity was evident in my ability to develop complex stories and ideas. I wanted to use this creativity to write original stories and poems, wanting the stories in my head to come alive.

## Middle School: Signs of a Learning Disability

Middle school was quite an experience for me at Le Conte Junior High School in Hollywood, California. The two-story brick school was located between television studios and working-class homes and apartments. Seventh and eighth grade was the time of Led Zeppelin, Pink Floyd, the movies *Tommy* and *Star Wars*. But it also was the time of angel dust, the cold war, and disco. School was chaos. I was not very interested in academics, often feeling separate and different from my peers, ultimately finding solace with a small group of friends who seemed to accept me. I learned quickly that smoking marijuana and drinking helped tremendously with fitting in. Yes, I was one of those middle school kids who used drugs at school, after school, and on weekends. But, my story is not much different from other kids today when school becomes frustrating and unaccepting.

Education slowly dimmed from my interest as the work became more difficult. Since I performed well on annual standardized assessments but did not do well in my classes, teachers labeled me an average student. Instead of focusing on the work given to me in class, I would write stories that teachers would not understand while dismissing and ignoring their criticism. My grades were also passing by my completing extra credit, participating in class, and doing the minimum. I was one of those kids they called "lazy, but with potential."

During ninth grade, I became inspired by my English teacher, Ms. Stonehill, who made me feel comfortable enough to share with her my stories and one poem I had written, which she submitted to a competition. Ms. Stonehill, however, was often frustrated by my constant talking and class disruptions. During one of her research and writing assignments, I chose to write about Edgar Allen Poe. Little did Ms. Stonehill know that the assignment took me numerous hours to complete. Consumed with Poe, I discussed his writing with friends and my mother. I turned the assignment in, proud that I had completed it and enjoyed the process.

After reading my essay, Ms. Stonehill pulled me aside and told me that I was clearly smarter than I was acting. Teachers cannot teach the insights I had into literature, she said. She wrote on my essay, "We have already spoken, Janeen. Your feel for literature is very fine. Your 'sentence sense' is pretty poor. You must start to care enough about yourself to care about your writing!" Although I received a C as a final grade in her class, Ms. Stonehill referred me to honors classes for high school.

## High School: Hitting the Wall

On the first day of enrollment at Hollywood High School, at the corner of Sunset and Highland, I was committed to changing my ways and doing well in school. I had stopped drinking alcohol and doing drugs. I thought that maybe whatever Ms. Stonehill saw in me might mean I could possibly go to college. Maybe I could have others see what I have in my head, and the boredom and frustration with school would stop.

My honors classes were a disaster; I failed almost all of them. With no understanding of how to study, when I would sit down to read for class, I would quickly get bored and stop altogether. When I was asked to write for my English class, I avoided my assignments, feeling completely overwhelmed.

The best example of my experience in honors classes was biology with Mr. Koslucher. I would get the assignment and try to read on the bus on my way to school. Although the class was organized and had daily assignments, the process made me lost and frustrated. I started arriving to class late or missed class entirely. After that semester, I decided to rely on instinct, since my intellect was letting me down. My escape was a social relationship, a boyfriend, rather than school. Given my failures, I resigned to abandon my studies, learn a trade, and move on.

Transferring into the alternative program at Hollywood High School during my second semester of tenth grade allowed me to take classes three days a week. All I wanted to do was be a writer; I no longer cared for the formalities and requirements of public instruction. I continued to pour my frustrations into my writing as reflected in this poem I composed at the time:

Today I will stay home
And tomorrow I will go
For I will miss nothing
Till tomorrow's show
Today is my tomorrow
And I am all too behind
While as I try here to make up my work
I am still blind to all that will come
For as I know my tomorrow will show
And the laziness in me will keep me from today
Tomorrow is coming
And I will be left behind

In the eleventh grade I enrolled in the Regional Occupational Program for Cosmetology on Hollywood Boulevard for four days a week with school credit. This time was exciting. With college out of the question, I was finally going to learn a trade and make it. School during this time was secondary for me. In order to pass my English classes, all I had to do was turn in recycled essays and stories. I could argue my way through passing my government classes, and my school counselor used my cosmetology and work credit to count as social studies and electives. It was clear that I was learning the art of manipulation.

By my senior year, I had earned enough credits to graduate early. Unclear exactly how this happened, I walked into the principal's office and asked to transfer to adult school. With no objections from the principal, I dropped out of Hollywood High and enrolled in the adult school to finish my credits and received my diploma in 1981. In 1982, I received my license as a cosmetologist and started working at a small salon. Feeling separate from others in the profession who wanted to build a clientele and learn new styles, I escaped as I had in school by going to nightclubs and engaging in risky behavior. After quitting my job as a hairdresser, I spent several years living a life with no direction. I tried welding, bartending, and real estate school yet never finished the required training. At one point, I quit a waitressing job at an upscale Beverly Hills restaurant when I could not understand how to use the American Express machine.

## The Journey to Intellect: The College Years

All I had wanted to be was a writer. Hitting rock bottom, living with friends and unemployable, I had no other option but to face the demon once again, and that was school. I enrolled in a beginning creative writing class during the spring of 1988 at Long Beach City College (LBCC). I passed the course and enrolled full time in the fall. In my first full semester, I enrolled in English 1 with Professor Gary Nagy. My first assignment went poorly; I received a C. The second assignment was a compare-and-contrast essay where I compared bars and gyms as places to pick up a date. My thoughts of this humorous satire backfired when my paper came back without a grade, only a note: "Janeen, please see me about this. We need to discuss the paper." Professor Nagy referred me to the Offices of Students with Disabilities to be tested for a learning disability.

In December 1988, I met with Marvin Mastros, a learning disability specialist at Long Beach City College, who discussed my teacher's concerns. Not knowing what he could do about my struggles, I explained why I was told to meet with him. I had no knowledge what it meant to have a learning disability. Mr. Mastros conducted an evaluation showing I had superior ability in the areas of visual perceptual speed, written language ability, and written aptitude. I was at a fourth-grade level in reasoning and at an eighth-grade level for memory. He did not believe that the diagnostic testing alone showed a learning disability, but his review of my writing did. Mr. Mastros diagnosed me with having a writing disorder with severe difficulties with written expression, including fluency, congruent thought, adequate paragraph organization, and continuity. He noted in his report, "Even though her content, grammar, spelling and punctuation are adequate, she is unable to unify all of her subtopics into a coherent paper."

The diagnosis was exciting. It explained so much of my life, and I realized that it wasn't me; it was my brain. Willing to do anything to learn how to learn, I met with a writing tutor on a weekly basis at school and worked diligently with him. The tutor reviewed my initial drafts, and I learned the art of rewriting and revising. Learning the formula for writing was critical because I did not know how to write a proper essay or even a paragraph. But writing was simple with the correct formula. I received a B in Mr. Nagy's class and an A on the final research project.

A lot happened to me and for me at the community college. As a person who previously had hated school, I was becoming an active participant in school politics, ultimately becoming student body president in the spring of 1990. I won numerous awards for my activities, including a writing schol-arship in 1989, which meant the most to me at the time. In June 1990 I received my associate degree from Long Beach City College and decided to transfer to a four-year university to study creative writing. In spring 1991, I transferred to San Francisco State University (SFSU) as a creative writing major. I immediately went to the Office for Students with Disabilities (OSD) to explain my disability and request accommodations.

On enrollment and after my interview with OSD, the uni-versity offered me additional accommodations for my classes, including a note taker, extended time on exams and assign-ments, and the use of a computer for my assignments and tests. In addition, given the severity of my writing disability and my major of creative writing, OSD hired a scribe for me. This scribe worked with me twenty hours a week for most of my education at SFSU. The scribe wrote as I dictated, and I learned by watching the words flow on the computer screen how to rewrite my own writing. My accommodations did not give me an upper hand in school, as some people would argue, or any advantage over other students. For me to be able to access higher education, I required these accommodations to put me on an even playing field with my peers.

Through my earlier experiences as a writer, I truly did not believe that I could make it as a writer—that writing was merely my passion, not a career. Realizing that the law had given me my voice, I contemplated studying the law. This frightened me, since in my mind, only smart people went to law school, and I was not smart. I was afraid even to mention the idea to anyone for fear of hearing them confirm my sus-picions and self-doubt. John Curtain, a professor of criminal justice who mentored several students at SFSU, helped me realize that I could become a lawyer. I enrolled in his class, became his teaching assistant, and took his externship class at the district attorney's office. He believed in my ability to be a lawyer, and I started to believe it as well.

To prepare for the Law School Admissions Test (LSAT), I enrolled in a class. This would be my first formal standardized test, since I had not taken the SAT or ACT in high school. Some of the practice tests were on tape, and other practice exams were given in class. I found that I scored much higher on the taped tests than the ones I took in class. I discussed this discrepancy in my performance with the OSD. After taking a reading assessment, the learning disability specialist found a severe reading deficit. My aptitude on this test was average, but my reading comprehension scores were in the severely impaired range. The specialist explained I had been compensating with other abilities, but that I had a true reading disability. This finally explained why I could never connect with or understand text.

The OSD provided me with books on tape and the option of a reader for exams. The first time I used books on tape was like watching a film through words. I finally understood when people would describe their experiences reading wonderful literature. All I ever saw in my mind from visual reading was the basic information, never the details. It all made sense why my papers in literature never described my insights: I wasn't getting all the information from the written word.

## Finding My Voice: Law School and Learning Rights

I was accepted into UCLA Law School for the fall of 1996. I could not believe that I enrolled in a top law school, but I was ready. As a creative writing major, I had not had extreme deadlines, and my eccentricities were usually dismissed as artistic. So beginning a new journey through law school was worrisome, prompting me to meet with a psychiatrist to work through feelings of extreme depression and self-judgment. Through these sessions, I explained my concerns about my learning disability and my ability to complete the work in law school. I explained my disorganized style, often getting lost and distracted by the world around me. My psychiatrist tested me for attention deficit disorder (ADD) and found I was a very severe case.

I know that many of you reading this are thinking: *Another disability?* Well, yes. This is my story. I believe when I was tested in college, the specialists evaluated only those issues I experienced in my classes; they were not looking to evaluate every possible disorder. I was not hyper, which is why I believe my ADD went undiagnosed. I think I also was perceived by others as an artist and dismissed as eccentric.

What does my ADD look like? I can do several things at once; I have ideas flowing in my head all at the same time and at random; I get lost going to the same place; I am very creative and can work on two to three paintings at once or two to three stories at once; I have the unique ability to listen to the TV and study at the same time; I cannot have any talking in the background at all when I am studying; I cannot focus on one conversation when another is in the background; I lose my keys; I forget to get directions before going to new places; and I thrive on chaos and deadlines.

Ultimately the psychiatrist prescribed Ritalin for me to try the summer before law school. I found myself organizing my files and reading and reviewing materials for my summer course. I put the dishes away. I hung up my clothes. Who was I? Everything fell into place, but I was on a drug. I learned that this was what I needed to focus.

Law school was perfect for me: everyone felt like me, lost and confused. Nothing can prepare anyone for law school. It was a constant final. I received accommodations throughout law school including extended time on exams, a quiet room, use of a computer, books on tape, and a note taker. For one exam, the school hired a stenographer because I had developed carpal tunnel from typing so much in class. I read on tape to and from school in my car, and everywhere I went, my books went with me. My world revolved around law school and my computer. I downloaded cases on my computer and used technology that read the text aloud. I enlarged the text, because this helped me read. Law school was all about the formula: issue, reasoning, application, and conclusion (IRAC). Everything in law school is IRAC.

I was never quiet about my learning disability. As an active member of the Disability Law Society, disclosing my disability was important to reduce the stigma associated with learning disabilities, especially in graduate programs. While in law school, I started to research on my own the laws for students with disabilities. I took the Education and Law course and worked on a project regarding desegregation and special education.

Law school was difficult, but the California Bar Exam was something entirely unexplainable. The accommodations I required included extended time, use of a computer, and a quiet place to take the exam. Yet before I could receive accommodations, I had to complete additional testing to confirm my learning disability. I went to the Department of Rehabilitation to see if they could help me, met with an intake person, and filled out the information for the interview. Here is a brief description of this interview:

> *Interviewer:* Why are you here?
>
> *Janeen:* I am graduating from UCLA Law School and am preparing to take the California Bar Exam and need retesting for my learning disability and was told I should come to the Department of Rehabilitation.
>
> *Interviewer:* People with learning disabilities don't go to law school.
>
> *Janeen:* Well, I *am* in law school and have a learning disability.
>
> *Interviewer:* You know, looking at your handwriting, you'll never pass the bar exam. How did you get into law school?

*Janeen:* The same as everyone else. [I explained that law
school was very difficult, as it is for everyone else, and I
required accommodations for my disability.]

*Interviewer:* If law school is so hard, why don't you just go
back to hairdressing or become a paralegal?

*Janeen:* I am in my last year of UCLA Law School. I need
help with getting the right computer equipment for the
practice of law.

*Interviewer:* I work with a lot of students with disabilities,
and they can't really read and would never make it to
law school.

*Janeen:* Can I have your supervisor?

I did receive the accommodations I needed for the bar
exam and passed on my third attempt.

Being a lawyer is easier than law school. I'm on my own
time. If I need more time to finish a project, brief, or research,
then I take it. I use a computer, keep a calendar, and close
my door when I need to concentrate. I have the uncanny ability to scan text and find the important pieces of information.
So the problem I had in reading actually became an advantage in the law. But when I need to learn a new area of law
I need to review it by using technology.

I graduated law school in 1999, and I was driven to dedicate my legal career to education law with a focus on ensuring
that students with learning disabilities have access to the public education system. I received the prestigious Echoing Green
Fellowship for Social Entrepreneurs to start Learning Rights
Law Center (LRLC), a nonprofit agency providing legal services to children with disabilities and their families.

The LRLC's mission is to ensure that all students have
equitable access to public education. LRLC focuses its efforts
on these categories of low-income K-12 students: those at risk
or involved in the child welfare or juvenile justice system;
those with emotional or physical disabilities or learning

difficulties; those with health and medical needs; Native Americans; and students who, because of language difficulties, homelessness, sexual orientation, or gender identity, have insufficient access to the public education services and classroom support to which they are legally entitled.

To bring about change in the public education system, families need a place to receive information about their education rights. Students need representation to enforce current laws that forbid segregating students with disabilities or denying them equal participation in the public education system. LRLC works with other socially aware professionals such as education professors, doctors, social workers, probation officers, and teachers to collaborate and build alliances to improve school systems. Attorneys have the skills to facilitate social change by representing and educating the community about education issues and legal requirements. I am excited about the opportunity—and the ability—to do this work.

## Recommendations and Final Thoughts

In 2004 Congress recognized that special education programs have "been impeded by low expectations, and an insufficient focus on applying replicable research on proven methods of teaching and learning for children with disabilities" (20 U.S.C. 1400(c)(4)). Congress went on to establish that students with disabilities are to be ensured "access to the general education curriculum in the regular classroom, to the maximum extent possible, in order to (i) meet developmental goals and to the maximum extent possible, the challenging expectations that have been established for all children; and (ii) be prepared to lead productive and independent adult lives" (20 U.S.C. 1400 (c)(5)). Although the law is clear, schools continue to provide substandard services, receive inadequate funding from the government for those services, and educate, graduate, and exit students with disabilities unable to live as independent, confident, skilled individuals.

To address these challenges, teachers need to learn best practices for teaching students with disabilities, research current methods, attend conferences, and demand support for these efforts from their administrators. Schools should establish open and collaborative relationships with local universities, eliciting their assistance. In the classroom, teachers must recognize that students with learning disabilities can be creative individuals with the ability to manage complex projects. On occasion these students may lack the patience to handle the often mundane tasks of more traditional instructional methods. However, students with learning disabilities have the same dreams, aspirations, and desires as other students; we just learn in different ways. Teachers should discern students' strengths, provide them with the skills to access the curriculum, and unearth their interests in order to facilitate learning and prepare them for their future.

Parents of children with learning disabilities need to accept that their child's disability does not imply parental failure of any kind. They must learn about their child's disability and understand the ongoing and sometimes confusing nature of this learning process. They should assist their child to discover his or her gifts and ways of making sense of the world. As parents begin to pay better attention to their child's abilities and disabilities, they become more knowledgeable advocates for their child's educational program. Asking questions of professionals and educators should become routine as a way to access essential services better suited to their child's needs. Parents are ultimately the most important teachers and advocates their child will ever have throughout their child's experience within the educational system.

Students with learning disabilities should understand exactly how they learn differently and be able to explain to others what those differences entail. Understanding one's disability will assist students to better advocate for personal accommodations and services. Students with learning disabilities should, whenever possible, learn from experienced mentors with disabilities and gain insight from their challenges and methods for working through those challenges. And given the often unfair treatment of students with disabilities by nondisabled peers and adults, students should learn advocacy skills, including how to handle the potential discrimination they may face.

Each individual must demand better educational outcomes for students with disabilities. We should no longer accept substandard results when developing educational programs for students. Maximizing potential requires attention to students' strengths as well as their needs. Currently students with learning disabilities more frequently drop out of school and face high rates of incarceration, drug addiction, and unemployment. It took hard work, resources, and supportive educators for me to become the successful attorney I am today. These services and supports will bring new artists, lawyers, doctors, judges, teachers, and other individuals with disabilities into our communities.

# FROM THE FIELD: BUILDING ACADEMICS, LEADERSHIP, AND COMMUNITY

## Sandi Drinkward

I am the teacher-director of a recently established small learning community of approximately four hundred students in Los Angeles, California. The three personal statements related in this chapter describe the incredible journeys students with disabilities commonly face, and their accounts caused me to reflect on the vision of our new school and our three pillars: Academics, Leadership, and Community (ALC). The ALC is one of three small learning communities and one autonomous school, all sharing a single public school campus. Eighty-seven percent of our students are Hispanic; an additional 12 percent consist of students from a combination of African American, Filipino, Asian, and

American Indian backgrounds; and 1 percent identify themselves as white. Our school has its own office and teaching staff, master schedule, assistant principal, and counselor, while sharing a principal with the other learning communities. We believe that by developing a community of support, students with and without disabilities will reach their academic potential, develop necessary leadership skills, and like the individuals in this chapter, enjoy fulfilling careers and lives well matched to their individual strengths.

I began my career as a high school special education teacher in a large, comprehensive high school with more than five thousand students, working in a self-contained classroom serving students identified with mild to moderate disabilities. I had a strong connection with my students and saw many of them show the personal determination and resiliency to meet their goals, but I was frustrated by the lack of support they received and the limited opportunities for them to be included in classes and activities with typically functioning peers.

After attending a graduation ceremony where only 628 students graduated (approximately one-third of the original freshman class) and only 32 successfully completed the necessary college requirements, I decided to help develop a program that would empower students to prepare for college. Three years later, my husband and I, along with other teachers and students, worked diligently to develop the Academic Leadership Community (ALC). The lives of Sue Rubin, Ollie Cantos, and Janeen Steel are excellent examples of why our three pillars are so important to ensure positive outcomes for students with and without disabilities.

## Academics

The goal of our school community is to challenge all students, yet allow them to feel confident about their abilities and potential. The most daunting challenge schools face is to offer a rigorous curriculum to a diverse body of learners. Similar to other high schools, we are challenged by the myriad of graduation requirements, state content standards, standardized tests, and college entrance requirements, each with its own set of academic requisites. Although we recognize these requirements are extremely important for our students' success after they graduate, we believe academic excellence includes a wider skill set than traditional content areas often assume. I genuinely believe that if we focus exclusively on teaching content, we fail to meet the individual learning needs of the students we teach. We must focus on teaching students to become academics, not merely teach academic content. Academics should address learning how to learn, question, and critique. It should encourage students to make connections between content areas and to access and engage with the world outside of the classroom. All of the individuals in this chapter sought to become academics when they saw a purpose for learning, and each has taken what he or she has learned and used it to improve their communities.

In order to better prepare and empower our students to think about their learning, we expanded on a previous program and created a course called Pathways so that all students have a class during the day where the curriculum is learning, goal setting, and academic support. We have found success by teaching students explicitly how to take notes, get organized, work collaboratively, ask higher-level thinking questions, and assess their own learning strengths and needs. We also recognize the power of offering students a teacher mentor and a cohort of friends who are also developing academic goals.

Janeen Steel is a prime example of a student who needed guidance in learning how to express her thoughts and ideas in meaningful ways. Given her tremendous difficulties with reading and writing, her academic potential was left unrealized when she completed high school. Her future was placed at risk because no one was there to help her identify how she learned best. Although she demonstrated the ability to think critically and through oral argument was able to express herself thoughtfully, her teachers were quick to conclude that her continued academic failure was the result of chronic laziness. I have counseled numerous students with similar stories and have found that when they are offered the proper tools to access curriculum and facilitate their learning, supposed laziness becomes genuine interest and a sense of personal satisfaction in realizing their academic potential.

Sue Rubin's journey toward accessing her academic potential began once she was introduced to facilitated communication. Due to the severity of her disability, her early education focused exclusively on maximizing basic life skills and controlling antisocial behaviors. Once she began using facilitated communication, she wanted to learn academic content provided to students without disabilities. She went further academically than her teachers expected because she was given access to the tools she needed. Finding her voice through facilitated communication was the beginning of her journey toward higher education and college. In my English classes, I encourage students to find their voice through their writing, and when they do express themselves, they feel empowered. One of my students beautifully expressed that finding her voice through writing journals and essays had helped her life outside of the classroom—with her family, in her relationships with peers, and in her work within the community. It is so important to move beyond simply teaching tasks, such as essay writing, and instead teach students to develop lifelong skills.

Teaching academics involves much more than teaching and assessing students' knowledge of discrete skills and their mastery of content. It means helping students assess their learning styles; seek supports, tools, and strategies to facilitate their learning; and collaborate with others to become better learners. Teaching academics means teaching students to question and make connections between their experiences and previous knowledge with new information about their world. In short, addressing academics in school programs is about offering students the opportunity to enhance their full learning potential and all that entails.

## Leadership

In the Academic Leadership Community, we seek to create student leaders, teaching them to work collaboratively with peers and adults while learning how to support others in the process. After years of working closely together, our students begin to help their peers identify strengths and overcome struggles. If a group of students is working on a question and knows another student is strong in math, the group will consult with that student. If they notice a student's grade dropping in a specific subject area, they will push their peer to get assistance. Our students regularly serve as speakers and tutors, providing assistance in other classes to help and support peers. At the ALC, we currently have five teenage mothers who are working not only to get their high school diploma but are preparing to attend college. Two of them are currently taking Advanced Placement courses. These students have served as speakers, candidly sharing with the entire school the difficulties of being a young parent, encouraging their peers to be careful and wait to have children until they can support themselves.

Leadership is about learning how to advocate for yourself and others. Leaders become role models and make decisions that affect their lives and the lives of others. Ollie Cantos was strong academically but needed his peers to encourage him to become a school leader. As is often the case, our friends see our talents much more readily than we do. It was crucial for him to find mentors and persons with disabilities experiencing success. He made the point that people with disabilities do not have to be restricted in their choice of career or future path but should consider positions in education, medicine, the law, or any other area they feel most compelled to pursue.

Janeen Steel's account shows us how important it is for students to take leadership roles in their own lives. After finishing high school and pursuing various jobs unsuccessfully, she took charge of her life and went back to school. The majority of her previous academic experiences permitted her to see only her inadequacies and imperfections. But in college, she advocated for herself through her undergraduate degree and law school experience. Her attempt to access accommodations for the bar exam demonstrated her evolved sense of self-advocacy. This is the type of leadership we want all of our students to embrace. Once students begin advocating for themselves, their journey as a leader has begun. They will no longer allow others to define or place limits on their future but can move forward to discover and realize their dreams.

As teachers and school staff, we need to provide students with opportunities to demonstrate their leadership potential in school. This will help us create a learning environment that is responsive to students' needs, allowing students to take ownership and develop skills. Schools will improve with diversified leadership and student ownership of the school's vision; more important, students will become empowered as they see the possibilities for their futures grow. It is extremely important that all students envision themselves as capable leaders and decision makers and that we as educators are conscious of empowering student leaders, especially students with disabilities, who traditionally have been excluded from decisions about their own education.

## Community

Each of the three authors spoke about the people who either supported or did not support them on their journey. In our school, we define *community* as the students, families, staff, and community partners who must work together for the success of our students. Community defined holistically is the foundation of a great school and the key to its success.

The first and most important stakeholder in the school community is the individual student. Although our students know they need an education, they become more concerned with the desire to fit in and become part of the school community. I hear my students' voices within Rubin's, Cantos's, and Steel's words throughout the chapter. Cantos describes many times his desire to fit in: "I learned that the biggest obstacle to my disability of blindness was not the disability itself but rather what people thought about it." He describes being taunted by his sighted peers and the accompanying feelings of rejection. And when peers defended or accepted him, his confidence and enjoyment in school soared. Similarly, Steel describes her need to fit in and the behaviors she exhibited to make this happen. Becoming the class clown and resorting to drugs are not uncommon ways students try to find acceptance. It has been my experience with high school students with and without identified disabilities that all students want to feel validated by their peers and supported by their teachers.

At ALC we strive to provide all students with the support they need to succeed. An example of this effort is Jonathan, a ninth-grade student with autism. His teachers worked hard to help Jonathan fit in, including educating his classmates about the nature of his disability, including him within collaborative groups, and conferencing with individual students. Although his peers tolerated him, Jonathan had no real friends. Things changed dramatically when our English class read a short story, "The Scarlet Ibis," in which a young boy helps raise his brother who has a disability. As we discussed the story, the mood in the classroom was tense while Jonathan remained silent. As I watched him further withdraw from the conversation, I decided to ask him directly; "Jonathan, what is it like having a disability?" His response was, "It stinks!" He went on for about ten minutes sharing openly what it was like being stared at and feeling stupid. Students gained the courage to ask him additional questions. At lunch two or three students approached him to continue the conversation. We began noting a marked change in other students' attitudes toward Jonathan while his own confidence grew. Jonathan's peers learned valuable lessons from him about the nature of autism, the importance of compassion, and the true definition of intelligence. When we are intentional about including all students in our community, all students benefit.

Families are the next most important stakeholders in educational communities. Rubin and Cantos acknowledge the supreme importance of their families in their education. It is the family that first knows, loves, and advocates for their child, making sure the child's basic needs for food, clothing, health care, recreation, and education are met. When a child comes to school, those first advocates need to be highly respected, whether or not they are versed in advocating for their child in an educational setting.

Many parents make it their mission to learn about educational options and thus become advocates for their children. Unfortunately some school staff assume they know their students' educational needs better than parents do. This was the case when Rubin was in middle school and the principal did not believe that she could handle academic classes. Her mother intervened and found a way to transfer her daughter to the high school, a more inclusive environment that would better meet Rubin's academic needs. In Steel's case, although she now recognizes the importance of family in her life, her immediate family was not equipped to advocate for her educational needs while going through the school system. In these cases, school professionals must empower students and their parents with the necessary information and support to make the best educational decisions. In the ALC, we recognize the importance of building relationships with parents. For secondary schools, this becomes a constant challenge often due to students' apprehension of working with their parents and other adults.

In order to build relationships with parents, the ALC has developed a parent committee and instituted a monthly Coffee House. We invite parents and students to the school for coffee, snacks, and informal conversation. Sometimes we talk about students or school events, and sometimes we merely share our lives and families with one another. In high schools, parents and teachers often communicate only when there are problems concerning a student regarding homework, discipline, exams, or personal trauma. We hope to change this unfortunate practice and invite parents, students, and staff into healthier conversations and relationships.

As educators, our role in the community is to offer a rigorous curriculum and empower students to succeed. The best way to accomplish this is by developing positive relationships with students and their families. It is our job to focus not only on academic teaching and learning, but also on environment, socialization, and the individual gifts and needs of each student. All three of the authors describe the ups and downs of their educational experiences. In short, there were those students, teachers, and staff who believed in and empowered them to move forward, and unfortunately, there were others, however well intentioned, who kept them from recognizing their strengths and achieving their goals. In the end, we appciate how much easier it is to merely teach content than it is to truly nurture and respect individual students by creating an educational community for lifelong learning.

## Final Thoughts

The Individuals with Disabilities Education Act (IDEA) was built on the belief that every child and youth is capable of great things "regardless" or "because of" their individual abilities and disabilities. As I reflect on the three personal statements in this chapter, I am reminded once more of what individuals can do when given the opportunity to succeed and develop their passions and dreams. I have watched many resilient students navigate a complex and often unsupportive educational system, move forward, and accomplish amazing things. While their stories are inspiring, I believe their ability to overcome the challenges they faced is unique. We need educational communities that support and encourage resiliency in our students. More important, we must emphasize academics, leadership, and community to genuinely empower students who lack the support and skills to move forward.

# Appendix

## DISCUSSION QUESTIONS

The following questions can be used by university faculty with undergraduate and graduate students, and by workshop leaders in discussions with education professionals, parents, and advocates to promote critical conversations about issues related to the education and support of students with disabilities and their families. Questions can also serve as prompts for course or workshop projects and reflections, allowing individuals to delve more deeply into the issues raised throughout this book. When responding to questions, readers should make meaningful connections between chapter content and their own personal and professional experiences.

### Chapter One: The Promise and Practice of the Individuals with Disabilities Education Act

1. What was the original purpose of the Education for All Handicapped Children Act of 1975 (P.L. 94–142)?

2. How did *Brown* v. *Board of Education* contribute as a landmark case to the passage of P.L. 94–142? Which issues did they share in common, and how were they different?

3. Why is it still necessary to have laws like the Individuals with Disabilities Education Act (IDEA) for students with disabilities?

4. Describe some of the problematic issues regarding special education programs the author identifies. Discuss whether these issues remain applicable today.

5. Define, describe, and critique the major principles of IDEA as discussed by the author.

6. Describe and discuss the major issues related to the discipline of students with disabilities in public education as described in the law.

7. What are the benefits and continuing challenges of special education legislation for families with children with disabilities?

8. How can schools increase their expectations for students with disabilities and improve the education they receive? What must schools do in order to make these outcomes possible?

9. How can general education and special education teachers be better prepared to support students with disabilities within inclusive settings?

10. How can educational professionals and advocates support families of varying linguistic, cultural, and socioeconomic backgrounds in understanding and exercising their rights and responsibilities on behalf of their children with disabilities? What issues must be considered when assisting these populations in the most compassionate and effective manner?

11. How does Marlene Canter's perspective in "From the Field" support, refute, or expand on the chapter's content related to the law?

## Chapter Two: The Evolving Relationship Between Families of Children with Disabilities and Professionals

1. How can schools assist parents in becoming better advocates for their children?

2. Describe what constitutes *family-professional partnerships*. How is this different from establishing ongoing home-school collaboration?

3. Describe the potential needs of culturally and linguistically diverse families who have children with special needs.

4. How might schools interact with or support families from varying linguistic, cultural, or socioeconomic backgrounds?

5. Describe the ideal training for educational professionals to work more effectively with families who have children with disabilities. How might a practitioner modify this training when considering culturally and linguistically diverse families? Who should be involved, and what would be covered?

6. Describe the barriers to successful home-school collaboration. How might they differ when considering families who have children with and without disabilities?

7. Why is it so important to involve parents in the decision-making process related to special education services for their child?

8. How does Virginia Victorín's perspective in "From the Field" support, refute, or expand on the chapter's content related to family partnerships?

## Chapter Three: Inclusion of Students with Disabilities in General Education

1. How do Menzies and Falvey define the term *inclusion*?

2. The term *inclusion* is defined in multiple ways. Why is this? How can this be problematic for schools, students, and families trying to implement inclusive practices? With which definition of inclusion do you agree?

3. What are some arguments for and against inclusion?

4. What are some ways to strengthen collaboration and communication between general and special education in order to implement and promote successful inclusive practices?

5. What factors need to be considered in order to support successful inclusive experiences for students with disabilities?

6. How can the effective implementation of inclusive practices be monitored?

7. Explain how disability is part of the human condition and is related to issues involving diversity. How can this view of disability be discussed with students with and without disabilities?

8. What cultural, linguistic, or socioeconomic factors may contribute to successful and unsuccessful inclusive experiences of students with disabilities and their families?

9. How does Robert Farran's perspective in "From the Field" support, refute, or expand on the chapter's content related to inclusion?

## Chapter Four: Gaining Access to the Schoolhouse

1. Describe the purpose of the Chanda Smith Consent Decree.

2. Describe and discuss Richard Cohen's perspective regarding the inclusion of children with disabilities in general education programs. How does his perspective relate to your own definition of inclusion?

3. Discuss whether the issues described in the chapter are unique to the particular district or are also relevant to other districts and schools.

4. How might schools foster or hinder parents' advocacy?

5. Describe how the students in the chapter advocated for themselves and others. How can educational professionals help students with and without disabilities develop self-advocacy skills?

6. How does Cohen portray parents in the chapter? How are the parents described in the chapter similar to or different from the families you interact with at your site?

7. Why are district and school administrators so important in facilitating effective special education programs?

8. How can film and other media facilitate change?

9. What specific issues does Cohen raise related to culturally and linguistically diverse students and their families? How do these issues compare with your experiences with schools?

10. How does Sandra Rentería's perspective support, refute, or expand on the chapter's content related to the substance of the documentary?

## Chapter Five: Reducing Disproportionate Representation in Special Education: Overview, Explanations, and Solutions

1. Why is the overidentification of minorities within special education programs such a problematic issue? How does the issue of overrepresentation affect students, schools, families, and communities? What individual and societal implications does the overrepresentation of students of color in special education programs ultimately have?

2. In what ways are students of color disproportionately represented in certain disability categories?

3. What do the authors indicate as contributing to the disproportionate representation of minorities in special education?

4. How do individual, familial, institutional, and community factors and larger sociopolitical considerations affect student learning? Why is it important to consider these factors when determining whether a student has a disability?

5. How do factors such as social interaction, interpersonal relationships, and organizational features of special settings affect student learning? What role could these factors play when determining whether a student has a disability?

6. Special education has traditionally focused on the remediation of specific cognitive and learning problems of individual students. What may be problematic about this approach?

7. What must be considered in order to create, implement, and research the most effective interventions for culturally and linguistically diverse students?

8. Why is it important for educators to use culturally responsive teaching practices when teaching culturally and linguistically diverse students?

9. How might a response-to-intervention approach address disproportionate representation? What are some critical challenges with this approach?

10. Define the roles that school psychologists, counselors, teachers, parents, therapists, and administrators have in addressing the disproportionate representation of minorities in special education.

11. How does Alnita Rettig Dunn's perspective in "From the Field" support, refute, or expand on the chapter's content related to the disproportionate representation of minorities in special education?

## Chapter Six: Early Intervention for Students in General Education: Promoting Academic Achievement for All

1. What are the major problems with the IQ–achievement discrepancy model when identifying students with learning disabilities?

2. Describe the structure of response-to-intervention (RTI) models.

3. What is the relationship between student study teams or teacher assistance teams and RTI models?

4. What is the role of RTI in assisting in the identification of learning disabilities?

5. Why aren't teacher referrals the best way to begin identifying students for learning disabilities?

6. Describe the roles of educational professionals and parents within an early intervention/RTI program.

7. How might early intervention help to prevent the misidentification of students?

8. Why should early intervention, such as student success teams, teacher assistance teams, or RTI, be the responsibility of general education programs? How might special education professionals assist in this effort?

9. What might be some challenges or obstacles to successful implementation of RTI models of early intervention?

10. What are potential cultural and linguistic factors to consider when developing or implementing an early intervention program for diverse student populations in need of support?

11. How does Jo Ann Isken's perspective in "From the Field" support, refute, or expand on the chapter's content related to early intervention?

## Chapter Seven: Differentiated Instruction: Legislative Support and Classroom Practices

1. How do IDEA and NCLB promote the use of differentiated instruction (DI) practices?

2. How do the authors define DI?

3. How does DI differ from individualized instruction?

4. Define and describe the *essential elements* and how they apply to DI.

5. Provide practical examples of how to differentiate content, process, and product based on students' levels of readiness, interests, and learning profiles.

6. How can educators help students define their own learning needs as they get older? How would this understanding help them become more successful learners within classrooms implementing DI practices?

7. What might be the roles of collaboration and technology in the successful implementation of DI?

8. What are some ways to support classroom teachers in infusing differentiated strategies into classroom practice? What is the role of professional development in this process?

9. How does Savina Woodyard's perspective in "From the Field" support, refute, or expand on the chapter's content related to differentiated instruction?

## Chapter Eight: Transition Services and Education for All

1. Describe and discuss the author's definitions of *transition*.

2. What are the major differences and similarities among the Individuals with Disabilities Education Act, the Americans with Disabilities Act, the Family Educational Rights and Privacy Act, and Section 504 of the Rehabilitation Act of 1973?

3. What does the author say is the most appropriate age at which to begin transition planning? Do you agree or disagree? Explain your answer.

4. How can schools better prepare students to understand the program and service options available to them after leaving high school? What areas should be considered?

5. What are a few examples of some appropriate postsecondary goals in training education, recreation, employment, and independent living skills?

6. How can the school and individualized education program team increase student participation in decisions about transition planning?

7. How should transition coordination with outside agencies be managed? What areas need to be considered?

8. Why is it important to track the outcomes and placement of high school students once they leave a special education program?

9. What factors should be considered when developing appropriate transition plans for culturally and linguistically diverse students with disabilities?

10. How does Gina Semenza's perspective in "From the Field" support, refute, or expand on the chapter's content related to transition?

## Chapter Nine: Personal Experiences with Disability and Special Education

1. What role did education play in influencing the future of Sue Rubin, Olegario Cantos, and Janeen Steel?

2. Describe and discuss the importance of family to the three authors.

3. Describe and discuss how each individual became actively involved in the decision-making process regarding educational and life decisions.

4. How did the three authors' peers without disabilities view or interact with each of these individuals?

5. What can educational professionals do to facilitate active and healthy relationships between students with and without disabilities?

6. All three of the authors are strong role models for students with disabilities. How might their journeys inspire students without disabilities?

7. What impact does a professional's expectation have on the learning outcomes of students with disabilities? Cite examples from the personal statement of each author and from your own experience.

8. How might familial and cultural background contribute to how students with disabilities understand their disability and their own potential? How can educational professionals take into account familial and cultural background when supporting students with disabilities in the school and classroom?

9. How does Sandi Drinkward's perspective in "From the Field" support, refute, or expand on the chapter's content?

# References

Abramson, M., Willson, V., Yoshida, R. K., & Hagerty, G. (1983). Parents' perceptions of their learning disabled child's educational performance. *Learning Disability Quarterly, 6,* 184–194.

Adams, M. J. (1990). *Beginning to read: Thinking and learning about print.* Cambridge, MA: MIT Press.

American Academy of Pediatrics. (2000). *Joint statement on the impact of entertainment violence on children. Congressional Public Health Statement.* www.aap.org/advocacy/releases/jsmtevc.html.

Americans with Disabilities Act of 1990, P.L. 101–336, 42 U.S.C. sec. 12101 et seq.

Ames, C. (1990). Motivation: What teachers need to know. *Teachers College Record, 91,* 409–421.

Andrews, J., Carnine, D. W., Coutinho, M. J., Edgar, E. B., Forness, S. R., Fuchs, L. S., et al. (2000). Bridging the special education divide. *Remedial and Special Education, 21*(5), 258–260, 267.

Arends, R. (2000). *Learning to teach* (5th ed.). New York: McGraw-Hill.

Armbuster, B., Lehr, F., & Osborn, M. (2006). *Put reading first: The research building blocks for teaching children to read: Kindergarten through grade 3.* Champaign, IL: Center for the Improvement of Early Reading Achievement.

Artiles, A. J. (2002). Culture in learning: The next frontier in reading difficulties research. In R. Bradley, L. Danielson, & D. P. Hallahan (Eds.), *Identification of learning disabilities: Research to policy* (pp. 693–701). Mahwah, NJ: Erlbaum.

Artiles, A. J. (2003). Special education's changing identity: Paradoxes and dilemmas in views of culture and space. *Harvard Educational Review, 73*(2), 164–202.

Artiles, A. J., & Ortiz, A. A. (2002). *English language learners with special education needs: Identification, assessment, and instruction.* McHenry, IL: Center for Applied Linguistics and Delta Systems.

Artiles, A. J., Harry, B., Reschly, D. J., & Chinn, P. C. (2002). Over-identification of students of color in special education: A critical overview. *Multicultural Perspectives, 4*, 3–10.

Artiles, A., & Rueda, R. (2002). General guidelines for monitoring over-representation in special education. *CASE: The Newsletter for the Council of Administrators of Special Education, 43*(5), 5–6. http://www .casecec.org/Newsletter/IN_CASE_MARCH02.pdf.

Artiles, A. J., Rueda, R., Salazar, J., & Higareda, I. (2002). English-language learner representation in special education in California urban school districts. In D. J. Losen & G. Orfield (Eds.), *Racial inequality in special education* (pp. 265–284). Boston: Harvard Education Press.

Artiles, A. J., Rueda, R., Salazar, J., & Higareda, I. (2005). Within-group diversity in minority special education disproportionate representation: The case of English language learners in California's urban school districts. *Exceptional Children, 71*(3), 283–300.

Artiles, A. J., & Trent, S. C. (1994). Overrepresentation of minority students in special education: A continuing debate. *Journal of Special Education, 27*, 410–437.

Artiles, A. J., & Trent, S. C. (2000). Representation of culturally/linguistically diverse students. In C. R. Reynolds & E. Fletcher-Jantzen (Eds.), *Encyclopedia of special education 1* (2nd ed., Vol. 1, pp. 513–517). Hoboken, NJ: Wiley.

Association for the Care of Children's Health. (1989, Spring). *Family Support Bulletin.*

Au, K. (1995). Multicultural perspectives on literacy research. *Journal of Reading Behavior, 27*, 85–100.

August, D., & Shanahan, T. (2006). *Developing literacy in second-language learners: Report of the National Literacy Panel on Language Minority Children and Youth.* Mahwah, NJ: Erlbaum.

August, D., & Siegel, L. S. (2006). Literacy instruction for language-minority children in special education settings. In D. August & T. Shanahan (Eds.), *Developing literacy in second-language learners: Report of the National Literacy Panel on Language Minority Children and Youth* (pp. 523–553). Mahwah, NJ: Erlbaum.

Bailey, D. B., & Winton, P. J. (1987). Stability and change in parents' expectations about mainstreaming. *Topics in Early Childhood Special Education, 7*, 73–88.

Baker, J., & Zigmond, N. (1990). Are regular education classes equipped to accommodate students with learning disabilities? *Exceptional Children, 56*, 515–526.

Bartolome, L. I. (1994). Beyond the methods fetish: Toward a humanizing pedagogy. *Harvard Educational Review, 64*, 173–194.

Beach Center on Disability, University of Kansas. (2006). *Definition of self-determination.* Lawrence, KS. www.beachcenter.org/?act = view&type = General%20Topic&id = 10.

Bennett, T., Deluca, D., & Bruns, D. (1997). Putting inclusion into practice: Perspectives of teachers and parents. *Exceptional Children, 64,* 115–131.

Biklen, D. (1992). *Schooling without labels: Parents, educators, and inclusive education.* Philadelphia: Temple University Press.

Blue-Banning, M. J., Summers, J. A., Frankland, H. C., Nelson, L. L., & Beegle, G. (2004). Dimensions of family and professional partnerships: Constructive guidelines for collaboration. *Exceptional Children, 70*(2), 167–184.

Board of Education v. Rowley, 458 U.S. 176 (1982).

Boesch, E. E. (1996). The seven flaws of cross-cultural psychology: The story of a conversion. *Mind, Culture, and Activity, 3,* 2–10.

Bond, H. M. (1969). *Negro education in Alabama: A study in cotton and steel.* New York: Octagon Books.

Borthwick-Duffy, S. A., Palmer, D. S., & Lane, K. L. (1996). One size doesn't fit all: Full inclusion and individual differences. *Journal of Behavioral Education, 6,* 311–329.

Braaten, S., Kauffman, J. M., Braaten, B., Polsgrove, B., & Nelson, C. M. (1988). The regular education initiative: Patent medicine for behavioral disorders. *Exceptional Children, 55,* 21–27.

Bricker, W. A., & Bricker, D. D. (1976). The Infant, Toddler, and Preschool Research and Intervention Project. In T. D. Tjossem (Ed.), *Intervention strategies for high risk infants and young children* (pp. 545–572). Baltimore, MD: University Park Press.

Brightman, A. J., & Sullivan, M. (1980). *The impact of Public Law 94–142 on parents of disabled children: A report of findings.* Washington, DC: Bureau of Education for the Handicapped. (ERIC Document Reproduction Service No. ED18817)

Bronfenbrenner, U. (1979). *The ecology of human development.* Cambridge, MA: Harvard University Press.

Brown v. Board of Education of Topeka, 348 U.S. 886, 72S. Ct. 120 (1954).

Brown, W., Thurman, S. K., & Pearl, L. F. (Eds.). (1993). *Family-centered early intervention with infants and toddlers: Innovative cross-disciplinary approaches.* Baltimore, MD: Brookes Publishing.

Bullivant, B. M. (1993). Culture: Its nature and meaning for educators. In J. A. Banks & A. M. Banks (Eds.), *Multicultural education: Issues and perspectives.* Needham Heights, MA: Allyn and Bacon.

Bundschuh, K., & Basler-Eggen, A. (2000). *Abschlussbericht zur Studie, getutzte Kommunication bei Menschen mit schwern Kommunikationasstorwigen.*

Munich: Bayerisches Staatsministerium fur Arbeit und Sozialor-
dunung, familie, Fauen und Gesundheit.

Cairney, T. H. (1997). Acknowledging diversity in home literacy practices:
Moving towards partnership with parents. *Early Child Development
and Care, 127–128*, 61–73.

Calculator, S. N., & Singer, K. M. (1992). Letter to the editor: Preliminary
validation of facilitated communication. *Topics in Language Disorders,
12*(4), ix–xvi.

California Department of Education. (1999). *Reading/language arts framework for California public schools, kindergarten through grade twelve.*
Sacramento: California Department of Education.

Cardinal, D., Hanson, D., & Wakeham, J. (1996). Investigation of authorship
in facilitated communication. *Mental Retardation, 34*(4), 231–242.

Carlo, M. S., August, D., McLaughlin, B., Snow, C. E., Dressler, C., Lippman,
D., et al. (2004). Closing the gap: Addressing the vocabulary needs
of English language learners in bilingual and mainstream classrooms.
*Reading Research Quarterly, 39*(2), 188–215.

Cass, M., Cates, D., Smith, M., & Jackson, C. (2003). Effects of manipulative
instruction on solving area perimeter problems by students with
learning disabilities. *Learning Disabilities Research and Practice, 18*(2),
112–120.

Chalfant, J. C., & Pysh, M. V. (1989). Teacher assistance teams: Five
descriptive studies on 96 teams. *Remedial and Special Education, 10*,
49–58.

Cole, M. (1998). Can cultural psychology help us think about diversity? *Mind,
Culture, and Activity, 5*(4), 291–304.

Cole, M., & Engestrom, Y. (1993). A cultural-historical approach to dis-
tributed cognition. In G. Salomon (Ed.), *Distributed cognitions:
Psychological and educational considerations* (pp. 1–46). Cambridge:
Cambridge University Press.

Cruickshank, D., Jenkins, D., & Metcalf, K. (2003). *The act of teaching* (3rd
ed.). New York: McGraw-Hill.

Cummings, C. (2002). *Winning strategies for classroom management.* Alexandria,
VA: Association for Supervision and Curriculum Development.

Cunningham, J. W., & Fitzgerald, J. (1996). Epistemology and reading. *Reading
Research Quarterly, 31*, 36–60.

Daniel R.R. v. State Board of Education, 874 F.2d. 1036 (1989).

Darling-Hammond, L. (2006). *Powerful teacher education.* San Francisco:
Jossey-Bass.

Delpit, L. (2003). No kinda' sense. In L. Delpit & J. K. Dowdy (Eds.), *The
skin that we speak: Thoughts on language and culture in the classroom*
(pp. 31–48). New York: New Press.

Diamond, K. E., & LeFurgy, W. G., (1994). Attitudes of parents of preschool children toward integration. *Early Education and Development, 5,* 69–77.

Diana v. California State Board of Education (1970). No. C-70, RFT, Dist. Ct. No. Cal.

Donovan, S., & Cross, C. (2002). *Minority students in special and gifted education.* Washington, DC: National Academy Press.

Drapeau, P. (2004). *Differentiated instruction: Making it work: A practical guide to planning, managing, and implementing differentiated instruction to meet the needs of all learners.* New York: Scholastic.

Dunst, C. J., Trivette, C. M., & Deal, A. G. (Eds.). (1994). *Supporting and strengthening families.* Cambridge, MA: Brookline Books.

DuPaul, G. J., & Stoner, G. (2003). *AD/HD in the schools: Assessment and intervention strategies* (2nd ed.). New York: Guilford Press.

Education for All Handicapped Children Act of 1975, P. L. 94–142, 20 U.S.C. 1410.

Education for the Handicapped Act Amendments of 1983, P. L. 98–199, 97 Stat., 1357–1377.

Eggen, P. & Kauchak, D. (2006). *Educational Psychology: Windows on classrooms* (6th ed.). Upper Saddle River, NJ: Pearson.

Egyed, C., & Short, R. (2006). Teacher self-efficacy, burnout, experience and decision to refer a disruptive student. *School Psychology International, 27*(4), 462–474.

Elementary and Secondary Education Act of 1965 (ESEA), originally 20 U.S.C. Secs. 3801–3900, now U.S.C. 7801.

Engestrom, Y. (1999). Expansive visibilization of work: An activity theoretical perspective. *Computer Supported Cooperative Work, 8,* 63–93.

Erwin, E. J., & Soodak, L. S. (1995). "I never know I could stand up to the system": Families' perspectives on pursuing inclusive education. *Journal of the Association for Severe Handicaps, 20*(2), 136–145.

Erwin, E. J., Soodak, L. S., Winton, P. J., & Turnbull, A. P. (2001). "I wish it wouldn't all depend upon me": Research on families and early childhood inclusion. In M. J. Guralnick (Ed.), *Early childhood inclusion: Focus on change* (pp. 127–158). Baltimore, MD: Brookes Publishing.

Etscheidt, S. (2006). Issues in transition planning: Legal decisions. *Career Development for Exceptional Individuals, 29*(1), 28–47.

Falvey, M. A. (1995). *Inclusive and heterogeneous schools.* Baltimore, MD: Brookes Publishing.

Family Educational Rights and Privacy Act Amendments of 1997, 20 U.S.C. sec. 1232g, 34 C.F.R. part 99.

Fass, P. S. (1980). The IQ: A cultural and historical framework. *American Journal of Education*, 88(4), 431–458.

Field, S., Sarver, M. D., & Shaw, S. (2003). Self-determination: A key to success in postsecondary education for students with learning disabilities. *Remedial and Special Education*, 24(6), 339–349.

Finn, C., Rotherman, A., & Hokanson, C. (2001). *Rethinking special education for a new century*. Washington, DC: Fordham Foundation.

Fisher, D., Sax, C., & Grove, K. A. (2000). The resilience of changes promoting inclusiveness in an urban elementary school. *Elementary School Journal*, 100, 213–226.

Fletcher, J. M., Francis, D. J., Shaywitz, S. E., Lyon, G. R., Foorman, B. R., & Steubing, K. K. (1998). Intelligence testing and the discrepancy model for children with LD. *Learning Disabilities Research and Practice*, 13, 186–203.

Foorman, B. R., & Torgesen, J. (2001). Critical elements of classroom and small-group instruction promote reading success in all children. *Learning Disabilities Research and Practice*, 16(4), 203–212.

Foster, M. (1993). Educating for competence in community and culture: Exploring the views of exemplary African-American teachers. *Urban Education*, 27(4), 370–394.

Fox, N. E., & Ysseldyke, J. E. (1997). Implementing inclusion at the middle school level: Lessons from a negative example. *Exceptional Children*, 64, 81–98.

Frey, W. (2006). Immigration goes nationwide: The Brookings Institution Metropolitan Policy Program. In *Briefing Immigration Policy: Federal Debates and Local Realities, US Capitol Building Policy*. Washington, DC: Brookings Institution.

Fuchs, D., & Deshler, D. D. (2007). What we need to know about responsiveness to intervention (and shouldn't be afraid to ask). *Learning Disabilities: Research and Practice*, 22(2), 129–136.

Fuchs, D., Deshler, D. D., & Reschly, D. J. (2004). National Research Center on Learning Disabilities: Multimethod studies of identification and classification issues. *Learning Disability Quarterly*, 27, 189–195.

Fuchs, D., & Fuchs, L. (1994). Inclusive schools movement and the radicalization of special education reform. *Exceptional Children*, 60, 294–309.

Fuchs, D., & Fuchs, L. (2006a). Introduction to response to intervention: What, why, and how valid is it? *Reading Research Quarterly*, 41, 93–99.

Fuchs, L. S., & Fuchs, D. (2006b). *What is scientifically based research on progress monitoring?* Retrieved December 20, 2006, from http://www.ose-pideasthatwork.org.

Fuchs, D., Mock, D., Morgan, P. L., & Young, C. L. (2003). Responsiveness-to-intervention: Definitions, evidence and implication for learning disability construct. *Learning Disabilities Research and Practice, 18,* 157–171.

Fuchs, L. S., & Fuchs, D. (2007). The role of assessment within a multi-tiered approach to reading instruction. In D. Haager, S. Vaughn, & J. K. Klingner (Eds.), *Evidence-based reading practices for response to intervention.* Baltimore, MD: Brookes Publishing.

Fullan, M. (2006). *Turnaround leadership.* San Francisco: Jossey-Bass.

Gallimore, R., Weisner, R., Kaufman, S., & Bernheimer, L. P. (1989). The social construction of ecocultural niches: Family accommodation of developmentally delayed children. *American Journal of Mental Retardation, 94,* 216–230.

Gartner, A., & Lipsky, D. (1987). Beyond separate education: Toward a quality system for all students. *Harvard Educational Review, 57*(4), 367–395.

Gee, J. P. (1999). Critical issues: Reading and the new literacy studies: Reframing the National Academy of Sciences Report on Reading. *Journal of Literacy Research, 31,* 355–374.

Gee, J. P. (2001). A sociocultural perspective on early literacy development. In S. B. Neuman & D. K. Dickinson (Eds.), *Handbook of early literacy research* (pp. 30–42). New York: Guilford Press.

Gersten, R., & Baker, S. (2000). What we know about effective instructional practices for English-language learners. *Exceptional Children, 66,* 454–470.

Gersten, R., & Dimino, J. (2006). RTI (response to intervention): Rethinking special education for students with reading difficulties (yet again). *Reading Research Quarterly, 41,* 99–108.

Gersten, R., & Jiménez, R. (1994). A delicate balance: Enhancing literacy instruction for students of English as a second language. *Reading Teacher, 47*(6), 438–449.

Gilhool, T. (1997, Spring). Tom Gilhool speaks out on significant accomplishments of parents as political advocates. *Parent Movement: Reflections and Directions. Coalition Quarterly, 14*(1).

Glazer, N. (1997). *We are all multiculturalists now.* Cambridge, MA: Harvard University Press.

Good, R. H. III, & Kaminski, R. A. (2002). *Dynamic indicators of basic early literacy skills: Administration and scoring guide* (6th ed.). Eugene, OR: Institute for the Development of Educational Achievement. http://dibels.uoregon.edu.

Goodnow, J. J. (2002). Adding culture to studies of development: Toward changes in procedures and theory. *Human Development, 45,* 237–245.

Gould, S. J. (1981). *The mismeasure of man*. New York: Norton.

Graden, J. L. (1989). Redefining "prereferral" intervention as intervention assistance: Collaboration between general and special education. *Exceptional Children, 56,* 227–231.

Graden, J. L., Casey, A., & Christenson, L. L. (1985). Implementing a pre-referral intervention system: Part I: The model. *Exceptional Children, 51,* 377–384.

Green, A. L., & Stoneman, Z. (1989). Attitudes of mothers and fathers of nonhandicapped children. *Journal of Early Intervention, 13,* 292–304.

Green, S. K., & Shinn, M. (1994). Parent attitudes about special education and reintegration: What is the role of student outcomes? *Exceptional Children, 61,* 269–281.

Gregory, G., & Chapman, C. (2001). *Differentiated instructional strategies: One size doesn't fit all.* Thousand Oaks, CA: Corwin Press.

Gresham, F. M. (2002). Responsiveness to intervention: An alternative approach to the identification of learning disabilities. In R. Bradley, L. Danielson, & D. P. Hallahan (Eds.), *Identification of learning disabilities: Research to practice* (pp. 467–519). Mahwah, NJ: Erlbaum.

Guadalupe Organization v. Tempe Elementary School District No. 3, No. 71-435, 1973. U.S. Dist. Court, District of Arizona, consent decree.

Guckenberger v. Boston University. 974 F. Supp. 106 (D. Mass. 1997).

Gunn, B., Biglan, A., Smolkowski, K., & Ary, D. (2000). The efficacy of supplemental instruction in decoding skills for Hispanic and non-Hispanic students in early elementary school. *Journal of Special Education, 34*(2), 90–103.

Guralnick, M. J. (1994). Mothers' perceptions of the benefits and drawbacks of early childhood mainstreaming. *Journal of Early Intervention, 18,* 168–183.

Guralnick, M. J., Connor, R. T., & Hammond, M. (1995). Parent perspectives of peer relationships and friendships in integrated and specialized programs. *American Journal on Mental Retardation, 99,* 457–476.

Gutierrez, K., & Rogoff, B. (2003). Cultural ways of learning: Individual traits or repertoires of practice. *Educational Researcher, 32*(5), 19–25.

Haager, D., Hunt, N., & Windmueller, M. (2003, April). *Promoting teacher "buy-in" to pre-referral intervention for students at risk for reading failure.* Paper presented at the Annual Conference of the American Educational Research Association, Chicago.

Haager, D., & Klingner, J. K. (2005). *Differentiating instruction in inclusive classrooms.* Needham Heights, MA: Pearson Allyn and Bacon.

Haager, D., & Mahdavi, J. N. (2007). Teacher roles in implementing intervention. In D. Haager, J. K. Klingner, & S. Vaughn (Eds.), *Evidence-based reading practices for response to intervention* (pp. 245–263). Baltimore, MD: Brookes Publishing.

Haager, D., & Windmueller, M. (2001). Early literacy intervention for English language learners at-risk for learning disabilities: Student outcomes in an urban school. *Learning Disability Quarterly, 24,* 235–250.

Hall, T., Strangman, N., & Meyer, A. (2003). *Differentiated instruction and implications for UDL implementation: Effective classroom practices report.* Wakefield, MA: National Center on Accessing the General Curriculum.

Halpern, A. S. (1994). The transition of youth with disabilities to adult life: A position statement of the Division on Career Development and Transition, the Council for Exceptional Children. *Career Development for Exceptional Individuals, 17,* 115–124.

Halvorsen, A. T., & Neary, T. (2001). *Building inclusive schools.* Needham Heights, MA: Allyn & Bacon.

Hardcastle, B., & Justice, K. (2006). *RTI and the classroom teacher.* Horsham, PA: LRP Publications.

Hardman, M. L., Drew, C. J., & Egan, M. W. (2004). *Human exceptionality: School, community, and family* (8th ed.). Needham Heights, MA: Allyn & Bacon.

Harry, B. (1992). An ethnographic study of cross-cultural communication with Puerto Rican–American families in the special education system. *American Educational Research Journal, 29*(3), 471–494.

Harry, B., Allen, N., & McLaughlin, M. (1995). Communication versus compliance: African-American parents' involvement in special education. *Exceptional Children, 61,* 364–377.

Harry, B., & Klingner, J. K. (2006). *Why are so many minority students in special education? Understanding race and disability in schools.* New York: Teachers College Press.

Hasazi, S., Gordon, L., & Roe, C. (1985). Factors associated with the employment status of handicapped youth exiting from high school for 1979–1983. *Exceptional Children, 51,* 455–469.

Hollenbeck, A. F. (2007). From IDEA to implementation: A discussion of foundational and future responsiveness-to-intervention research. *Learning Disabilities: Research and Practice, 22*(2), 137–146.

Honig v. Doe, 484 U.S. 305 (1988).

Horn, L., & Berktold, S. (1999). *Students with disabilities in postsecondary education: A profile of preparation, participation and outcome.* Washington, DC: U.S. Department of Education, National Center for Education Statistics.

Horn, L., & Nevill, S. (2006). *Profile of undergraduates in U.S. postsecondary education institutions: 2003–2004: With a special analysis of community college students*. Washington, DC: U.S. Department of Education, National Center for Education Statistics.

Hunt, P., & Goetz, L. (1997). Research on inclusive educational programs, practices, and outcomes for students with severe disabilities. *Journal of Special Education, 31*, 3–29.

Individuals with Disabilities Act, 20 U.S.C. Sec. 1400 et seq., 34C.F.R. 300 et seq.

Institute of Education Sciences. (2006). *What Works Clearinghouse.* http://www.whatworks.ed.gov/whoweare/overview.html#tag.

Intellectual Disability Review Panel. (1989). *Investigation into the reliability and validity of the assisted communication technique.* Melbourne, Australia: Department of Community Services, Victoria.

Jacob-Timm, S., & Hartshorne, T. S. (1998). *Ethics and law for school psychologists.* Hoboken, NJ: Wiley.

Jiménez, T. C. (2006). *Special education for culturally and linguistically diverse learners.* Position statement for the California Association for Bilingual Education, Multicultural Educator.

Johnson v. San Francisco Unified School District, 339 F. Supp. 1315 (N.D. Cal. 1971).

Johnson, D. R., Stodden, R. A., Emanuel, E. J., Luecking, R., & Mack, M. (2002). Current challenges facing secondary education and transition services: What research tells us. *Exceptional Children, 68*, 519–531.

Kalyanpur, M., & Rao, S. S. (1991). Empowering low-income black families of handicapped children. *American Journal of Orthopsychiatry, 61*, 523–532.

Karnes, M. B., & Teska, J. A. (1980). Toward successful parent involvement in programs for handicapped children. In J. J. Gallagher (Ed.), *New directions for exceptional children: Parents and families of handicapped children* (Vol. 4, pp. 85–109). San Francisco: Jossey-Bass.

Katsiyannis, A., Yell, M. L., & Bradley, R. (2001). Reflections on the 25th anniversary of the Individuals with Disabilities Education Act. *Remedial and Special Education, 22*, 324–334.

Kauffman, J. M. (1993). How we might achieve the radical reform of special education. *Exceptional Children, 60*, 7–17.

Kavale, K. (1979). Mainstreaming: The genesis of an idea. *Exceptional Children, 26*(1), 3–21.

Kavale, K. A., & Forness, S. R. (2000a). History, rhetoric, and reality: Analysis of the inclusion debate. *Remedial and Special Education, 21*, 279–296.

Kavale, K., & Forness, S. (2000b). What definitions of learning disability say and don't say: A critical analysis. *Journal of Learning Disabilities, 33*(3), 239–256.

Kennedy, F. (1942). The problem of social control of the congenital defective: Education, sterilization, euthanasia. *American Journal of Psychiatry, 99*, 13–16.

Keough, B., & MacMillan, D. L. (1996). Exceptionality. In D. C. Berliner & R. C. Calfee (Eds.), *Handbook of educational psychology* (pp. 311–330). New York: Simon & Schuster.

Kincheloe, J., & Steinberg, S. (1997). *Changing multiculturalism*. Bristol, Pa.: Open University Press.

Klingner, J. K., & Artiles, A. J. (2006). English language learners struggling to learn to read: Emergent scholarship on linguistic differences and learning disabilities. *Journal of Learning Disabilities, 39*(5), 386–389.

Klingner, J. K., Artiles, A. J., Kozleski, E., Harry, B., Zion, S., Tate, W., et al. (2005). Addressing the disproportionate representation of culturally and linguistically diverse students in special education through culturally responsive educational systems. *Education Policy Analysis Archives, 13*(38). http://epaa.asu.edu/epaa/v13n38/.

Klingner, J. K., & Edwards, P. (2006). Cultural considerations with response to intervention models. *Reading Research Quarterly, 41*, 108–117.

Klingner, J., & Harry, B. (2006). The special education referral and decision-making process for English language learners: Child study team meetings and placement conferences. *Teachers College Record, 108*, 2247–2281.

Klingner, J. K., McCray Sorrells, A., & Barrerra, M. T. (2007). Considerations when implementing response to intervention with culturally and linguistically diverse students. In D. Haager, J. K. Klingner, & S. Vaughn (Eds.), *Evidence based practices for response to intervention* (pp. 223–244). Baltimore, MD: Brookes Publishing.

Klingner, J. K., & Solano-Flores, G. (2007). Cultural responsiveness in response-to-intervention models. In C. C. Laitusis and L. L. Cook (Eds.), *Large-scale assessment and accommodations: What works?* (pp. 229–241). Arlington, VA: Council for Exceptional Children and Educational Testing Service.

Kolstoe, O. P. (1970). *Teaching educable mentally retarded children*. New York: Holt.

Kovaleski, J. F., Gickling, E. E., Morrow, H., & Swank, P. R. (1999). High versus low implementation of instructional support teams: A case for maintaining program fidelity. *Remedial and Special Education, 20*, 170–183.

Kozol, J. (1991). *Savage inequalities: Children in America's schools*. New York: Crown.

Kozol, J. (2005). *The shame of the nation: The restoration of apartheid schooling in America*. New York: Crown.

Ladson-Billings, G. (1995). Toward a theory of culturally relevant pedagogy. *American Educational Research Journal, 32*, 465–491.

Lake, J. F., & Billingsley, B. S. (2000). An analysis of factors that contribute to parent-school conflict in special education. *Remedial and Special Education, 21*(4), 240–251.

Lane, K. L., Mahdavi, J. N., & Borthwick-Duffy, S. A. (2003). Teacher perceptions of the prereferral intervention process: A call for assistance with school-based interventions. *Preventing School Failure*, *4*, 148–155.

Lapkoff, S., & Li, R. M. (2007). Five trends for schools. *Educational Leadership*, *64*(6), 8–15.

Larry P. v. Riles, 343 F. Supp. 1308 (N.D. Cal. 1972).

Lau v. Nichols, 414 U.S. 563 (1974).

Lawrence-Brown, D. (2004). Differentiated instruction: Inclusive strategies for standards-based learning that benefit the whole class. *American Secondary Education*, *32*(3), 34–62.

Lee, C. D. (2001a). Toward a framework for culturally responsive design in multimedia computer environments: Cultural modeling as a case. *Mind, Culture and Activity*, *10*, 42–61.

Lee, C. (2001b). Is October Brown Chinese? A cultural modeling activity system for underachieving students. *American Educational Research Journal*, *38*, 97–141.

Lee, C. (2002). Interrogating race and ethnicity as constructs in the examination of cultural processes in developmental research. *Human Development*, *45*, 282–290.

Lieberman, L. M. (1996). Preserving special education...for those who need it. In W. Stainback & S. Stainback (Eds.), *Controversial issues confronting special education* (pp. 3–15). Needham Heights, MA: Allyn & Bacon.

Linan-Thompson, S., Vaughn, S., Hickman-Davis, P., & Kouzekanani, K. (2003). Effectiveness of supplemental reading instruction for second-grade English language learners with reading difficulties. *Elementary School Journal*, *103*(3), 221–238.

Lipsky, D. K. (1985). A parental perspective on stress and coping. *American Journal of Orthopsychiatry*, *55*(4), 614–617.

Lipsky, D. K., & Gartner, A. (1997). *Inclusion and school reform: Transforming America's classrooms*. Baltimore, MD: Brookes Publishing.

Logan, K., Hansen, C., Nieminen, P., & Wright, E. (2001). Student support teams: Helping students succeed in general education classrooms or working to place students in special education? *Education and Training in Mental Retardation and Developmental Disabilities*, *36*(3), 280–292.

Luckasson, R., Borthwick-Duffy, S., Buntinx, W.H.E., Coulter, D. L., Craig, E. M., Reeve, A., et al. (2002). *Mental retardation: Definition, classification, and systems of supports* (10th ed.). Washington, DC: AAMR.

MacMillan, D. (1982). *Mental retardation in school and society* (2nd ed.). New York: Little, Brown.

Madaus, J. W., & Shaw, S. (2006). The impact of the IDEA 2004 on transition to college for students with learning disabilities. *Learning Disabilities Research and Practice, 21*(4), 273–281.

Mamlin, N. (1999). Despite best intentions: When inclusion fails. *Journal of Special Education, 33,* 36–49.

Manset, G., & Semmel, M. I. (1997). Are inclusive programs for students with mild disabilities effective? A comparative review of model programs. *Journal of Special Education, 31,* 155–180.

Martin, E. W., Martin, R., & Terman, D. (1996). The legislative and litigation history of special education. *The Future of Children: Special Education for Students with Disabilities, 6*(1), 35–39.

Martin, J., Huber-Marshall, L., & Sale, P. (2004). A three-year study of middle, junior high, and high school IEP meetings. *Exceptional Children, 70,* 285–297.

Martin, J., Mithaug, D., Cox, P., Peterson, L., Van Dyke, J., & Cash, M. (2003). Increasing self-determination: Teaching students to plan, work, evaluate, and adjust. *Exceptional Children, 69,* 431–446.

Mastropieri, M. A., & Scruggs, T. E. (2007). *The inclusive classroom: Strategies for effective instruction* (3rd ed.). Upper Saddle River, NJ: Pearson Merrill Prentice Hall.

McCook, J. E. (2006). *The RTI guide: Developing and implementing a model in your schools.* Horsham, PA: LRP Publications.

McEneaney, J. E., Lose, M. K., & Schwartz, R. M. (2006). A transactional perspective on reading difficulties and response to intervention. *Reading Research Quarterly, 41,* 117–128.

McLoughlin, J. A., Edge, A., Petrosko, J. M., & Strenecky, B. J. (1981). P. L. 94–142 and information dissemination: A step forward. *Journal of Special Education Technology, 4*(4), 50–56.

McNamara, K., & Hollinger, C. (2003). Intervention-based assessment: Evaluation rates and eligibility findings. *Exceptional Children, 69,* 181–193.

Medterms. (2006). *Definition of eugenics.* http://www.medterms.com/script /main/art.asp?articlekey=3335.

Mehlinger, H. (1995). *School reform in the information age.* Bloomington: Indiana University, Center for Excellence in Education.

Mellard, D. F., Byrd, S. E., Johnson, E., Tollefson, J. M., & Boesche, L. (2004). Foundations and research on identifying model responsiveness-to-intervention methods. *Exceptional Children, 71,* 445–463.

Menzies, H. (2005). *Instructor's manual and test bank for Haager & Klingner's differentiating instruction in inclusive classrooms: The special educator's guide.* Needham Heights, MA: Allyn & Bacon.

Meyen, E. L., & Skrtic, T. M. (Eds.). (1995). *Special education and student disability.* Denver, CO: Love Publishing Company.

Mills v. District of Columbia Board of Education, 348 F. Supp. 866 (D.D.C. 1972).

Miramontes, O., Nadeau, A., & Commins, N. L. (1997). *Restructuring schools for linguistic diversity: Linking decision-making to effective programs.* New York: Teachers College Press.

Mithaug, D., Horiuchi, C., & Fanning, P. (1985). A report on the Colorado statewide follow-up survey of special education students. *Exceptional Children, 51,* 397–404.

Mlynek, S., Hannah, M. E., & Hamlin, M. A. (1982). Mainstreaming: Parental perceptions. *Psychology in the Schools, 19,* 354–359.

Moll, L. (1999). Foreword. In J. Paratore, G. Melzei, & B. Krol-Sinclair (Eds.), *What should we expect of family literacy? Experiences of Latino children whose parents participate in an intergenerational literacy project* (p. xiii). Chicago: National Reading Conference.

Montgomery, W. (2001). Creating culturally responsive, inclusive classrooms. *Exceptional Children, 33,* 4–9.

Monzo, L., & Rueda, R. (2001). *Constructing achievement orientations toward literacy: An analysis of sociocultural activity in Latino home and community contexts.* Ann Arbor: Center for the Improvement of Early Reading Achievement, University of Michigan.

Morris, V. G., & Morris, C. L. (2000). *Creating caring and nurturing educational environments for African American children.* Westport, CT: Bergin and Garvey.

National Center for Education Statistics. (2006). *The condition of education.* Washington, DC: U.S. Department of Education.

National Institute of Child Health and Human Development. (2000). *Report of the National Reading Panel. Teaching children to read: An evidence-based assessment of the scientific research literature on reading and its implications for reading instruction.* Washington, DC: U.S. Government Printing Office.

National Reading Panel. (2000). *Report of the National Reading Panel: Teaching children to read: An evidence-based assessment of the scientific research literature on reading and its implications for reading instruction.* Washington, DC: National Institute of Child Health and Human Development.

Nelson, L. L., Summers, J. A., & Turnbull, A. P. (2004). Boundaries in family-professional relationships: Implications for special education. *Remedial and Special Education, 25*(3), 153–165.

Neubert, D. (2000). Transition education and services guidelines. In P. L. Sitlington, G. M. Clark, & O. P. Kolstoe (Eds.), *Transition education and services for adolescents with disabilities* (pp. 39–69). Needham Heights, MA: Allyn & Bacon.

No Child Left Behind Act of 2001, P.L. 107–110, 20 U.S.C. 6301 et seq.

O'Connor, C., & Fernandez, S. D. (2006). Race, class, and disproportionality: Reevaluating the relationship between poverty and special education placement. *Educational Researcher, 35*(6), 6–11.

Ogletree, B., Hamtil, A., Solberg, L., & Scoby-Schmelzle, S. (1993). Facilitated communication: A naturalistic validation method. *Focus on Autistic Behavior, 8*(4), 1–10.

Olenchak, F. R. (2001). Lessons learned from gifted children about differentiation. *Teacher Educator, 36*, 185–198.

Olney, M. (1995). *A controlled evaluation of facilitated communication.* Unpublished doctoral dissertation, Syracuse University.

Olney, M. (2001). Other research: Evidence of literacy in individuals labeled with mental retardation. *Disability Studies Quarterly, 21*(2), 111–122.

O'Neil, M. (2005, October). *A perfect fit: People with disabilities building assets.* World Institute on Disability Equity. http://www.wid.org/publications/?page=equity&sub=200510&topic=fa.

Oswald, D. P., Coutinho, M. J., & Best, A. M. (2000, November 17). *Community and school predictors of overrepresentation of minority children in special education.* Paper prepared for the Harvard University Civil Rights Project Conference on Minority Issues in Special Education, Cambridge, MA.

Oswald, D., Coutinho, M. J., Singh, N., & Best, A. (1998). Ethnicity in special education and relationships with school related economic and educational variables. *Journal of Special Education, 32*, 194–206.

Owen, F., Griffiths, D., Stoner, K., Gosse, L., Watson, S. L., Tardif, C. Y., et al. (2003). Multi-level human rights training in an association for community living: First steps toward systemic change. *Journal on Developmental Disabilities, 10*, 43–64.

Palmer, D. S., Borthwick-Duffy, S. A., & Widaman, K. (1998). Parent perceptions of inclusive practices for their children with significant cognitive disabilities. *Exceptional Children, 64*, 271–282.

Paredes, A. (1984). On ethnographic work among minorities: A folklorist's perspective. In R. Romo & R. Paredes (Eds.), *New directions in Chicano scholarship* (pp. 1–32). Santa Barbara, CA: Center for Chicano Studies.

Parents and the I.E.P. (1979). *Exceptional Parent, 9*(4), 10–13.

Parents in Action in Special Education (PACE) v. Hannon, U.S. District Court, 1980, 506 F. Supp. 831 (N.D. Ill.)

Park, J., Turnbull, A. P., & Park, H. S. (2001). Quality of partnerships in service provision for Korean parents of children with special needs: A qualitative inquiry. *Journal of the Association for Persons with Severe Disabilities, 26*(3), 158–170.

Park, J., Turnbull, A. P., & Turnbull, H. R. (2002). Impacts of poverty on quality of life in families of children with disabilities. *Exceptional Children, 68*(2), 151–170.

Parrish, T. (1994). *National agenda for achieving better results for children and youth with serious emotional disturbance.* Washington, DC: U.S. Department of Education.

Pennsylvania Association for Retarded Children (PARC) v. Commonwealth of Pennsylvania, 334 F. Supp. 1257 (E.D. Pa. 1971).

Piggott, A. (2002). Putting differentiation into practice in secondary science lessons. *School Science Review, 305,* 65–73.

Plunge, M. M., & Kratochwill, T. R. (1995). Parental knowledge, involvement, and satisfaction with their child's special education services. *Special Services in the Schools, 10,* 113–138.

President's Commission on Excellence in Special Education. (2002, July). *A new era: Revitalizing special education for children and their families.* http://www.ed.gov/inits/commissionboards/whspecialeducation/reports/letter.html.

Pruitt, P., Wandry, D., & Hollums, D. (1998). Listen to us! Parents speak out about their interactions with special educators. *Preventing School Failure, 42*(4), 161–166.

Public Agenda. (2002). *When it's your own child: A report on special education from the families who use it.* New York: Author.

Pugach, M. (1995). On the failure of imagination in inclusive schooling. *Journal of Special Education, 29,* 212–223.

Pugach, M. C. (2005). Research on preparing general education teachers to work with students with disabilities. In M. Cochran-Smith & K. M. Zeichner (Eds.), *Studying teacher education: A report of the AERA panel on research and teacher education* (pp. 549–643). Washington, DC: American Educational Research Association.

Rea, P. J., McLaughlin, V. L., & Walther-Thomas, C. (2002). Outcomes for students with learning disabilities in inclusive and pullout programs. *Exceptional Children, 68,* 203–222.

Rehabilitation Act of 1973, P.L. 93–112, Sec. 504, 29 U.S.C. 794 et seq.

Reschly, D. J. (1997a). Diagnostic and treatment utility of intelligence tests. In D. P. Flanagan, J. L. Genshaft, & P. L. Harrison (Eds.), *Contemporary intellectual assessment: Theories, tests and issues.* New York: Guilford Press.

Reschly, D. J. (1997b). *Disproportionate minority representation in general and special education: Patterns, issues, and alternatives.* Des Moines: Iowa Department of Education.

Roach, V. (1995). *Winning ways: Creating inclusive schools, classrooms and communities.* Alexandria, VA: National Association of the State Boards of Education.

Rock, M. L., & Zigmond, N. (2001). Intervention assistance: Is it substance or symbolism? *Preventing School Failure, 45,* 153–161.

Roe v. Wade, 410 U.S. 113 (1973).

Rogers, D., & Bowman, M. (2003). *A history: The construction of race and racism.* Portland, OR: Western States Center.

Rogoff, B. (2003). *The cultural nature of human development.* New York: Oxford University Press.

Rogoff, B., & Angelillo, C. (2002). Investigating the coordinated functioning of multifaceted cultural practices in human development. *Human Development, 45,* 211–225.

Roncher v. Walter. 700 F.2d 1058, 1063, cert. denied, 464 U.S. 864 (6th Cir. 1983).

Rose, E., Rainforth, B., & Steere, D. (2002). Guiding principles for the education of children and youth with severe and multiple disabilities. In F. Obiakor, C. Utley, & A. Rotatori (Eds.), *Advances in special education: Psychology of effective education for learners with exceptionalities.* Stamford, CT: JAI Press.

Rueda, R., MacGillivray, L., Monzo, L., & Arzubiaga, A. (2001). *Engaged reading: A multilevel approach to considering sociocultural factors with diverse learners.* Ann Arbor: Center for the Improvement of Early Reading Achievement, University of Michigan.

Rueda, R., Monzo, L., Shapiro, J., Gomez, J., & Blacher, J. (2005). Cultural models of transition: Latina mothers of young adults with developmental disabilities. *Exceptional Children, 71*(4), 401–414.

Rueda, R., & Windmueller, M. P. (2006). English language learners, LD, and overrepresentation: A multiple-level analysis. *Journal of Learning Disabilities, 39,* 99–107.

Ruiz, N. (1998). Instructional strategies for children with limited-English proficiency. *Journal of Early Education and Family Review, 5,* 21–22.

Ryndak, D. L., Downing, J. E., Jacqueline, L. R., & Morrison, A. P. (1995). Parents' perceptions after inclusion of their children with moderate or severe disabilities. *Journal of the Association for Persons with Severe Handicaps, 20,* 147–157.

Safran, S. P., & Safran, J. S. (1996). Intervention assistance programs and prereferral teams: Directions for the twenty-first century. *Remedial and Special Education, 17,* 363–369.

Salend, S. J. (in press). *Creating inclusive classrooms: Effective and reflective practices.* Upper Saddle River, NJ: Pearson Merrill Prentice Hall.

Salett, S., & Henderson, A. (1980). *A report on the Education of All Handicapped Children Act: Are parents involved?* Columbia, MD: National Committee for Citizens in Education.

Sax, C., Noyes, D., & Fisher, F. (2001). High school inclusion+seamless transition=desired outcomes. *TASH Connections, 27,* 17–20.

Schaffer v. Weast, 126S. Ct. 528 (2005).

School Committee of the Town of Burlington v. Department of Education of Massachusetts, 471 U.S. 359 (1985).

Scott, B., Vitale, M. R., & Masten, W. G. (1998). Implementing instructional adaptations for students with disabilities in inclusive classrooms. *Remedial and Special Education, 19*, 106–119.

Scruggs, T. E., & Mastropieri, M. A. (1996). Teacher perceptions of mainstreaming/inclusion, 1958–1995: A research synthesis. *Exceptional Children, 63*, 59–75.

Selden, S. (1999). *Inheriting shame: The story of eugenics and racism in America.* New York: Teachers College Press.

Shapiro, J. (1994). *No pity.* New York: Three Rivers Press.

Shaw, S. (2006). Legal and policy perspectives on transition assessment and documentation. *Career Development for Exceptional Individuals, 29*(2), 108–113.

Shearer, M. S., & Shearer, D. E. (1977). Parent involvement. In J. B. Jordan, A. H. Hayden, M. B. Karnes, & M. M. Wood (Eds.), *Early childhood education for exceptional children* (pp. 208–235). Reston, VA: Council for Exceptional Children.

Sheehan, C., & Matuozzi, R. (1996). Validation of facilitated communication. *Mental Retardation, 34*(2), 94–107.

Shriner, J. G., & Destefano, L. (2003). Participation and accommodation in state assessment: The role of individualized education programs. *Exceptional Children, 69*, 147–161.

Simon, E. W., Toll, D. M., & Whitehair, P. M. (1994). A naturalistic approach to the validation of facilitated communication. *Journal of Autism and Developmental Disorders, 24*(5), 647–657.

Sindelar, P. T., Shearer, D. K., Yendol- Hoppey, D., & Liebert, T. W. (2006). The sustainability of inclusive school reform. *Exceptional Children, 72*, 317–331.

Singer, A. (2003). The new U.S. demographics. Brookings Institution Center on Urban and Metropolitan Policy. Presentation to Funders Network on Population, Reproductive and Health Rights.

Sitlington, P. (2003). Postsecondary education: The other transition. *Exceptionality, 11*(2), 103–113.

Smith, J. D., & Polloway, E. D. (1993). Institutionalization, involuntary sterilization, and mental retardation: Profiles from the history of the practice. *Mental Retardation, 31*, 208–214.

Snow, C. S., Burns, S. M., & Griffin, P. (1998). *Preventing reading difficulties in young children.* Washington, DC: National Academy Press.

Soodak, L. C., & Erwin, E. J. (2000). Valued member or tolerated participant: Parents' experiences in inclusive early childhood settings. *Journal of the Association for Persons with Severe Handicaps, 25*(1), 29–41.

Southeastern Community College v. Davis, 442 U.S. 397 (1979).

Speece, D. L., & Case, L. P. (2001). Classification in context: An alternative approach to identifying early reading disability. *Journal of Educational Psychology, 93*, 735–749.

Stainback, W., & Stainback, S. (1984). A rationale for the merger of regular and special education. *Exceptional Children, 51,* 102–112.

Stanovich, K. (1991). Discrepancy definitions of reading disability: Has intelligence led us astray? *Reading Research Quarterly, 26*(1), 7–29.

Steere, D. E., Rose, E., & Cavaiuolo, D. (2007). *Growing up: Transition to adult life for students with disabilities.* Needham Heights, MA: Allyn & Bacon.

Steere, D. E., Rose, E., & Fishbaugh, M.S.E. (1999). Integration in the secondary school for students with severe disabilities. In M. Coutinho & A. C. Repp (Eds.), *Inclusion: The integration of students with disabilities.* Belmont, CA: Wadsworth.

Stodolsky, S. S., & Grossman, P. L. (2000). Changing students, changing teachers. *Teachers College Record, 102,* 125–172.

Strangman, N., Hall, T., & Meyer, A. (2003). *Graphic organizers and implications for universal design for learning: Curriculum enhancement report.* Wakefield, MA: National Center on Accessing the General Curriculum.

Strom, R., Rees, R., Slaughter, H., & Wurster, S. (1980). Role expectations of intellectually handicapped children. *Exceptional Children, 47*(2), 144–147.

Super, C., & Harkness, S. (1986). The development niche: A conceptualization at the interface of child and culture. *International Journal of Behaviour Development, 9,* 1–25.

Swanson, H. L., Harris, K. R., & Graham, S. (Eds.). (2003). *Handbook of learning disabilities.* New York: Guilford Press.

Szymanski, E. M. (1994). Transition: Life span and life space considerations for empowerment. *Exceptional Children, 60,* 402–410.

Thousand, J., & Villa, R. (1990). Strategies for educating learners with severe disabilities within their local home schools and communities. *Focus on Exceptional Children, 23,* 1–24.

Tomlinson, C. A. (2001). Differentiated instruction in the regular classroom: What does it mean? How does it look? *Understanding Our Gifted, 14,* 3–6.

Tomlinson, C. A. (2003a). *Hallmarks of quality differentiation: How do we know if we're on the right track?* [Differentiated instruction in Action CD-ROM]. Alexandria, VA: Association for Supervision and Curriculum Development.

Tomlinson, C. A. (2003b). *Fulfilling the promise of the differentiated classroom: Strategies and tools for responsive teaching.* Alexandria, VA: Association for Supervision and Curriculum Development.

Tomlinson, C. A. (2005a). *How to differentiate instruction in mixed-ability classrooms.* (2nd ed.) Upper Saddle River, NJ: Pearson Education.

Tomlinson, C. A. (2005b). *The differentiated classroom: Responding to the needs of all learners.* Upper Saddle River, NJ: Pearson Education.

Tomlinson, C. A., & Eidson, C. C. (2003a). *Differentiation in practice: A resource guide for differentiating curriculum, grades K-5.* Arlington, VA: Association for Supervision and Curriculum Development.

Tomlinson, C. A., & Eidson, C. C. (2003b). *Differentiation in practice: A resource guide for differentiating curriculum, grades 5–9.* Arlington, VA: Association for Supervision and Curriculum Development.

Tomlinson, C. A., Brighton, C., Hertberg, H., Callahan, C. M., Moon, T. R., Brimijoin, K., et al. (2003). Differentiating instruction in response to student readiness, interest, and learning profile in academically diverse classrooms: A review of the literature. *Journal for the Education of the Gifted, 27,* 119–145.

Tomlinson, C. A., & McTighe, J. (2006). *Integrating differentiated instruction and understanding by design: Connecting content and kids.* Alexandria, VA: Association for Supervision and Curriculum Development.

Tomlinson, C. A., & Strickland, C. A. (2005). *Differentiation in practice: A resource guide for differentiating curriculum, grades 9-12.* Arlington, VA: Association for Supervision and Curriculum Development.

Torgesen, J. K. (2000). Individual differences in response to early interventions in reading: The lingering problem of treatment resisters. *Learning Disabilities Research and Practice, 10*(1), 55–64.

Townsend, B. L., & Patton, J. M. (2000). Reflecting on ethics, power, and privilege. *Teacher Education and Special Education, 23,* 32–33.

Turnbull, A., Turnbull, R., Erwin, E., & Soodak, L. (2006). *Families, professionals and exceptionality: Positive outcomes through partnership and trust.* Upper Saddle River, NJ: Pearson/Merrill Prentice Hall.

Turnbull, H. R., Huerta, N. E., & Stowe, M. J. (2006). *The Individuals with Disabilities Act as amended in 2004.* Columbus, OH, and Upper Saddle River, NJ: Pearson/Merrill-Prentice Hall.

Turnbull, H. R., Stowe, M. J., & Huerta, N. E. (2007). *Free Appropriate Public Education: The Law and Children with Disabilities* (7th ed.). Denver, CO: Love Publishing Company.

Tyack, D. (1993). School governance in the United States: Historical puzzles and anomalies. In J. Hannaway & M. Carnoy (Eds.), *Decentralization and school improvement: Can we fulfill the promise?* (pp. 1–32). San Francisco: Jossey-Bass.

Tyack, D., & Hansot, E. (1982). *Managers of virtue: Public school leadership in America, 1820–1980.* New York: Basic Books.

U.S. Congress. Committee on Education and Labor. Select Subcommittee on Education. Hearing. 93rd Cong., 1st sess., 1973.

U.S. Department of Education. (2002). *A new era: Revitalizing special education for children and their families.* Washington, DC: Author.

U.S. Department of Education. (2003). *Identifying and implementing educational practices supported by rigorous evidence: A user-friendly guide.* Washington, DC: U.S. Department of Education.

U.S. Department of Education. National Center for Education Statistics. (2006). *The condition of education 2006.* http://nces.ed.gove/programs/coe/2006/pdf/07_2006.pdf.

U.S. Department of Education, Office of Special Education and Rehabilitative Services, Office of Special Education Programs. *Data analysis system,* 1976–2004. https://www.ideadata.org/docs/PartBTrendData/B1.html.

Varenne, H., & McDermott, R. (1999). *Successful failure: The school America builds.* Boulder, CO: Westview Press.

Vaughn, S., Gersten, R., & Chard, D. I. (2000). The underlying message in LD intervention research: Findings from research syntheses. *Exceptional Children, 67,* 99–114.

Vaughn, S., & Klingner, J. K. (2007). Overview of the three-tier model of reading intervention. In D. Haager, J. K. Klingner, & S. Vaughn (Eds.), *Evidence-based reading practices for response to intervention.* Baltimore, MD: Brookes Publishing.

Vaughn, S., & Linan-Thompson, S. (2003). What is special about special education for students with learning disabilities? *Journal of Special Education, 37*(3), 140–147.

Vaughn, S., Linan-Thompson, S., & Hickman, P. (2003). Response to instruction as a means of identifying students with reading/learning disabilities. *Exceptional Children, 69,* 391–409.

Vaughn, S., Wanzek, J., Woodruff, A. L., & Linan-Thompson, S. (2007a). A three-tier model for preventing reading difficulties and early identification of students with reading disabilities. In D. Haager, S. Vaughn, & J. K. Klingner (Eds.), *Evidence-based reading practices for response to intervention.* Baltimore, MD: Brookes Publishing.

Vaughn, S., Wanzek, J., Woodruff, A. L., & Linan-Thompson, S. (2007b). Prevention and early identification of students with reading disabilities. In D. Haager, J. Klingner, & S. Vaughn (Eds.), *Evidence-based reading practices for response to intervention* (pp. 11–27). Baltimore, MD: Paul H. Brookes.

Vazquez, C. A. (1994). Brief report: A multitask controlled evaluation of facilitated communication. *Journal of Autism and Developmental Disorders, 24*(3), 369–379.

Vellutino, F. R., Scanlon, D. M., Sipay, E., Small, S., Pratt, A., Chen, R., et al. (1996). Cognitive profiles of difficult-to-remediate and readily remediated poor readers: Early intervention as a vehicle for distinguishing between cognitive and experiential deficits as basic causes of specific reading disability. *Journal of Educational Psychology, 88,* 601–638.

Villa, R. A., & Thousand, J. S. (Eds.). (2005). *Creating an inclusive school.* (Eds). Alexandria, VA: ASCD.

Vygotsky, L. S. (1987). *Problems of general psychology.* New York: Plenum.

Wagner, M. (1989). Youth with disabilities during transition: An overview of descriptive findings from the national longitudinal transition study. In *Project Director's Fourth Annual Meeting.* Champaign, IL: Secondary Transition Effectiveness Institute.

Wagner, M., Newman, L., Cameto, R., Garza, N., & Levine, P. (2005). *After high school: A first look at the postschool experiences of youth with disabilities.* Menlo Park, CA: SRI International.

Walker, V. S. (1999). Culture and commitment: Challenges for the future training of education researchers. In E. C. Lagemann & L. Shulman (Eds.), *Issues in education research: Problems and possibilities* (pp. 224–244). San Francisco: Jossey-Bass.

Walker, V. S. (2005). After methods, then what? A researcher's response to the report of the National Research Council. *Teachers College Record, 107,* 30–37.

Wallace, T., Anderson, A. R., Bartholomay, T., & Hupp, S. (2002). An ecobehavioral examination of high school classrooms that include students with disabilities. *Exceptional Children, 68,* 345–359.

Wang, M., Mannan, H., Poston, D., Turnbull, A. P., & Summers, J. A. (2004). Parents' perspectives of advocacy activities and their impact on family quality of life. *Research and Practice for Persons with Severe Disabilities, 29*(2), 144–155.

Wang, M. C., & Birch, J. W. (1984). Effective special education in regular classes. *Exceptional Children, 50,* 391–398.

Wehman, P. (2001). *Life beyond the classroom* (3rd ed.). Baltimore, MD: Brookes Publishing.

Wehmeyer, M. (1996). Self-determination as an educational outcome: Why is it important to children, youth, and adults with disabilities? In D. Sands & M. Wehmeyer (Eds.), *Self-determination across the lifespan: Independence and choice for people with disabilities* (pp. 17–36). Baltimore, MD: Brookes Publishing.

Wehmeyer, M. L., & Schwartz, M. (1997). Self-determination and positive adult outcomes: A follow-up study of youth with mental retardation or learning disabilities. *Exceptional Children, 63*(2), 245–255.

Weiss, M.J.S., Wagner, S. H., & Bauman, M. L. (1996). A validated case study of facilitated communication. *Mental Retardation, 34*(4), 220–230.

West, M., Kregel, J., & Revell, W. (1993–1994, Winter). A new era of self-determination, *Impact, 6,* 13–21.

Whitten, E., & Dieker, L. (1995). Intervention assistance teams: A broader vision. *Preventing School Failure, 40,* 41–45.

Wiley, T. G. (1996). Literacy and language diversity in sociocultural contexts. In T. G. Wiley (Ed.), *Literacy and language diversity in the United States.* Washington, DC: Center for Applied Linguistics and Delta Systems.

Williams, J. M., & O'Leary, E. (2001). What we've learned and where we go from here. *Career Development for Exceptional Individuals, 24,* 157–169.

Winton, P. J., Turnbull, A. P., Blacher, J. B., & Salkind, N. (1983). Mainstreaming in the kindergarten classroom: Perspectives of parents of handicapped and nonhandicapped children. *Journal of the Division of Early Childhood, 6,* 14–20.

Wisniewski, Z. G., & Smith, D. (2002). How effective is TouchMath for improving students with special needs academic achievement on math addition mad minute timed tests? (ED469445). Retrieved October 23, 2006, from http://www.touchmath.com.

Wolfensberger, W. (1972). *The principle of normalization in human services.* Toronto: National Institute on Mental Retardation.

York, J., & Tundidor, H. (1995). Issues raised in the name of inclusion: Perspectives of educators, parents, and students. *Journal of the Association for Persons with Severe Handicaps, 20,* 31–44.

Yoshida, R. K., Fenton, K. S., Kaufman, M. J., & Maxwell, J. P. (1978). Parental involvement in the special education pupil planning process: The school's perspective. *Exceptional Children, 44*(7), 531–534.

Ysseldyke, J., Nelson, J. R., Christenson, S., Johnson, D. R., Dennison, A., Triezenberg, H., et al. (2004). What we know and need to know about the consequences of high-stakes testing for students with disabilities. *Exceptional Children, 71,* 75–94.

Ysseldyke, J., Thurlow, M., Bielinski, J., House, A., Moody, M., & Haigh, J. (2001). The relationship between instructional and assessment accommodations in an inclusive state accountability system. *Journal of Learning Disabilities, 3,* 212–220.

Zehr, M. A. (2007). State guidance on English-language learners lags. *Education Week,* 20–21.

Zirkel, P. A. (2005). Does *Brown v. Board of Education* play a prominent role in special education law? *Journal of Law and Education, 34*(2), 255–271.

Zoints, L. T., Zoints, P., Harrison, S., & Bellinger, O. (2004). Urban African American families' perceptions of cultural sensitivity with the special education system. *Focus on Autism and Other Developmental Disabilities, 18*(1), 41–50.

Zollers, N. J., Ramananthan, A. K., & Yu, M. (1999). The relationship between school culture and inclusion: How an inclusive culture supports an inclusive education. *International Journal of Qualitative Studies in Education, 12,* 157–174.

# Index

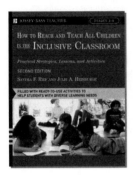

# How To Reach and Teach All Children in the Inclusive Classroom
*Practical Strategies, Lessons, and Activities*
*Second Edition*

**Sandra F. Rief & Julie A. Heimburge**

Paper | 480 pp.
ISBN: 978-0-7879-8154-9
www.josseybass.com

"Rief and Heimburge's new work provides the novice/beginning and experienced professional educator with a plethora of valuable ideas and techniques for promoting prosocial behaviors in school and raising the academic achievement of all learners." —**Dr. Bob Bayuk**, school psychologist and past president of Wyoming School Psychology Association

"Rief and Heimburge have included ideas for students with a wide array of learning challenges such as bipolar disorders, nonverbal LD, Asperger's Syndrome, and ODD. Teachers will find this book invaluable in the classroom!" —**Dr. William N. Bender**, author, *Differentiating Math Instruction: Strategies That Work for K–8 Classrooms*

This thoroughly updated edition of the best-selling book gives all classroom teachers, special educators, and administrators an arsenal of adaptable and ready-to-use strategies, lessons, and activities. *How to Reach and Teach All Children in the Inclusive Classroom* is a comprehensive resource that helps teachers reach students with varied learning styles, ability levels, skills, and behaviors. The authors offer a team approach that includes parents, colleagues, and learning specialists, enabling teachers to guide diverse groups of students in grades 3–8 toward academic, social, and emotional success.

This book is an invaluable resource for educators who want to successfully reach and teach all of the children in a mainstream general education classroom. Topics include how to:

- Effectively differentiate instruction
- Make accommodations and modifications for students based on their learning styles, abilities, and behaviors
- Engage reluctant readers and writers
- Motivate all students to be successful mathematicians
- Increase communication and collaboration between home and school
- Build students' organization, time management, and study skills
- Implement positive behavioral supports and interventions
- Create classroom and school-wide programs designed to enhance students' resiliency and self-esteem

**Sandra F. Rief**, M.A., is an internationally known speaker, teacher trainer, consultant, and author of several best-selling books including *How to Reach and Teach All Children Through Balanced Literacy*. She lives in San Diego, California.

**Julie A. Heimburge**, M.A., coauthor of the best-selling *How to Reach and Teach All Children Through Balanced Literacy*, is a veteran classroom teacher, with extensive experience as a staff developer, curriculum writer, and literacy coach. She lives in San Diego, California.

## Revealing Minds
*Assessing to Understand and Support Struggling Learners*

**Craig Pohlman**
**Foreword by Mel Levine, M.D.**

Paper | 352 pp
ISBN: 978-0-7879-8790-9
www.josseybass.com

"Any clinician, advocate, parent, or educator who wants to truly understand and help children who struggle in school should read this book and will want to return to it often." —**Paul B. Yellin**, M.D., FAAP, Director, Yellin Center for Student Success and Associate Professor of Pediatrics, New York University School of Medicine

"Pohlman provides us with a cogent, step-by-step guide to conducting assessments." —**Katherine Balisterri Howard**, M.A., NCSP, school psychologist, Old Trail School, Bath, Ohio

"Draws the essential connections between theory and practice that can enable every teacher to be 'smart' about assessing student learning—not just of those who struggle, but all students." —**Peter Gow**, Director of College Counseling and Special Programs, Beaver Country Day School

"Delivers a wealth of insights for understanding students who struggle with learning." —**Douglas Bouman**, Director, Psychological Services, CLC Network, Grand Rapids, Michigan

*Revealing Minds* is a practical, hands-on guide to assessing learning problems, based on the approach of All Kinds of Minds, the groundbreaking nonprofit institute co-founded by Mel Levine. Whereas most assessments of struggling learners focus on what is "broken" within a student and needs to be fixed, All Kinds of Minds has adopted a more positive and comprehensive approach to the process. Rather than labeling children or categorizing them into certain pre-defined groups, their optimistic and helpful path creates a complete picture (or "profile") of each student, outlining the child's assets along with any weaknesses, and identifying specific breakdown points that lead to problems at school.

The process of assessment should be able to answer a question such as, "Why is my son struggling with reading?" with a better answer than, "Because he has a reading disability." *Revealing Minds* shows how to discover hidden factors—such as language functioning, memory ability, or attention control—that are impeding a student's learning. It goes beyond labels and categories to help readers understand what's really going on with their students and create useful learning plans.

Providing scores of real-life examples, definitions of key terms, helpful diagrams, tables, and sample assessments, Pohlman offers a useful roadmap for educators, psychologists, and other professionals to implement the All Kinds of Minds approach in their own assessments.

**Craig Pohlman**, Ph.D., NCSP, is a licensed psychologist at All Kinds of Minds, a nonprofit institute helping struggling learners improve their success in school and in life. He has conducted and supervised thousands of assessments of students from kindergarten through college.

# Other Jossey-Bass Books of Interest

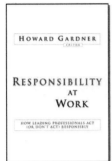

## Responsibility at Work
*How Leading Professionals Act (Or Don't Act) Responsibly*

**Howard Gardner, Editor**

Cloth | 368 pp.
ISBN: 978-0-7879-9475-4
www.josseybass.com

"In this remarkable collection of essays, Gardner and his colleagues have given us an astonishing array of penetrating insights into the responsibilities, meaning, and ethics of work. Everyone, anyone, in any organization, can learn and profit from the wisdom in these pages." —**Warren Bennis**, Distinguished Professor of Business and University Professor at the University of Southern California and author of *On Becoming a Leader*

"Gardner and his colleagues boldly confront the ever-present tensions between professional action and professional responsibility with superbly crafted individual case studies as well as broad theoretical arguments. Taken together, the writers deepen our understanding of the challenges of leadership—from classical ethical dilemmas to the seemingly mundane question of how to allocate one's time." —**Lee S. Shulman**, President, The Carnegie Foundation for the Advancement of Teaching

Most persons strive to produce work that is of excellent technical quality, is pursued in an ethical and socially responsible way, and has the qualities of being engaging and meaningful. How can we attain this ideal of good work in a world that changes so rapidly and all too often features an ethically compromised milieu?

Filled with original essays by Howard Gardner, William Damon, Mihaly Csikszentmihalyi, and Jeanne Nakamura, among others, and based on a large-scale research project, the GoodWork® Project, *Responsibility at Work* reflects the information gleaned from in-depth interviews with more than 1,200 people from nine different professions—journalism, genetics, theatre, higher education, philanthropy, law, medicine, business, and pre-collegiate education. The book reveals how motivation, culture, and professional norms can intersect to produce work that is personally, socially, and economically beneficial. At the heart of the study is the revelation that the key to good work is responsibility—taking ownership for one's work and its wider impact.

The authors examine how responsibility for work is shaped by both personal and professional components and explore the factors that cause a sense of responsibility, the obstacles that lead to compromised work, and the educational interventions that can lead to a greater sense of responsibility. Most important, this volume provides strategies for cultivating greater responsibility in both seasoned workers as well as the young people who will one day enter the workplace.

**Howard Gardner** is the Hobbs Professor of Cognition and Education at the Harvard Graduate School of Education. He is the author of more than twenty books translated into twenty-four languages. Gardner also holds positions as adjunct professor of psychology at Harvard University, adjunct professor of neurology at Boston University, and senior director of Harvard Project Zero.

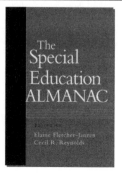

## The Special Education Almanac

**Elaine Fletcher-Janzen & Cecil R. Reynolds, Editors**

Paper | 576 pp.
ISBN: 978-0-471-67797-0
www.josseybass.com

*An essential resource for anyone working in the field of special education*

*The Special Education Almanac* serves as a practical, comprehensive reference that supports the everyday needs of professionals working in the field. Written by recognized experts from various areas of special education, this handy resource puts up-to-date information covering a wide range of special education topics and applications into a single, accessible toolbox filled with summaries, tips, examples, best practices, and references to the latest research.

Topics covered include:

- Special education teaching strategies
- Educational and psychological measurement and testing, including test descriptions and reviews
- Crisis intervention and students with special needs
- Special education case law
- Childhood disorders
- Special education associations, publishers, web sites, acronyms, journals, and other resources
- Special education biographies
- Positive behavioral support
- Self-determination for the special education student
- Creativity and the special education student
- Individualized education programs
- Psychoactive medications
- Instruction and assessment of culturally and linguistically diverse students

An essential guide for anyone working in special education or planning a career in this challenging field, *The Special Education Almanac* is an important resource for today's proven practices and critical information.

**Elaine Fletcher-Janzen**, EdD, NCSP, teaches at the University of Colorado, Colorado Springs, and consults to area school districts. She also serves as a trainer for American Guidance Service, a publisher of clinical assessment instruments for school psychologists. She has written or edited more than a dozen books on special education, school psychology, and child neuropsychology.

**Cecil R. Reynolds**, PhD, ABPN, is Professor of Educational Psychology and Professor of Neuroscience at Texas A&M University. He has written or edited more than thirty-four books, and is the author of several widely used psychological assessment instruments.